Foreword

Europe can no longer afford to wait. The world race against the clock in which our countries are already participating and playing for survival, requires a greater ability to adapt and take initiative from all, while demanding that our strengths and our energies be united. Following the proposal by the European Commission, the Community has resolved to establish by 1992 a genuinely common and cohesive European economic space which will, by virtue of its size, offer European enterprises new possibilities for expansion and cooperation. It has also decided to develop its scientific and technological programmes, which have already demonstrated that Europeans can aspire to the first rank as soon as they put together their resources and unite their talents.

The single market is a challenge. In the sphere of telecommunications, it will offer a new framework of regulation and management, on a higher level, favouring research and development, and the establishment of high capacity networks which will be an essential dynamic element of our productive capacity. It is an opportunity that must be grasped for the sake of employment and the future of European technology.

Jacques DELORS
President of the Commission
of the European Communities

COMMISSION OF THE EUROPEAN COMMUNITIES

Telecommunications in Europe

Free choice for the user in Europe's 1992 market

The challenge for the European Community

by Herbert UNGERER
with the collaboration of Nicholas COSTELLO

Foreword by J. DELORS
Preface by K. H. NARJES
Introduction by M. CARPENTIER

THE EUROPEAN PERSPECTIVES SERIES
BRUSSELS

Notice

This publication is designed to contribute to public debate on European integration. The views expressed are those of the authors alone, and do not necessarily reflect the opinion of the Commission of the European Communities.

This publication is also available in:

ES ISBN 92-825-8205-1
DA ISBN 92-825-8206-X
DE ISBN 92-825-8207-8
GR ISBN 92-825-8208-6
FR ISBN 92-825-8210-8
IT   ISBN 92-825-8211-6
NL ISBN 92-825-8212-4
PT ISBN 92-825-8213-2

Cataloguing data appear at the end of this publication

Luxembourg: Office for Official Publications of the European Communities, 1988

ISBN 92-825-8209-4

Catalogue number: CB-PP-88-009-EN-C

Preface

Telecommunications has become a key element of any strategy for economic and social revival. Esoteric acronyms such as ISDN — the Integrated Services Digital Network — and IBC — Integrated Broadband Communications — are now taking on a real economic meaning. The integration of telecommunications and computers is creating the new telematics market, and at the same time, a fundamental transformation of the regulatory, industrial, and political conditions dominating this sector.

Telecommunications are at the meeting point of services and high technology. The advanced telecommunications network that has started to develop will be as strong a driving force for change in the 21st century as the electricity network and the motorway system have been for the 20th.

These changes will go to the very root of our society and values. They will test our future attitudes towards new technology, new opportunities, and new growth. They will test Europe's willingness and ability to remain one of the leading actors in the world economy.

There can only be two options: either to participate in the dynamic transformation of the world economy, or to become a second-rank player and to accept the loss of wealth and prosperity which this would mean for every European citizen.

I am confident. The Single European Act, adopted by all national Parliaments in the Community, and which entered into force on 1 July 1987, has created a strong framework to lead us to the Single European Market in 1992; it has established the European Technology Community; and it has strengthened the principle of solidarity between the rich and the poor regions in the Community, without which a Community-wide market cannot be achieved.

But we will be called upon to take clear positions if we want successfully to mobilize Europe's forces:

(i)   we must say 'yes' to the principle of free consumer choice which is a fundamental conviction underlying the Treaty of Rome: independent individuals, free to buy what they want; suppliers free to provide what is desired; and a Community-wide market to satisfy needs, at the lowest cost and with the highest benefit. This — the underlying

5

theme of the Green Paper on telecommunications — is the main topic of this book and defines a framework for European policy;

(ii) *we must say 'yes' to technology, carefully selected and properly used, if we want to maintain a strong European position in the world. With the adoption of the Community's framework programme for research and development in September of last year, the Community has taken a major step. The RACE programme is a centre-piece in this context. It harnesses the explosive growth of telecommunications through one overall — but open — scheme, Integrated Broadband Communications. After its final adoption in December 1987, the major companies in Europe are now working together within this framework on Europe's future telecommunications system;*

(iii) *we must say 'yes' to equitable access to the new technologies for all regions of the Community. The Community's STAR programme, adopted in autumn 1986 and funded by the European Regional Development Fund, which brings advanced telecommunications to the peripheral regions of the Community, is a first step.*

We will have to take account of legitimate social concerns. But we should keep in mind that adjustment to inevitable change is easier in a climate of growth than in a climate of decline.

We will have to develop in Europe a common understanding on the future position of the individual in an environment which will be substantially richer in information than before. But while measures for protecting the private life of the individual will be required, they must not halt change which will bring above all more freedom of access to information for everyone.

Finally, we will have to accept measures which may be inconvenient for some but which are necessary for the well-being of all: opening national procurement is indispensable for the creation of a Europe-wide market base.

The European Council of 11 and 12 February 1988 cleared the way. It gave the Community an acceptable agreement on the Community's future finances, the harnessing of agricultural expenditure and the increase of the structural funds available to help the Community's less favoured regions. The Community can now concentrate fully on building the 1992 market. Telecommunications will be a key area.

Over the past four years, the Commission has developed the basis of the Community's telecommunications policy. This success has been due in large part to the dedication of Michel Carpentier, Director-General for Telecommunications, Information Industries, and Innovation and to his Telecommunications Directorate. This book testifies to the progress up to now, and outlines the future challenges.

K.H. NARJES
Vice-President of the Commission
of the European Communities

Acknowledgements

Telecommunications is a complex and multi-faceted issue; it follows that our work has necessarily drawn on materials and studies from a wide variety of sources. Our thanks go especially to our colleagues in the Directorate-General for Telecommunications, Information Industries and Innovation of the European Commission, and to our colleagues in the other departments of the Commission, in particular the Directorate-General for Competition. Of course responsibility for the final contents lies with the authors. We wish furthermore to thank our secretaries, who have contributed to the production of this work with great diligence and patience.

The occasion of the first English edition has been used to update the figures to the latest available.

September 1988

Contents

List of figures

12

List of tables

List of boxes

15

Introduction

The telecommunications sector is undergoing fundamental change. Change represents a challenge but also new opportunities. Europe has the competence, the potential and the know-how to confront change.

Ten years after the publishing of the seminal report by Nora and Minc [1] which introduced the concept of 'telematics' to Europe, the convergence of telecommunications and data processing has created a conglomerate sector of the management and transport of information representing more than 500 000 million ECU for the world as a whole. With telecommunications services near 300 000 million ECU world-wide and with a telecommunications world equipment market reaching 90 000 million ECU, telecommunications accounts for far more than half of this total.

Access to information has become the key to prosperity and growth. Information is of an all-pervasive nature. It is the basic input of the emerging service economy, it is at the base of new growth in industry; and it links industry, services and markets together.

The challenge is enormous. The digitization of the telephone network is changing the basis of telecommunications. A wide range of technical advances lie ahead: the digital network, optical fibres, satellites. A broad spread of new forms of communications and access is emerging: widespread use of portable telephones and car telephones over coming years; transmission of moving images combined with the telephone by the start of the 1990s; and innumerable combinations of computers and telecommunications in the office and — more and more — in the home. New services are being developed every day.

With its 320 million inhabitants, a highly qualified work-force and a strong starting position in industry and services, Europe unites all the conditions to be able to benefit fully from the new potential and the new growth, for new jobs and for a better quality of life.

But the cost of 'non-Europe' has been high in telecommunications. By the early 1980s, Europe had a substantial lag in two respects:

(i) with regard to information technology and in particular the highly integrated circuit components — the famous chips — which form the heart of this new 'intelligent' technology;

---

[1] *L'informatisation de la société*, La documentation française, Paris, 1978.

(ii) with regard to the adaptation of regulation, the opening of the telecommunications sector to the new opportunities.

In the telecommunications sector, no national market in Europe accounts for more than 6% of the world market. The United States accounts for more than 35%, Japan 11%. For industry and for the new services, concentrating on the purely national base will not be enough.

Europe is faced with dynamic development in the United States and Japan. Only united will Europe be able to secure its share of the future markets.

Since the early 1980s, Europe has shown its capability to act together — once the need is clearly perceived. In 1984, the Council of the European Communities adopted the ESPRIT programme, the European Strategic Programme for Research and development in Information Technologies; in 1985, the first phase of the RACE programme, research and development in advanced communications technologies for Europe, was started. In 1987, the adoption of the Community's framework programme for research and development created a stable base: the RACE main phase has been launched, ESPRIT II has been budgeted.

In both programmes the major European companies in information technologies and telecommunications and many small companies and university laboratories — many thousands of European researchers — are now working together on strengthening Europe's technological base, in a unique new transnational experiment.

In parallel, since 1984, work has started at the Community level — together with the SOG-T, the Senior Officials Group on Telecommunications — on adapting the telecommunications sector to the new conditions: work on network coordination, on standards, and with the publication of the Green Paper in June 1987, on regulatory adjustment. All Member States envisage change. The Green Paper on telecommunications sets out a programme for the Community, based on national developments, foreseeing an open environment by 1992, the overriding deadline set by the Single European Act.

By January 1988, more than 45 organizations in the field, both at Community and national level, had responded to the Green Paper: the users; the telecommunications administrations ; the European telecommunications, data processing and services industries; and the trade unions and other organizations which represent the social interest in this field.

On the basis of this consensus, on 9 February 1988 the Commission submitted a programme to the Council, the European Parliament and the Community's Economic and Social Committee, which will constitute a determined effort to lead telecommunications in Europe to the 1992 goal — the Europe-wide market which the European user needs.

This book aims to set out the background, the achievements to date and the future challenge of this process. The overall aims of Community telecommunications policy were set out at the start of the process in 1984:

18

(i) promoting the creation of an advanced European telecommunications infrastructure;

(ii) contributing to the creation of a Community-wide market for services and equipment;

(iii) contributing to the competitiveness of European industry and service providers.

The Community has the will to act to achieve these goals. During the past 18 months alone, the Council has taken, following proposals by the Commission, eight major decisions.

In order to appreciate fully the importance of the goals, they must be seen in context. They must be seen in the context of the other policies of the Community leading up to the overriding 1992 objective, as set out in the parallel publications of this series of *European perspectives.* Telecommunications will be a major contributor to these policies and will also draw major benefits from them. They must be seen in the context of the fundamental goal of linking the Member States closer together: the basic aim of European cohesion confirmed in the Single European Act. They must be seen in the context of the social aspirations and desires of the European citizen.

This last goal must be at the centre of all considerations. It lies at the root of the 1992 goal and is its ultimate justification. As the Commission states in its Green Paper, 'the overriding aim is to develop the conditions for the market to provide European users with a greater variability of telecommunications services of better quality and at lower cost, affording Europe the full internal and external benefits of a strong telecommunications sector'.

It is with this central theme in mind that the reader should approach this publication.

M. Carpentier
Director-General for Telecommunications,
Information Industries and Innovation in the
Commission of the European Communities

I — Telecommunications: a crucial element for the completion of the Community's internal market

Telecommunications have become one of the major challenges for the completion of the internal market of the Community by 1992. Rapid technological change has made telecommunications a spearhead of future market development.

Over the last few years, the European telecommunications scene has been undergoing a fundamental transformation owing to the impact of changes in technology, and of deregulation in the United States and Japan.

Nearly all Member States of the European Community have either already undertaken regulatory reform or are currently reviewing their regulatory situation.

Telecommunications services took 140 years to grow from a single service — telegraphy — to more than a dozen different types of service by the start of this decade. By the year 2000, this figure is expected to have doubled or tripled (Figure 1).

It is the management of this dramatic service differentiation which is the basic challenge for telecommunications administrations and policy makers world-wide — and particularly in the Community, given the inherent complexity of the Community's situation in telecommunications.

The trend towards the integration of telecommunications, data processing and the audio-visual media is accelerating. It is this trend which transforms telecommunications into an all pervasive force making it the base of a broad range of future economic, social and cultural activities.

The rapid broadening of telecommunications services into the infrastructure of a wide variety of services has given to telecommunications a new role in the economy and society. Telecommunications is developing into one of the basic inputs of our future communications-based society.

Telecommunications will be a major factor in structuring the Community-wide services market in 1992. It will determine, to a large extent, Europe's future position in high technology.

It is within this overall picture that the European Community has conceived its policy in this field since 1984.

FIGURE 1

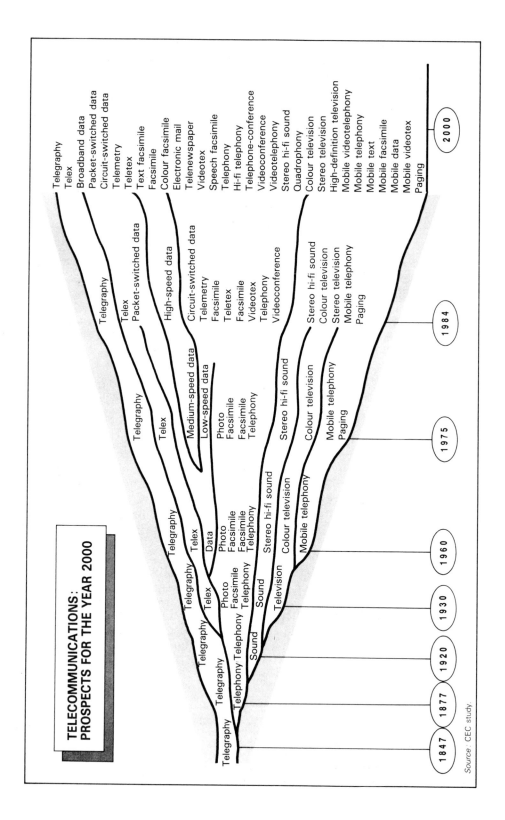

The overall framework was set out by the Commission of the European Communities in two major policy documents which are the source of most Community telecommunications policy at this stage:

(i) The 1984 Community action programme on telecommunications. [1]
(ii) The 1987 Green Paper. [2]

This publication is structured around these two comprehensive policy statements which set out the framework of the telecommunications policy of the European Community to date. It refers to these documents and to studies carried out for the Commission of the European Communities where appropriate. It describes the technological and market trends which are the background to telecommunications policy in Europe. It gives an account of achievements to date and of plans announced for the future.

But this publication endeavours above all to demonstrate the overall thinking behind Community telecommunications policy which links it so closely to the general goal of the completion of the Community's internal market by 1992.

In the White Paper from the Commission to the Milan European Council of 28 and 29 June 1985, setting out the basic objective of the completion of the Community's internal market by 31 December 1992, the Commission stated that:

'It is no exaggeration to see the establishment of a common market in services as one of the main preconditions for a return to economic prosperity ...'

and emphasized that:

'The development of new technologies has led to the creation and development of new cross-border services which are playing an increasingly important role in the economy. However, these services can develop their full potential only when they serve a large, unobstructed market. This applies equally to audio-visual services, information and data-processing services and to computerized marketing and distribution services ...'. [3]

In the Green Paper, the Commission puts this in greater detail:

'A technically advanced, Europe-wide and low-cost telecommunications network will provide an essential infrastructure for improving the competitiveness of the European economy, achieving the internal market and strengthening Community cohesion — which constitute priority Community goals reaffirmed in the Single European Act. Telecommunications have a great influence not only on services in general, such as financial services, transport and tourism, but also on trade in goods and on European industrial cooperation.'

---

[1] 'Progress report on the thinking and work done in the field of telecommunications and initial proposals for an action programme', COM(84) 277, 18 May 1984.
[2] 'Towards a dynamic European economy — Green Paper on the development of the common market for telecommunications services and equipment', COM(87) 290, 30 June 1987.
[3] Communication from the Commission to the Council, COM(85) 310, 14 June 1985.

Community telecommunications policy is now dominated by two fundamental considerations:

(i) The entering into force of the Single European Act, on 1 July 1987, involving the completion of the internal Community-wide market by 1992; the creation of the European Technology Community; the development of a forward-looking competition policy; and promotion of regional cohesion.

(ii) The dynamics — and economic and social requirements — which have been introduced by the rapid technological change in what has become one single sector of information movement and management — telecommunications and information technology.

By the end of this century, the competitiveness and security of up to 60 million jobs in the European Community will depend largely on the emerging information technologies.

Telecommunications will become a critical factor in Europe's future economic, social and cultural development.

The European Community and its Member States have to face up to this challenge. This is the central theme addressed in this publication.

II — A silent revolution during the 1970s: the telephone becoming generally available at home and at work

During the 1970s, Europe experienced a silent revolution, away from the spotlight of public attention. The use of and dependence on information underwent dramatic changes both in the business and in the household sector.

1. Rapid increase of telephone penetration during the 1970s: the telephone develops into a general facility for the European citizen

Since the late 1960s, the telephone has developed from a service restricted mainly to business and emergency use to a feature present in two out of every three households in the European Community.

Over the period 1976-86 telephone penetration grew at an accelerated speed in Europe (Table 1), with France an outstanding example, showing an increase from 16 connections per 100 inhabitants in 1976 to 42 connections per 100 inhabitants in 1986.

It is now easy to forget that the telephone only became a mass consumer item very recently.

Together with the parallel spread of television it is this new role of the telephone, as an everyday item, which has modified fundamentally the communications base of Europe's society. This silent revolution has, unperceived by many, already brought the European economy to the threshold of the future information society.

TABLE 1

Development of penetration of main lines (1976-86)
for France, Germany, Italy and the United Kingdom

	1976	1977	1978	1979	1980	1981	1982	1983	1984	1985	1986
	Main lines (thousands)										
France	8 444	10 060	12 010	13 959	15 898	17 743	19 478	20 942	22 086	23 031	23 911
FR Germany	14 212	15 748	17 305	18 917	20 535	21 769	22 713	23 550	24 603	25 589	26 399
Italy	10 166	10 778	11 456	12 172	13 017	13 860	14 698	15 601	16 521	17 396	18 253
United Kingdom	13 962	14 059	15 173	16 462	17 696	18 523	19 083	19 550	20 193	20 921	21 654
	Growth rate (% per year)										
France	18.9	19.1	19.4	16.2	13.9	11.6	9.8	7.5	5.5	4.3	3.8
FR Germany	8.3	10.8	9.9	9.3	8.6	6.0	4.3	3.7	4.5	4.0	3.2
Italy	5.2	6.0	6.3	6.3	6.9	6.5	6.0	6.1	5.9	5.3	4.9
United Kingdom	5.5	0.7	7.9	8.5	7.5	4.7	3.0	2.4	3.3	3.6	3.5
	Main lines (per 100 inhabitants)										
France	15.6	18.5	22.0	25.5	28.9	32.1	35.0	37.4	39.3	40.8	42.2
FR Germany	23.1	25.6	28.2	30.8	33.4	35.3	36.9	38.3	40.3	41.9	43.2
Italy	18.0	19.0	20.2	21.3	22.8	24.6	25.9	27.4	28.9	30.4	31.8
United Kingdom	25.0	25.2	27.2	29.5	31.7	33.1	34.1	34.8	35.8	37.1	38.3

2. The telecommunications administrations enter the ranks of the Community's largest enterprises and employers

The same revolution of consumer behaviour has propelled Europe's telecommunications administrations to become some of Europe's largest enterprises and employers (Table 2).

TABLE 2

Telecommunications administrations in the European Community Member States

Belgium

Régie des télégraphes et des téléphones (RTT) (public corporation).

Denmark

The General Directorate of P&T carries out the functions of the Ministry on a delegated basis in the posts and telecommunications sector.

The regional concessionary enterprises, Copenhagen Telephone Company, Jutland Telephone Company, Funen Telephone Company and the State enterprise South Jutland Telecom, are in charge of all regional communications activities, including customer contact, each within its own geographical area.

Another State enterprise, Telecom Denmark, is responsible for international and nationwide telecommunications between the regional companies.

France

France Télécom (formerly 'DGT').

The French PTT is a State organization responsible to the PTT minister. The 'Administration des postes et télécommunications' comprises two directorates-general, one for posts and the other — 'France Télécom' — for telecommunications.

France Télécom has two principal areas of responsibility:

(i) network and services provision for the whole of the country;

(ii) entrepreneurial activities, such as provision of customer premises equipment and advanced services.

'Télédiffusion de France' (TDF) operates a specialized network for broadcasting and television purposes. TDF has recently introduced a paging service.

Federal Republic of Germany

Deutsche Bundespost (DBP).

In the Federal Republic of Germany, telecommunications is a government responsibility. Both regulatory and operational tasks are currently fulfilled in a uniform way by the Federal Minister of Posts and Telecommunications and by the Bundespost he manages, taking into account the aims of government policy.

A bill for the restructuring of the Bundespost is before Parliament.

Greece

Hellenic Telecommunications Organization SA (OTE).

Publicly owned but financially autonomous (OTE statute).

Ireland

Telecom Eireann (State-owned company).

Italy

Services are provided primarily by the State organizations in the Ministry of Posts and Telecommunications and by subsidiaries of the state-owned IRI/STET holding company. The three subsidiaries are SIP, Italcable and Telespazio.

Together these constitute the public operating companies.

A bill on the institutional reorganization of the sector has been proposed. Its main points are as follows:

(i) telecommunications to be operated by companies of the IRI/STET State holding group;

(ii) the Ministry of Posts and Telecommunications to become the 'planning and control body' for the whole sector.

Luxembourg

Telecommunications services are provided by the Luxembourg PTT, 'Administration des postes et des télécommunications' (P&T).

Netherlands

The Netherlands PTT is a State-owned organization under the political responsibility of the Ministry.

Spain

Telefonica (formerly CTNE) is the major service provider.

It has the status of a private company; 31% of shares in Telefonica are directly held by the government and a further 15% are the property of government-owned institutions.

Portugal

The Portuguese PTT (CTT) is a public company under the political authority of the Ministry.

CTT provides all postal services and all telecommunications services apart from the following, which are provided under government concessions to two other carriers:

(i) Telefones de Lisboa e Porto (TLP) — a public company — provides telephony in Lisbon and Oporto;

(ii) Companhia Portuguesa Radio Marconi (CPRM) provides intercontinental telephone and telex services; international telegraphy (apart from Spain); and intercontinental links for new services such as the data network.

CTT and TLP share a board, nominated by the government.

United Kingdom

Fourteen organizations are licensed as public telecommunications operators (PTOs):

(i) British Telecommunications plc (BT), which is a company with 51% private ownership, 49% government ownership;

(ii) Mercury Communications Limited (Mercury), privately owned;

(Both these companies are licensed to run nation-wide fixed networks.)

(iii) Racal Vodafone

(iv) Telecoms Securicor Cellular Radio Ltd (Cellnet)

only for mobile cellular radio telephone systems;

(v) City of Kingston upon Hull: a fixed network only for its own area;

(vi) 9 cable operators, full range of telecommunications services and cable TV in their franchise areas.

The telecommunications administrations in the European Community now represent a combined income from telecommunications services of 64 800 million ECU (1986); combined total employment of 922 000; and combined annual investment of more than 22 000 million ECU (Table 3).

The extension of the telephone network into a general communications infrastructure over the two decades has made the telephone network the biggest interconnected machine ever built by humanity.

World-wide, telecommunications networks now represent an asset value of more than 500 000 million ECU. Within the Community, the value of the network installed can be estimated at close to 200 000 million ECU. This means that the current telecommunications networks are by far the greatest Community asset in information technology. It makes the economic management and the financing capability of the telecommunications administrations for its renewal and extension a primary policy concern in the sector in Europe.

TABLE 3

Revenues, investment and employment of telecommunications administrations in the European Community

	1986	1986 growth over 1985
Telephone sets connected to the public network (million)	173.0	3.9%
Number of main lines (million)	117.7	4.1%
Total staff in telecommunications services	922 000	−1.8%
Total income from the telephone service (1 000 million ECU)	54.8	5.2%
Total income from all telecommunications services (1 000 million ECU)	64.8	5.4%
Total annual gross investment in telecommunications excluding land and buildings (1 000 million ECU)	22.5	8.8%
Annual gross investments in telephone switching equipment (1 000 million ECU)	5.1	6.8%
Telephone main lines per 100 inhabitants (average)	35.8	4.1%
Telephone stations (sets) of all kinds per 100 inhabitants (average)	52.6	3.8%

Source: International Telecommunications Union *Yearbook of common carrier statistics* (1988) and CEC studies.

Country	No of telephone sets connected to the public network (1 000)	Main lines (1 000)	Total staff in telecommunications services (1 000)	Total income from all telecommunications (million ECU)
Belgium	4 556	3 257	27	1 546
Denmark	4 195	2 683	17[2]	1 297
France	35 659[1]	23 911	165	15 488
FR Germany	39 128	26 399	214	16 585
Greece	3 920	3 292	30	737
Ireland	1 006[1]	751	15	687
Italy	26 874	18 253	110	9 393
Luxembourg	252[3]	162	0.8	79
Netherlands	9 080	6 029	30	2 880
Portugal	1 936	1 512	23	868
Spain	14 748	9 801	63	2 672
United Kingdom	31 653[1]	21 654	227	12 518
EEC	173 007	117 704	922	64 753

Source: International Telecommunications Union *Yearbook of common carrier statistics* (1988) and CEC studies.
Reference year: 1986.

[1] *Estimate.*
[2] *Source:* Statens Teletjenste; figure for 1985.
[3] *Source:* Luxconsult; figure for 1985.

3. The strategies of the 1970s

The task of placing the telephone within the reach of every consumer and business user, independent of status, geographic location and frequency of use, has made the public service mandate the overriding business objective of telecommunications administrations in Europe. The task of providing telephone services (and telex) to the whole national territory on reasonably equal conditions has deeply influenced the strict regulatory regimes under which the sector has traditionally operated in all Member States and the mandate, ethics and enterprise culture of the telecommunications administrations.

The emphasis on a public service goal mainly interpreted as general telephone coverage has led in all European countries (and worldwide) to an extended monopoly regime in the past for the provision of the network, telephone and telex service and telephone sets, with the aim of ensuring the financing of the general network and of telephone penetration.

In most European countries, rentals and connections are heavily subsidized by usage-related charges (call charges), in order to encourage telephone penetration. In all European countries, long-distance rates have served to subsidize local rates. In a number of European countries postal services are subsidized from telecommunications services.

While the dominating fact during the 1970s has been the rapid catching up of Europe, there continue to persist substantial differences in general telephone service penetration, both between leading European countries and the world leaders in telephone penetration, but particularly so within the European Community between the central and peripheral regions. Table 4 and Figure 2 compare telephone and telex penetration for Community Member States.

TABLE 4

Telephone and telex penetration per Member State

Country	Telephone connections (1 000)	Telephone connections per 100 inhabitants	Telex subscriber lines (1 000)	Telex subscriber lines per 100 inhabitants
Belgium	3 257	33.0	28	0.28
Denmark	2 683	52.4	13	0.13
France	23 911	42.2	134	0.24
FR Germany	26 399	43.2	165	0.27
Greece	3 292	33.0	22	0.22
Ireland	751	21.2	7	0.20
Italy	18 253	31.9	69	0.12
Luxembourg	162	45.3	2	0.63
Netherlands	6 029	41.3	40	0.27
Portugal	1 512	14.8	21	0.21
Spain	9 801	25.2	40	0.10
United Kingdom	21 654	38.3	105	0.18
EEC	117 703	35.8	646	0.20

Source: International Telecommunications Union *Yearbook of common carrier statistics* (1988) and CEC studies.
Reference year: 1986.

FIGURE 2

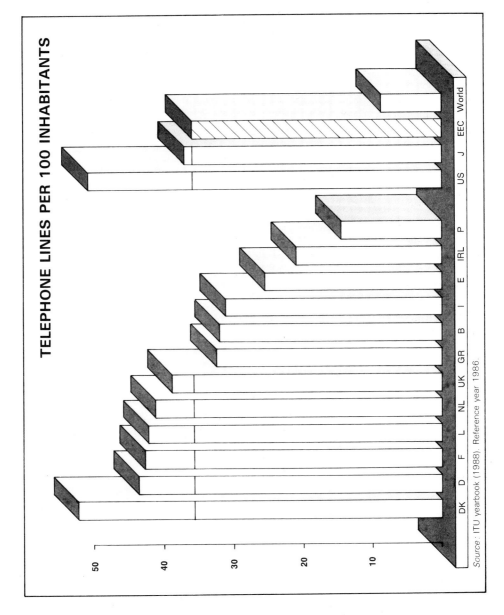

TELEPHONE LINES PER 100 INHABITANTS

Source : ITU yearbook (1988). Reference year 1986.

31

Telephone penetration can be taken essentially as an indication of the current penetration of private households by telecommunications: telex has traditionally been aimed at the business community.

Therefore, while Member States near the geographical centre of the Community have begun since the end of the 1970s to experience declining growth rates in telephone connections — with the result that they are searching more and more for new growth opportunities in fields other than telephone services — the public-service goal of providing broad public telephone coverage remains a preponderant concern for a number of peripheral Member States in the Community.

This leads to an inherent divergence of telecommunications administrations' strategies which must be taken into account in policy formulation at the European level.

As regards the telecommunications equipment industry in the Community, its structure was deeply marked by the period of close cooperation which developed during the rapid build-up of the network in most European countries between the national telecommunications administrations and a small number of national suppliers, specializing in the particularities of national network technology.

The telecommunications administrations in Europe have been traditionally by far the largest buyers of telecommunications equipment, with a share of more than 70% of total purchases. The natural cooperation developed during network build-up between the national telecommunications administrations and suppliers, often for reasons of specific national network technology and standards, has encouraged governments further to reinforce the closing of national markets by using the nationally focused closed-off telecommunications sector as the starting point for nationally oriented industrial policies.

TABLE 5

Size of national markets relative to world markets

	% of world total
Belgium	0.7
Denmark	0.4
France	5.1
Ireland	0.1
Italy	3.4
FR Germany	5.6
Greece	0.3
Netherlands	0.7
Portugal	0.2
Spain	1.7
United Kingdom	4.2
Community total	22.4

Source: Estimates based on Arthur D. Little and TIR.

Although Europe has demonstrated a high degree of competitivity in the telecommunications sector, the fact remains that the European telecommunications industry is extremely fragmented. Estimates for the percentage of the global market for each country vary according to different sources and depending on the exchange rate basis used for comparisons, but the picture that emerges from looking at a range of sources is that no individual Member State's market represents more than about 6% while the US market represents more than 35% and the Japanese about 11%. The European market as a whole, however, accounts for about 20% of the global market.

No national Community market represents more than 6% of the world's telecommunications market. Table 5 illustrates the national market sizes. The USA represents 35% while Japan accounts for 11%. The European telecommunications industry has been operating on a fragile market base compared to its US and Japanese competitors.

Europe has thus inherited from the period of accelerated build-up of the telephone networks a fragmented nationally focused telecommunications industrial structure, with national markets largely closed to other Member States and with national industry focused on national network requirements.

4. The balance at the end of the 1970s: general telephone coverage achieved but telecommunications nationally fragmented — the cost of 'non-Europe'

The balance sheet of the rapid build-up of telephone penetration in the European Community during the 1970s is thus mixed.

On the one hand, the telephone became an everyday tool for the consumer, with high quality networks optimized for telephone provision and planned according to national technologies which only changed slowly over time. Achieving general telephone availability brought Europe to the threshold of the information age.

But on the other hand, these systems had developed largely with a purely national focus.

During the rapid growth of telephone penetration over the last decade, governments and telecommunications administrations had come to be deeply influenced, with regard to their strategic vision for the telecommunications sector, by the ethics and the goal of general provision of national public telephone services — with 85 to 90% of telecommunications revenues, by far the main influence in revenue considerations.

The main concern was the economical management of a huge national network investment, characterized by a slowly moving technology and correspondingly long depreciation periods of 20 years and more.

Only loose international coordination mechanisms in the framework of the European Conference of Postal and Telecommunications Administrations (CEPT) and the International Telecommunications Union (ITU) had been established.

The organization of the sector was shaped by the aim of providing a very limited number of standard services and types of terminal equipment, mostly under strict monopoly regimes and mainly on a national basis. The whole, rapidly growing sector was thus withdrawn from the operation of market forces and its self-regulating influence — in the national market by the broad interpretation of monopoly provision, in the Community market additionally by the virtual closing off of Member States.

As will be seen later, the efforts of the Commission of the European Communities throughout the 1970s to open the telecommunications markets, in particular procurement and equipment markets, were unsuccessful up to the end of the decade — mainly because the prevailing opinion in the Member States was that the existing structures would be sufficient to attain public service goals.

The immediate costs of 'non-Europe' during this period were higher prices for telephone introduction than could otherwise have been achieved, and delayed and non-harmonized introduction of new services. The traditional loose coordination mechanisms between the European telecommunications administrations were only fully successful in ensuring international communications for the services at the centre of the public service goals of the time — the telephone and telex services.

The longer term price of 'non-Europe' has turned out to be higher. European telecommunications went into the technological revolution of the 1980s with a fragmented market structure, without the economic benefits of scale, cost-efficiency and flexibility which the larger Community market could have offered.

It was thus a nationally fragmented structure — adapted to national technology and closed-off markets and the provision of a very limited number of standard services — which was hit by the fundamental change of the technological base of communications in the beginning of the 1980s — the computerization of telecommunications.

Within a very few years, at an accelerating rate since 1980, telecommunications was propelled into the high technology field, subject to the characteristics developed by the computer market — rapid innovation, high degree of service differentiation, dynamic markets, substantially shorter depreciation times, economies of scale and scope, and aggressive international competitors.

III — The new technological base of telecommunications: the convergence of telecommunications and information technologies

The entry of computer intelligence into the network and terminals since the late 1970s has led to a fundamental change in communications. It means that — world-wide — the industry will completely change its technological and economic role within a single decade.

The integration of computers in the network — or digitization, i.e. the encoding, transformation and transmission of any information as bits — is creating a new 'telematics' market. 'Telematics' is a term used to describe the emerging combined sector of telecommunications and computing, in a world where it is less and less possible to say where one begins and the other ends.

The full introduction of new broadband transmission technologies — fibre optics, satellites, microwave — is the source of a further transformation: the merging of telecommunications with audio-visual/TV broadcasting technologies.

Together, these two transformations will lead to a new information era: for business at the start, but — as shown by Minitel in France — eventually for households as a whole. We are witnessing the establishment of the infrastructure which will give European society widespread access to information.

1. The service explosion

A broad range of telecommunications services will emerge (Box 1).

Box 1

The development of telecommunications — the service explosion

Conventional services

- Telephone
- Telex
- Telegraphy
- Low-speed packet-switched and circuit-switched data
- Low-speed facsimile (Group III, 1 minute for A4 page)
- Low-speed videotex
- Low-speed private lines (leased lines)
- Mobile telephones, often local only and with limited quality
- Paging, often local only and with limited quality
- Separate TV cable networks
- Very limited availability of satellite services

New services

To be delivered on a semi or fully digital basis, ultimately in the context of the ISDN
- Enhanced telephony (improved speech quality), with a broad range of features such as call transfer, etc.
- Circuit-switched data at 64 Kbit/s and enhanced package-switched data services
- Facsimile at 64 Kbit/s (Group IV, a few seconds for an A4 page)
- Teletex at 64 Kbit/s (about 100 times speed of telex)
- Alphageometric videotex
- Availability of mobile telephone and paging, on digital basis
- High-speed private lines (64 Kbit/s, 2 Mbit/s)
- Direct satellite television, extended availability of satellite business communications (2 Mbit/s)
- Emergence of a broad range of sophisticated value-added services

Advanced, high bandwidth services

- High-speed data (> 2 Mbit/s) for real-time high-speed computer links and file transfer
- Colour facsimile
- Videoconference
- Videotelephony
- Full integration of TV services, with higher quality: high-definition television (HDTV)
- Extended use of mobile voice and data, fully integrated in general telecommunications network
- Broad range of value-added services, combining narrow-band (voice/data), and broad-band (visual) information and intelligent data processing function (voice, data and video-messaging and retrieval)

Current services will continue to form the bulk of service provision for the time being but on a renewed and more cost-effective basis — telephony, telex, low-speed data transfer.

Based on the new intelligence of the network, a broad range of new services offering enhanced features will appear.

This introduction of a whole new range of high quality services will become fully effective with the full application of the advantages of digitization in the ISDN — the Integrated Services Digital Network. This concerns in particular services essential for the new telematics market and the working of businesses — digital enhanced telephony, high-speed telecopy (facsimile), high-quality videotex, and electronic messaging. At the same time a broad range of so-called value-added services will develop, which combine computing and telecommunications to allow the availability of the full sophistication of computer service functions at exactly the time and place they are needed: information in the right form (through computing) at the right time and place (through telecommunications).

Before the end of the decade, a new type of advanced service will fully enter the market, which will need both intelligence and higher bandwidth — digitization and fibre optics. This will essentially concern visual communication and high-speed computer communications: integration of current TV distribution into the general telecommunications network, with substantially higher quality; videoconferencing and videophones; high-speed colour facsimile and high-speed data links (Box 2).

Underlying this service explosion are four major technological changes which have most affected telecommunications:

(i)   micro-electronics, in particular the manufacture of complex circuits on a single integrated-circuit chip;

(ii)   digitization, i.e. the operation of telecommunications functions, both switching and transmission, in a digital form;

(iii) the introduction of stored programme control (SPC) exchanges;

(iv)   new transmission techniques: optical fibre, improvement in microwave and satellites and the revolution in communications and the audio-visual sector resulting from them.

The Commission has presented its analysis of these technological trends in both COM(84) 277 and the Green Paper. This vision of the changes in the telecommunications sector has influenced substantially the policy proposals at Community level since 1984.

The 'three generations' of telecommunications services — simplified presentation

	Traditional services (first generation)	New services (second generation)	Advanced services (third generation)
	Current basic telecommunications infrastructure	Enhancement of basic telecommunications infrastructure	New telecommunications infrastructure
Two-way communi-cations	• Telephony • Telex, teletex • Low-speed data • Mobile telephony • Low-speed facsimile	• Integrated basic services with some speed enhancement (ISDN) • Digitized voice • Textfax • Audiographic teleconferencing • Electronic mail • Wider availability of mobile telephony • Higher resolution videotex	• Videotelephony • Video-conferencing • Bulk document transfer • High-speed colour facsimile • High-speed data • On-line graphical design • Remote printing and publishing • Dynamic computer load-sharing • Burst-mode host-to-host transfer
Broadcast communi-cations	• Over-the-air radio • Over-the-air and cable TV	• Multichannel cable TV • Direct broadcasting by satellite (DBS)	• High definition television (HDTV)

2. Micro-electronics and digitization: a quantum leap towards new communications functions

Digitization — the encoding, transformation and transmission of any information, voice, data and visual, as bits — has been the major force in transforming the telecommunications sector since the late 1970s (Box 3).

Box 3

Technological developments: digitization — the computerization of telecommunications

The telecommunications system consists basically of three elements:

(i) transmission facilities;

(ii) switching facilities, at different 'hierarchical' levels, which establish communication between different subscribers;

(iii) terminals which allow access to the network.

The most well-known terminal is the simple voice telephone set.

Over recent years, all three elements have gone through an accelerating pace of technological innovation.

The major technological innovation has been the application of micro-electronics to transmission and switching. It has allowed the replacement of electrical signals in analogue form by transmission in the form of a stream of bits representing the information content — digitization.

Transmission

Ever since the invention of the telephone, networks have been constructed using analogue techniques, with an increasing range of active building blocks (amplifiers, frequency division multiplexers, etc.).

Transmission in digitized form offers a broad range of advantages: higher quality, easier handling in both multiplexing and switching, transmission of both voice and data in the same form.

Switching

The earliest automatic telephone exchanges (known as Strowger switches) employed rotary switches in order to establish connections physically between two subscriber lines.

The next major innovation in the development of the telephone exchange was the introduction of the 'cross-bar' exchange in which the cross-point itself was simplified to a single, non-moving pair of contacts, but each cross-bar matrix of contacts was provided with a logic controller constructed of electro-mechanical relays.

With the development of micro-electronics, the electromechanical control system was replaced by computer systems, known as stored program control (SPC). SPC switches are software controlled and have a broad range of advantages, extending from easy maintenance and reconfigurability to the addition and execution of a wide number of intelligent functions previously not possible, such as re-routeing of calls. The combination of SPC and digitization leads to fully digital exchanges where the physical cross-over matrix is replaced by a logical matrix which establishes the link between two subscribers by assigning particular time-slots to them ('time-division switching').

Digital exchanges now are huge computer installations, switching up to
100 000 lines and worth up to several tens of millions of ECUs. Major
public digital exchanges currently in use in Europe comprise amongst
others, the E10/12 and System 12 switches (Alcatel, France), the EWS-D
Switch (Siemens, Germany), the AXE switch (Ericsson), System X
(GEC/Plessey), and the ESS (ATT, Philips). The first time-division switching
systems in Europe were French.

Terminals

In addition to the conventional telephone and telex sets a broad range of
terminals has developed: sophisticated facsimile machines, teletex terminals, etc. Since the late 1970s data-processing installations, personal
computers and data terminals have been more and more connected to the
network: either via modems to the switched telephone network, or to the
emerging switched or private (leased line) specialized networks. Developments are moving towards the multi-functional computer-based terminal,
combining a broad range of intelligent functions to handle both voice and
data.

The main general impact of digitization has been due to the transmission of
information, both voice and data, in the form of bits which can be acted on
directly by the intelligence of computers, both inside the network as well as
in the subscriber terminal. This has led to a broad range of new functions
and activities which can be carried out both inside and outside the network.
It has opened the way towards the development of ISDN, the Integrated
Services Digital Network which will carry both voice and data, via one
single subscriber line.

The consequences have been three-fold:

(i)   first, the telecommunications networks themselves have been transformed into some
      of the biggest computer installations that presently exist. Given the transformation of
      the switching nodes of the telephone network into huge computer installations, the
      telephone network is transformed by digitization into a vast interconnected network
      of high-powered computers.

(ii) second, the telecommunications networks are becoming more and more software-
      based. Increased flexibility created by the change from hardware to software design
      leads to a multitude of new functions which can be carried out. This merger of
      telecommunications and computer functions is at the origin of the service explosion
      which the sector is currently experiencing.

(iii) third, the telecommunications network becomes the necessary complement of data-
      processing installations.

Data-processing installations are more and more hooked up via telecommunications links
into interconnected networks. Telecommunications networks add the dimension of
movement to the localized intelligence of traditional computer centres.

FIGURE 3

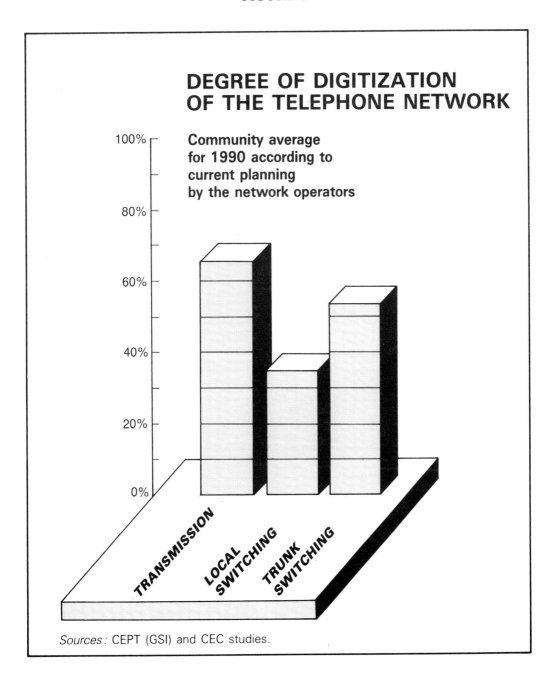

DEGREE OF DIGITIZATION
OF THE TELEPHONE NETWORK

**Community average
for 1990 according to
current planning
by the network operators**

Sources: CEPT (GSI) and CEC studies.

The combination of telecommunications and computer intelligence makes the telecommunications sector participate in the dynamics, efficiency increases and cost decreases of the computer sector. Average cost decreases of equipment in the computer sector have been 20 to 30% per annum. A micro-computer of today costs 50 times less than a mainframe computer in 1959, but is 100 times more powerful.

Telematics — the convergence of telecommunications and information technologies — is currently moving from the concept that it was at the end of the 1970s to becoming a tangible and dominant economic reality by the end of the 1980s.

Digitization of the telecommunications networks is proceeding rapidly in all Member States of the European Community. According to current plans, by 1990 in the European Community on average approximately 70% of transmission lines will be digitized, 50% of long-distance switching and 30% of local switching (Figure 3).

The Green Paper singles out as major consequences of this change in the technological base of telecommunications:

Growing 'intelligence' of network and terminals

First, the introduction of the digital network, controlled by sophisticated computers, has meant that many of the functions that were previously carried out inside the network (and thus could only be carried out by the controlling administration) can now be performed outside the network by the increasingly sophisticated terminal equipment.

Second, the range of services that can be offered by the switching systems is increasing. Telecommunications exchanges can now perform many additional functions in addition to switching simple calls.

The exchange can also store, process and retrieve information and can carry out electronic data-processing (EDP) functions.

Changes of network economics

The cost of technology has dropped dramatically in real terms over the last few years. Thus the cost of implementing a given function in hardware has fallen, or conversely, the level of sophistication available for a given unit cost has increased.

Major trends in telecommunications can be summarized as follows:

(i) the importance of the 'distance' cost factor has fallen compared with the 'usage time' or 'connection time' cost factors. Thus the cost of provision of long-distance communications has fallen much more than the cost of provision of local traffic;

FIGURE 4

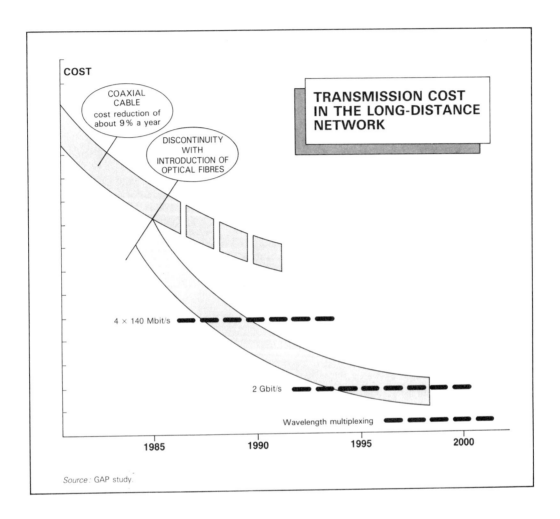

COST

COAXIAL CABLE
cost reduction of about 9% a year

DISCONTINUITY WITH INTRODUCTION OF OPTICAL FIBRES

TRANSMISSION COST IN THE LONG-DISTANCE NETWORK

4 × 140 Mbit/s

2 Gbit/s

Wavelength multiplexing

1985   1990   1995   2000

Source: GAP study.

(ii) the cost base of international, and in particular inter-continental traffic has fallen substantially in real terms;

(iii) the cost to the user of terminal equipment is declining, at the same time that the level of sophistication is increasing.

The cost of provision of long-distance communications has halved every seven years (Figure 4). The tariff structure has not followed this cost trend, leading to increasing imbalances in the network and increasing financial transfers.

Globally, financial transfers from long-distance telephone services can be approximately estimated to correspond to up to 25% of the overall telecommunications revenue of more than 60 000 million ECU in the Community, i.e. roughly 15 000 million ECU. As a result of this enormous transfer, the debate in Europe has inevitably focused more closely on this issue of long-distance tariffs.

Development of sophisticated terminals and PABXs

A single telephone or telex machine was a device with a very limited range of capabilities. Since the late 1970s, a range of sophisticated, more and more computer-based terminals have developed with high growth, providing a broad range of functions (Box 4).

Box 4

The broadening range of telecommunications terminals: new technical choices and opportunities for the telecommunications user

Telephone sets

By far the most widely used telecommunications terminal (EEC: over 170 million).

Trends: introduction of intelligence (microchips), cordless connection to the network and digitization at the standard bit rate of 64 Kbit/s will lead to greater ease of use, higher speech quality and integration of a large number of non-voice functions. Integration of images.

Telex/Teletex

Telex terminals are still the most widely used terminals for urgent business communications (EEC: about 650 000).

Trends: replacement of electromechanical equipment, integration with word-processing systems (personal computers) and the need for higher speed and sophisticated formats have led to the development of teletex for text transmission via digital networks. Interworking with telex is possible.

Facsimile

For telecopying of documents via the telephone network; high growth rates in all countries — EEC: about 250 000 in mid-1980s. In Germany alone nearly 200 000 new machines were sold in 1987 (up 150 % on 1986).

Trends: transition from Group III (1 minute per A4 page) to Group IV for higher speed and better quality. Future development to digital transmission (ISDN) at 64 Kbit/s (a few seconds per page, with colour option).

Modems

Equipment for the connection of data terminals to the telephone network; the most widely used method for present data communications.

Trends: development towards higher speeds (9.6 Kbit/s) and integration into the data terminal; future digital transmission (64 Kbit/s) will not require modems.

Data terminals

For sending, reception and processing of data.

Trends: because of its potential to be connected to the network by standardized interfaces any electronic data-processing system, in particular personal computers, could become a data terminal. Interconnection of customers' data terminals via 64 Kbit/s. ISDN links will create powerful data-processing systems with distributed intelligence.

Personal computers

Small, cheap but powerful electronic data-processing equipment for a large number of applications — EEC: about 4 million in mid-1980s. In 1987 alone, about 2.5 million new machines were sold in Europe, with sales growing at 30 % per annum.

Trends: very high growth rates. PCs will become the standard equipment of any white-collar work-place. A growing percentage of PCs will be connected to the telecommunications network. PCs are becoming the most widely used intelligent terminals in the Community.

Videotex terminals

Combination of a TV-type display and keyboard to access retrieval services and to allow data transmission via the telephone network.

Trends: services are established in various countries. The highest growth rates have been reached in France with the introduction of the Minitel terminal in homes (by end-1987: 3 million). Other European countries have concentrated on the business sector and introduced videotex business terminals, with sophisticated editing and presentation features, including colour display.

PABX

Private automatic branch exchanges for the interconnection of terminals at the customer's premises, providing access to the public networks; about 50% of business telephones are connected via PABXs.

Trends: digital multi-service PABXs with increasing intelligence and integration of network functions are developing; they will be connected to the future ISDN via a standardized interface (primary ISDN access; equivalent to 30 64-Kbit/s channels).

LAN

Local area networks, interlinking different types of text, data and video terminals (mainly personal computers) by high-capacity links on the customer's premises; specific structures (ring, bus) and interfaces.

Trends: large-scale introduction has just started. The future role of LANs relative to ISDN-PABXs will depend on the development of LAN gateways to the primary access of the ISDN.

Video terminals

For transmission and display of moving images via new communication services like videophony and videoconferencing.

Trends: conference studios (private or public) are being increasingly established in all European countries; future development of small integrated workstations with image capability (screens) for business use. Videophone terminals are expected to penetrate progressively into private households during the next decade.

Since the early 1980s, the number of facsimile machines in the Community has been doubling each year. Prices decline 20% per annum. In the Community a total of over 4 million personal computers had been sold by the mid-eighties, with 10% estimated to be connected to the telecommunications network and thus converted into multi-functional sophisticated terminals. In the United States 25% of personal computers are estimated to be connected to the telecommunications network. By the beginning of 1988 about 3 million videotex Minitel data terminals had been distributed in France, giving access to the French videotex service.

At the same time, sophisticated private automatic branch exchanges (PABXs) have been developed. The shipment of digital PABXs was begun in 1985. It has been estimated that for the period 1985-90 roughly a third of all PABX lines ordered in Europe will be digital.

By the end of this decade, nearly 80% of large PABXs (500 extensions and more), 65% of medium-sized PABXs and 20% of small PABXs are projected to be digital.

3. The emergence of integrated business communications systems: a new basis for the productivity of the economic system

With digitization, the PABX is increasingly developing into an office system centre — going far beyond its original telecommunications role of linking a number of telephone sets on the users' premises via a private switch to the telephone network.

Modern PABXs provide many features on top of basic telephony requirements; for example the PABX will usually have a number of additional telephony-based features (ring back when free, diversion on busy, etc.) as well as providing access to word processing, electronic mail distribution, and other forms of data communications. The PABX acts more and more as the hub of sophisticated user premises networks via which a broad range of external telecommunications services are accessed.

While the PABX is developing in this way into an office system, the local area networks (LANs) — developing originally from a computer environment and designed to link up computers on the users' premises — are extending into fully fledged local communications networks, more and more connected to the public network.

PABXs and LANs together form the core of the new type of intelligent private networks which are revolutionizing the communications basis of business activity. Together they constitute the key locus of the two tendencies which dominate the current development of the communications system:

(i) the convergence of telecommunications with data-processing functions;

(ii) the blurring of the distinction between (public) network functions and (private) premises equipment functions.

Both are key elements in the move towards integration of functions.

In the terminal equipment market the trend towards integration of functions will show up strongly before the end of this decade. It is estimated that the integrated office systems market will be worth more than USD 200 000 million annually world-wide, with at least 20% of this accounted for by the Community (Figure 5). Recent surveys amongst major industrial companies in Europe show correspondingly large growth expectations for non-voice (data, information and text) communications of 25 to 40%.

A new telematics market is developing which will substantially influence the future productivity of Europe's entire economic system.

The growth of the new market will depend on Europe's ability to manage the two major trends resulting from digitization and the convergence of data-processing and telecommunications functions:

(i) the full use of digitization as providing a general network infrastructure able to carry integrated applications — the Integrated Services Digital Network (ISDN);

(ii) the diversification potential for services offered by the computerization of telecommunications — value-added services.

FIGURE 5

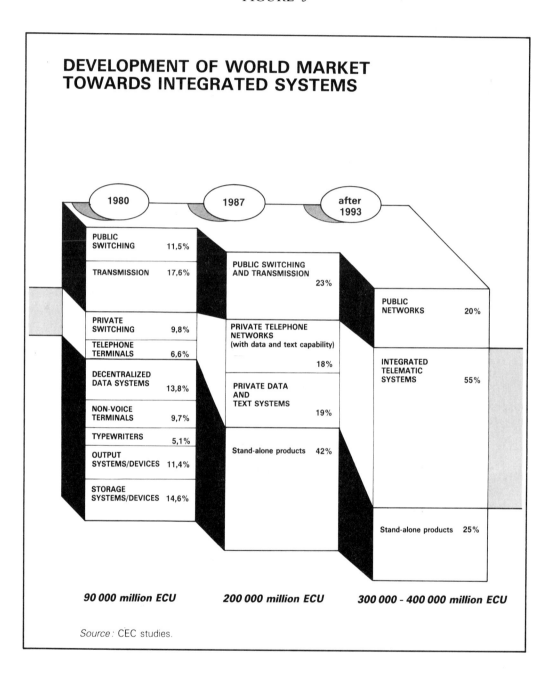

DEVELOPMENT OF WORLD MARKET
TOWARDS INTEGRATED SYSTEMS

1980 | 1987 | after 1993

PUBLIC SWITCHING 11,5%		
TRANSMISSION 17,6%	PUBLIC SWITCHING AND TRANSMISSION 23%	
		PUBLIC NETWORKS 20%
PRIVATE SWITCHING 9,8%	PRIVATE TELEPHONE NETWORKS (with data and text capability) 18%	
TELEPHONE TERMINALS 6,6%		INTEGRATED TELEMATIC SYSTEMS 55%
DECENTRALIZED DATA SYSTEMS 13,8%	PRIVATE DATA AND TEXT SYSTEMS 19%	
NON-VOICE TERMINALS 9,7%		
TYPEWRITERS 5,1%	Stand-alone products 42%	
OUTPUT SYSTEMS/DEVICES 11,4%		
STORAGE SYSTEMS/DEVICES 14,6%		Stand-alone products 25%

90 000 million ECU   **200 000 million ECU**   **300 000 – 400 000 million ECU**

Source: CEC studies.

4. ISDN — The Integrated Services Digital Network: an end-to-end digital infrastructure

The Integrated Services Digital Network is the natural consequence of digitization. It is a unique opportunity to operate Europe's network infrastructure to a new standard of quality, for both business and domestic users.

Digitization of the network was originally developed to allow efficient telephone operation. Current digitization mainly concerns digitization of the switching centres and the long-distance links between these centres. With limited additional investment in equipment at both ends of the subscriber line, the local link from the switching centre to the subscriber can be digitized.

The local links to the subscriber represent by far the largest capital item of the telecommunications network — the dug-in copper wires to the subscriber represent roughly one third of the asset value sunk in Europe's telecommunications network. Digitization of these existing lines by adding software and equipment — but without digging up streets and replacing wires — is estimated to cost 20 to 30% of investment additional to the ongoing digitization of switching and long-distance lines while doubling the transmission capacity of existing subscriber lines. The ISDN concept must therefore be seen, above all, as a unique opportunity to upgrade Europe's existing capital stock in telecommunications into a high-quality network infrastructure for multiple use for both voice and data (Box 5).

Box 5

The Integrated Services Digital Network (ISDN): putting the digital network infrastructure to full use

The general digitization of the telephone network offers the opportunity to use the existing telephone network infrastructure for a much broader range of services than up to now. The ISDN concept will support a wide range of services, all running on a single 'neutral' network.

The framework of the world-wide transition from the current telephone network and specialized data networks (telex, public switched data networks) has been worked out by the CCITT (the International Telephone and Telegraph Consultative Committee of the International Telecommunications Union) since the beginning of the 1980s.

The ISDN is defined by the CCITT as follows:

'The main feature of the ISDN concept is the support of a wide range of voice and non-voice applications in the same network. A key element of service integration for an ISDN is the provision of a range of services using a limited set of connection types and multi-purpose user network interface arrangements.

ISDN supports a variety of applications including both switched and non-switched connections. Switched connections in an ISDN include both circuit-switched and packet-switched connections and their combinations.'

A major boost for the ISDN concept was the discovery that it was possible — by adding software and electronic equipment — to convert existing local copper wiring to digital operation and to deliver digital services according to ISDN standards via existing cables. This meant that — together with the on-going digitization of switches and transmission — the existing telephone network could be transformed into an end-to-end (subscriber to subscriber) full-scale digital network infrastructure at incremental costs of 20 to 30 % of total investment.

ISDN offers a wide range of advantages for the support of the future telematics market:

(i)   a multitude of services via a single subscriber access;

(ii) simultaneous operation of two channels (equivalent to two telephone lines) via one 'basic access' (standard ISDN subscriber line); connection of up to eight terminals or telephone sets;

(iii) easy connection of digital PABXs via the ISDN 'primary access' facility at 2 Mbit/s (equivalent to 30 simultaneous channels).

ISDN will deliver the existing telephone service with a new quality and give access to a broad range of new services.

According to Recommendation 86/659/EEC [1] ISDN in Europe will offer:

(i)   digital telephony (high-quality 64 Kbit/s transmission) with a broad range of new functions for the user, notably:

    (a) call waiting: indicates to an engaged subscriber that a new calling subscriber is trying to reach him or her,

    (b) calling line identification: gives the number of the caller,

    (c) advice of charge: indicates to the user the call charge,

    (d) call diversion: possibility for a subscriber to be called on a line other than his or her own,

    (e) completion of call meeting busy: when the called subscriber is busy, the call is re-established as soon as this subscriber becomes free,

    (f) malicious call identification: facility to record the calling number of a call;

(ii) high-speed data communication at 64 Kbit/s, with special attention given to the connection of personal computers;

---

[1] See Chapter VI, Section 2.

(iii) a range of other advanced services: facsimile at 64 Kbit/s (transmission of one A4 page in a few seconds, 20 times more rapid than any currently available fax machine); teletex at 64 Kbit/s (100 times the speed of current telex); alpha-geometric and alpha-photographic (picture-quality) videotex at 64 Kbit/s (nearly instantaneous filling of screen, 30 times the speed of current videotex).

ISDN implementation in Europe is now fully under way. The Community aims at progressive implantation of ISDN from 1988 onwards, in line with current planning in the Member States. By the end of 1992, the conversion of roughly 5 million subscriber lines to ISDN should be achieved, corresponding to roughly 5% of the 118 million subscriber lines in the Community (out of which roughly a fourth are used for business purposes). 80% of subscribers should be within reach of an ISDN-capable exchange by the end of 1992.

Currently all telecommunications administrations in Europe are investing heavily in digitization of the telephone network to operate what represents the major part of their business in a future-oriented economic way. At the same time, they are faced with a confusing and growing number of special purpose networks (telex, public data communications networks, etc.), the economical operation of which seems uncertain. ISDN, with its basic user access, allowing the simultaneous use of a (high-quality) voice and data channel via the existing telephone copper wire, offers the opportunity of putting the operation of the whole network structure on a sound future-proof economic basis, for a limited additional cost.

ISDN coincides with the widespread economic needs of the most dynamic section of the user population — business communications. There is a clearly expressed and growing requirement for telecommunications networks which offer reliable and sophisticated support for integrated business communications systems.

It is estimated that by the early 1990s this market will reach the same order of magnitude as the conventional telecommunications market.

While ISDN will become an important instrument for the competitiveness of Europe's business sector, ISDN is also the first comprehensive — and under current conditions the only economically possible — attempt to bring the advantages of modern telecommunications systems not only to the business sector, but also to the much larger number of private subscribers.

The current network structure in the Community brings data services to less than 1% of the subscriber population, aimed nearly exclusively at the business sector with the exception of the recent distribution of Minitels in France (Table 6). Carrying data and high-quality services on the telephone network extending now in the Community to over 115 million subscribers and 170 million telephone sets, is the only way to allow Europe's citizens the opportunity in the future to use the new functions and services.

TABLE 6

**Current availability of data communications compared
to future projected ISDN availability**

Country	Public telephone network (main lines)	Telex	Number of private leased circuits	Number of data terminals connected to public data networks	ISDN penetration (1993) [1]
Belgium	3 257 000	28 000	93 600 [3]	1 000	140 000
Denmark	2 683 000	13 000	14 900 [2]	10 800	125 000
France	23 911 000	134 000	116 000 [2, 3]	166 200 [6]	1 100 000
FR of Germany	26 399 000	165 000	4 600 [3]	146 400 [3]	1 250 000
Greece	3 292 000	22 000	2 600	NA	170 000
Ireland	751 000	7 000	4 800	700	30 000
Italy	18 253 000	69 000	53 700 [2]	157 300	825 000
Luxembourg	162 000	2 000	400 [4]	200 [4]	7 000
Netherlands	6 029 000	40 000	11 200	NA	280 000
Portugal	1 512 000	21 000	5 600	500	60 000
Spain	9 801 000	40 000	44 600	32 600	420 000
United Kingdom	21 654 000	105 000	115 000 [5]	NA	1 000 000
EEC	117 703 000	646 000	NA [3]	NA [3]	5 407 000

Source: International Telecommunications Union *Yearbook of common carrier statistics* (1988) and CEC studies. Reference year: 1986.

[1] 5% of 1983 subscriber main lines (GAP report on ISDN).
[2] 1983.
[3] Leased circuit and data terminal statistics can vary significantly between different countries and periods according to the definitions employed.
[4] 1985.
[5] 1982.
[6] Excluding Minitels.
NA: not available.

According to the GAP report [1] on the coordinated introduction of the Integrated Services Digital Network in the Community [2] the ISDN is considered to be a natural evolution of the existing telephone network.

'Although the initial subscribers will be professionals — large and small — the ISDN should also be aimed at the residential population. Thus it should not be a network dedicated to a closed subscriber population.'

All Member States of the European Community are now actively engaged in implementation plans for ISDN. With Council Recommendation 86/659/EEC, the European Community has made the coordinated introduction of ISDN a fundamental objective. [3]

Traditionally in Europe, the development of telecommunications services has been supply-constrained. For telephone services, this has led to long waiting lists in the past, particularly in some Member States.

---

[1] Analysis and Forecasting Group of the CEC; see Chapter V, Section 5.
[2] Proposal for a Council Recommendation, COM(86) 205, 20 May 1986.
[3] See Chapter VI.

Since the 1970s, a major supply constraint has developed for the emerging new data services, due to the lag in most countries in the introduction of networks and the slow and insufficient availability of dedicated private lines leased for data transmission from the telecommunications administrations.

The introduction of ISDN can be seen as a comprehensive policy to give, for the first time, in Europe to the user — in particular to the small business user and the private household — a free choice to opt for access to the new services — without being subject to a supply constraint. ISDN will be able to fulfil this role if it evolves into an open network infrastructure for Europe on which the provision of services, according to user choice and demand, can develop.

The test case for this will be the provision of value-added services.

5. VAS — value-added services: adding value to suit users' needs

The convergence of telecommunications and data processing has made possible a new dimension of service diversification. Computer-handling of information — in computerized switches inside the network or by the computerized terminals connected to the network at the subscriber's site — allows for the first time in communications history the tailoring and packaging of information closely tuned to user needs. Value-added services imply 'intelligent delivery of information to the subscriber'. (Box 6).

Box 6

Value-added services — survey of functions

I — Enhancement of telecommunications functions

Protocol conversion, code conversion, format conversion, speed conversion

Error protection

Encryption, scrambling

Adaptation to quality requirements

Telex and teletex 'forwarding agencies'

II — Provision of computer capacity and information

Trade and industry information, 'yellow pages'

Product information

News, sports information, weather forecasts etc.

Directories

Time-sharing access to computer capacity

Software support

III — Transactional functions

Message storing and forwarding:

Mailbox systems and message handling

Automatic answering and recording facilities

Financial transactions, telebanking

Authorization of payments (smart cards)

Ordering of goods and services, teleshopping

Reservation of tickets, hotels, flights, cars etc.

Trade electronic data interchange

IV — Teleworking, security and control

Teletranslation

Telesoftware

Teledictation

Medical consultation

Tax consultation

Expert reports

Bookkeeping

CAD/CAM assistance

Training and education

Surveillance, alarm, registration

Telemetry, telediagnosis

Telecontrol, teleprocessing

Value-added services — leaving aside the definitional problem — represent the higher end of the new conglomerate of telecommunications and computer services. The precise communications component may vary widely — and is often difficult to determine — from 15% for information-based systems up to 90% for telex-forwarding agencies.

At present, the revenues attributable to value-added services are still a minute proportion of the total 64 800 million ECU derived in the Community from telecommunications services in 1986. According to estimates — depending on the definitions used — they amounted in 1986 to 800 to 900 million ECU in Europe — slightly more than 1% of total telecommunications services revenues — compared to voice telephony which accounted for 85 to 90% of income from telecommunications services.

But the emerging value-added services market is disproportionately important. Value-added services will be essential for the future functioning of European businesses.

They are projected in Europe to grow at 25 to 30% annually. According to the Green Paper, 'two facts stand out regarding these developing telecommunications markets: they are an essential part of the emerging information-based service economy; and they are specialized, innovative, and therefore very different from the centrally provided telecommunications of the past'.

Non-voice 'value-added/enhanced services' presently designated as such in Europe include services such as EDP time-sharing and database services, videotex services, ticket reservation, automatic bank tellers and other financial services, other retail services including teleshopping, electronic data interchange within industries for ordering, supply, etc., mailbox services, word-processing/facsimile/telex, interfacing/protocol conversion, telemetry and telecontrol services, etc. In addition to non-voice value-added services, new specialized telephony-like services such as conference calls, deferred transmission, and telephone message services, are emerging.

Within this plethora of services which value-added services incorporate, three lines of development currently stand out.

Information-related services

Information-related services, the high-value part of the new market, are closely related to the current information and communications needs of the business sector, with 85% of total value-added services revenues projected by 1990 to relate to credit/financial/economic and marketing information and to financial transactions. The rapid movements on the stock market in autumn 1987 have demonstrated the extent to which the financial sector now depends on telecommunications as a major competitive element. Reuters Holding — the best known European example — moves up to 100 000 million ECU via its service on a single day.

Videotex-based services

While videotex-based services are currently targeted in most European countries mainly at the business users, the success of the French Minitel strategy aimed at the public at large has demonstrated that value-added services are not limited by nature to serving the business sector (Box 7).

Box 7

The French Minitel — demonstrating demand and acceptance of information-based telecommunications services by the public at large

Since 1985, the French telecommunications administration — now called France Télécom — has installed three million Minitel videotex terminals in French homes. A Minitel terminal is a simple specialized terminal equipped with screen and keyboard. This has been more successful than anyone dared imagine. Figures only tell half the story: more than 4 000 services — offered by private service providers — accessible at the end of 1987, and about 10 000 jobs created. The other half of the story is that French videotex — the Télétel service — has become a part of everyday life for millions of people in France, and is starting to transform the citizen's ability to obtain information and to communicate.

Three key factors underlie this rapid growth of Minitel:

(i)   The French administration chose an easy-to-use version of videotex, allowing cheap terminal production. This permitted the distribution of a large number of terminals free of charge in place of the paper telephone directory. At the same time, on-line access via the Minitel screen and keyboard to the electronic directory which replaced the paper directory made millions of users acquainted with handling an electronic base of immediate use for them.

(ii) With this active introduction of electronic access and the wide availability of terminals, France Télécom created a large market for potential service providers. A very liberal policy, allowing other service providers to offer services via the videotex system (Télétel) quickly created a booming service environment.

(iii) Access to services was made simple for non-specialists. The Minitel itself was designed for ease of use; the 'Kiosque' system of payment, under which France Télécom passes payment on to service providers, made payment possible without any paperwork or special arrangements.

The following illustrates the range of services available by Minitel:

- Information-based services:

  General information:

  (i) electronic telephone directory;

  (ii) telematic newspapers/journals;

  (iii) general interest information;

  (iv) specialized interests (e.g. law, history, engineering);

  (v) data bases (e.g. catalogues, train/air timetables, exchange rates).

  Personal information:

  (i) state of bank account;

  (ii) position of orders passed to suppliers.

- Transaction services:

  Transactions:

  (i) home shopping;

  (ii) home banking;

  (iii) booking tickets (airline, theatre, etc.);

  (iv) games.

  Communications:

  electronic mail, used for a broad range of private communications.

  Computing:

  (i) access to specialized software;

  (ii) processing data in remote data bases.

The French videotex introduction strategy has proved that:

(i) the public is ready to accept and to demand telematics services if they are given a free hand in choosing services according to their preferences;

(ii) in order to adjust to user demand, a very flexible liberal service environment is needed. For example, quite unexpectedly, the Minitel service has seen a very rapid use of transactional services.

The Minitel approach in France is an example of the combination of a very active introduction policy by a strong network operator combined with a very liberal policy regarding use and offering of services via the network.

As a result, French videotex has taken a world lead, accounting at present for more than half of the installed videotex terminals in the world.

For the first time it was shown that private households demand and accept information-based services — if services are allowed to develop freely and to adapt to user needs, via the efficient working of the market. By the end of 1987, there were over 3 million terminals and 4 000 private Télétel services in France.

Trade electronic data interchange

Transactions now require the exchange of a vast volume of data between business partners and a high proportion of this is international.

Often the data exchange is more time consuming than the actual manufacture or delivery of the traded goods or provision of the traded services. Currently data exchange is carried out on paper and through a multiplicity of incompatible computer systems.

Standardized electronic data interchange (EDI) has therefore developed as one of the most promising lines of value-added services, based on cooperative ventures mainly established by industry associations (Box 8).

Box 8

Trade electronic data interchange: cutting down paperwork in the future information-based economy

In international trade, the costs related to paperwork are estimated to lie between 4% and 15% of the value of the merchandise. The financial repercussions of any reduction in paperwork are therefore enormous. In one example, a large company sends out 2 900 000 invoices per year. The cost of processing an invoice manually is estimated at 9.60 ECU. If electronic processing of the invoicing reduces the costs of the paperwork by 25%, this represents an estimated annual gain of 7 million ECU.

Electronic data interchange (EDI) is the solution to the problem of the paper mountain.

Electronic data interchange, or the electronic transfer of commercial and administrative data, involves the exchange of information and messages between trading partners or public administrators via electronic means of communications. To be able to communicate, the computers involved have to be taught a kind of electronic Esperanto.

EDI is carried out either from computer to computer, through the exchange of magnetic media (tapes, diskettes), or via switched telephone networks or leased lines.

These new possibilities for the transfer of commercial documents have a range of advantages: increased efficiency, reduced costs, improved competitiveness.

Comparison of transmission times and costs in Europe of a commercial document, depending on the method employed:

Letter	1 to 2 days	0.3 ECU
Telex	5 minutes	0.6 ECU
Computer to computer	13 seconds	0.01-0.1 ECU

It is imperative that international standards are used. Proper connections between all trading partners can only be achieved if everyone respects ISO standards, the European standards of the CEN and the recommendations of the United Nations with regard to international trade procedures.

Uniform treatment is also essential to avoid the formation of closed electronic networks and assure the possibility of communication between the various sectoral networks now in the development stage. All industries (automobile manufacturers, the chemical industries, electronics, etc.) must be able to exchange trade messages with freighters, suppliers, wholesalers, forwarding agents, distributors, customs, etc., not forgetting the insurance companies and the banks.

The transfer of trade messages must be effected without technical or procedural problems of any sort whatsoever along the entire length of the chain of trading partners.

The Commission of the European Communities has therefore drawn up a Community action programme — the TEDIS programme — to promote the electronic transfer of trade data. [1]

---

[1] See Chapter VI, Section 2.

Europe will have to act rapidly to enter the value-added services field. The potential will be enormous.

Interbank data transactions for example are provided on a world scale by Swift, now carrying 750 000 messages daily between 1 500 banks located in 64 countries. The airline information system SITA now covers 184 companies located in 90 countries and links data terminals in more than 1 000 cities around the world.

The data processing value-added services multinational EDS has a total annual turnover of USD 4 500 million, exceeding the turnover of most smaller European telecommunications administrations (Box 9).

Box 9

Major value-added services providers — examples

Reuters

The British firm Reuters is a good illustration of the ability of Europeans to establish themselves in the world value-added services market.

Reuters is a British group specializing in financial information services. Its activities in Europe and throughout the world have grown rapidly over the past few years.

In 1987 its turnover reached 1 200 million ECU, with profits standing at 254 million ECU; 60% of its sales are within Europe.

By the end of 1987 about 141 000 video terminals giving access to the Reuters information system had been installed throughout the world. The 'Equity 2000' service, which came on stream recently, offers on-line information on the prices of more than 100 000 shares, futures and raw materials.

SWIFT

In the early 1970s, a group of major European banks got together to study how to improve the functioning of international financial transactions. As a result, SWIFT was established in 1973 after American banks joined in. It is set up as a joint venture of all the world-wide banks which use the service. The headquarters are located in Brussels.

The first transactions took place in 1977, when 240 banks in 15 countries were members. By 1985, 1 275 banks in 46 countries had joined. The number of transactions has grown from about 55 000 in 1977 to 192 million in 1985. 1986 revenues were about 135 million ECU, about 20% up on 1985.

The main categories of SWIFT communications are customer transfers (30% of total volume), bank transfers (30%), statements and confirmations (25%).

The potential of the technology was perceived early. Electronic transactions are orders of magnitude less expensive to conduct than paper transactions.

To make a reality of international transactions, banks had to agree to a set of standards. The standards developed by SWIFT have now been sanctioned by international standards organizations, such as the ISO.

The service provided by SWIFT is extremely secure, in terms of both privacy and reliability. SWIFT developed their own encryption program, which is not known to have been broken to this day. SWIFT are sufficiently confident of their own system to accept liability for all losses through cheating, errors in their system, or interest losses due to delays in their system.

A further complicated problem that SWIFT had to solve was that of obtaining international telecommunications links. They needed to use leased lines, because their encryption technique were not compatible with use of packet-switched networks.

SWIFT therefore had to negotiate *ad hoc* agreements with the telecommunications administrations in each country where they operate, since there existed no regulatory framework for the provision of trans-border value-added services. This clearly led to delays and uncertainty about the conditions for the provision of services.

EDS

EDS (Electronic Data Systems) was set up in the United States in 1962 as a computing company. By 1984, EDS had also turned to offering value-added services, additional to its computing activities. Its turnover had reached USD 1 000 million and the workforce 14 000. In that year it was bought by General Motors, and took over responsibility for all GM electronic data processing (EDP). As a result its turnover and workforce rose to USD 4 500 million and 45 000 respectively.

EDS offers the service of managing all or part of other organizations' electronic data processing including telecommunications requirements and networking. Its most complete service is to take on all the customers' EDP requirements, a service known as 'facilities management'.

Major customers of EDS include:

(i)   Medicare and Medicaid in 16 US states;

(ii)   1 600 banks and 4 000 credit institutions in the USA;

(iii) AT & T and Western Union for some of their EDP;

(iv) several Bell operating companies, whose billing systems are run by EDS.

EDS is now also active in Europe offering a number of communications-related services.

In Europe, further major providers of services are DATEV, Germany, specializing in tax and accounting information; CCMC and GSI, France, providing a broad range of information and transactional services; GEIS, a subsidiary of US General Electric; and, of course, IBM.

After having penetrated the financial sector, value-added services will now increasingly enter the services related to the industrial sectors of the economy.

At this stage, with the exception of Reuters, which has obtained a major position in the supply of on-line financial information in Europe's and the world's financial markets, none of the main international European providers have so far become a major force on the world market — largely due to the regulatory restrictions prevailing for value-added services in Europe to this date.

For Europe to develop a strategy in this field, it will be important to fully understand the nature of this new business.

It is true that most value-added services have developed up to now on the basis of private networks constructed with lines leased from the telecommunications administrations.

This led to the original designation as VANS — value-added network services.

However, the main economic future for value-added services providers is the tailoring of the service package — by combining computer intelligence and telecommunications — provided via a suitable telecommunications network infrastructure.

In most cases, only 15% of the total cost of value-added services is accounted for by the communications network component.

VANS are in the service business. Most providers have constructed their own networks only because of the insufficient functions offered by the telephone network, or the specialised data networks of the time, because of their insufficient quality and tariff structures not adjusted to the needs of service providers.

The current lifting of the functional limitations through the digitization of the general network infrastructure — with its later enhancement by the ISDN — must therefore be seen not as a different development line but as the future basis of value-added services. The main consequence of digitization is that the future digital telecommunications network infrastructure will be more and more able to carry a broad range of services independent of the network operator and provided by operators outside the network. Increased functionality of the network will also allow the telecommunications administrations to offer value-added services and enter a broad range of new service activities.

This effect will be substantially amplified by the lifting of a second limitation: the limitations of transmission speed and capacity.

6. Fibre optics: lifting the limitations of speed and capacity

The amount of information which can be transmitted via a given 'carrier' depends on the ratio of the frequency of the signal relative to the frequency of the carrier. The conventional telephone voice channel works with a 'bandwidth' of 3.1 kHz. Microwave transmission systems work at 1 million times this frequency. Infra-red light has a frequency 100 000 million times greater than the conventional voice channel.

The discovery in the 1970s that infra-red light propagating within glass-fibres could be used economically — with attenuation and dispersion, i.e. signal deterioration, held within reasonable limits — was the second major step towards the information age, besides the introduction of the microprocessor into communications and computing.

Since then, telecommunications have started to move gradually but irreversibly from the copper age to the glass-fibre age — from the technology of electrical signals to the technology of light, opto-electronics (Box 10).

Box 10

Survey of transmission technologies: copper wire, coaxial cable, microwave, optical fibre

A cable can be thought of as a channel down which information can be sent. And channels vary according to the maximum amount of information that can be sent down them in a given period of time. For example, it may take 3 minutes to send an A4 page down one channel, but only one second down another channel. The first channel is said to have low or narrow bandwidth, and the second high or broad bandwidth. The bandwidth of a channel can be measured in terms of the number of bits of information that can be squeezed down it in one second — bits per second — or more often, the number of thousands of bits per second (Kbit/s), million bits per second (Mbit/s), or even thousand million bits per second (Gbit/s) that it can accommodate.

Since the beginning of telephony and until the early 1970s, modes of transmission were confined to pair cable (the copper wire running down from the local exchange to the subscriber), coaxial cable (concentric cables within which electro-magnetic waves propagate), and various methods of radio relay at microwave frequencies which transmit information via open-air targeted beams between remote antennas. Enhancement of these technologies has been continuous, leading to successively higher carrier frequencies, channel capacity and quality and reliability of transmission.

The major improvement was brought about through the introduction of transmission in digitized form via these media, by adding electronic equipment on both ends — PCM or pulse-code modulation. In ISDN, the local copper-pair cable will be used for digital transmission at a speed of 144 Kbit/s (two voice-grade channels of 64 Kbit/s plus 16 Kbit/s control channel).

A new quantitative step was taken with the introduction of light as a carrier propagating within optical wave guides, optical fibres. With its substantially higher carrier frequency, normally in the infra-red range, light offers a substantially higher channel bandwidth and can carry almost unlimited amounts of information.

An optical fibre consists of:

(i) a core made of either glass or plastic, of a diameter of a fraction of a millimetre, i.e. the thickness of a human hair, within which the light propagates. The light is contained within the core by continuous total reflection while propagating;

(ii) a cladding which surrounds the core, in order to reduce scattering losses;

(iii) a buffer coating for protection against physical damage, of a few millimetres' thickness.

The total transmission system consists of the fibre and light-emitting diodes and light-receiving detectors at both ends, which convert electronic signals into light pulses for transmission or light pulses into electronic signals for further amplification or use. The transmission capacity is determined by the capacity of the total electro-optical system.

The first generation optical-fibre systems had bit rates up to 140 Mbit/s and needed reamplification of the signal — repeaters — every 10 kilometres. The more modern so-called 'monomode' systems can carry 565 Mbit/s, equivalent to 8 000 simultaneous telephone conversations, via a single fibre pair, with repeater spaces of 30 kilometres or more. Conventional coaxial cables could only carry a few hundred voice channels with repeaters every few kilometres.

Research efforts are concentrating on the materials used for fibre and coating, the performance of sources and light detectors and optical switching and amplification which would make conversion into electronic signals for amplification and switching unnecessary. For the early 1990s single mode fibre systems with a transmission speed of 2.5 Gbit/s are expected, with repeater spacing as high as 100 kilometres. Embryonic heavy-metal fluoride fibre-optic cables promise very low loss and repeater spacing of 6 000 kilometres sometime later.

Prices of optical fibres have been decreasing rapidly in recent years — from 3 ECU/metre in 1977 to 0.3 ECU in 1988. Overall, over the last few years the total cost of transmission has been at least halving every 10 years.

Since the mid-1980s optical-fibre systems have been introduced extensively world-wide into the long-distance part of the network and into transnational links. The first transatlantic submarine optical fibre cable (TAT-8) will be completed in 1988 and will be able to carry 40 000 telephone calls simultaneously, compared to the capacity of current coaxial cables of 4 000 channels. The first transatlantic coaxial cable put into operation in 1956 (TAT-1) had a capacity of 36 telephone channels.

For the end of the decade, a number of additional submarine optical-fibre systems are planned in both the Atlantic and the Pacific. They will pose a serious competitive challenge for international satellite communications — the Intelsat system which currently carries more than two-thirds of transatlantic telephone calls.

In the local loop, it is expected that optical fibre will be gradually installed as replacement for the twisted pair copper cable on a large scale in the not too distant future, with a cost cross-over point expected for the early 1990s. While the quantum leap in bandwidth which optical fibre brings to the transmission system will lead to important cost savings in the operation of conventional (narrowband) services, such as voice telephony, their major impact is that they will allow for the first time the economic operation of broadband services such as video communications — the transmission of moving pictures — which, depending on the data conversion methods used, have bandwidth requirements of the equivalent of several hundred voice channels.

In Europe, France tried to take an early lead in the field with its 'plan câble' of the early 1980s, aimed at accelerated introduction of optical fibre into cable TV networks, at a time when the technology was still at an early stage of development and costs were high.

The market for opto-electronics will be a key element of the future information market. While about two thirds of fibre-optic systems are applied to the public telecommunications network, the applications to customer premises networks, in particular LANs, will rapidly grow in importance.

Europe's position in this key market segment is promoted by the RACE programme, within its general drive towards Integrated Broadband Communications.

This has great implications for the kinds of telecommunications services which can be expected in the future; and almost all of these implications derive from the greater bandwidth of glass-fibre or fibre-optic cable. The real interest of the higher bandwidth cable is that it will allow the introduction of a whole new range of services as fibre-optic cable starts to reach into the office and the home.

The introduction of high bandwidth capability into the network will for the first time make videocommunications via the general switched telecommunications network a technologically viable option. The transmission of high-quality pictures requires in general 'broadband' transmission above 2 Mbit/s.

At the moment fibre-optic cable is starting to be widely used in the trunk (long-distance) part of the telecommunications network with subscribers still being connected by copper wire. This 'last kilometre' connecting subscribers to the network accounts for a very high proportion of the total investment of the telecommunications network — of the order of 30% — and will take, starting from the early 1990s, a substantial period of time to upgrade.

FIGURE 6

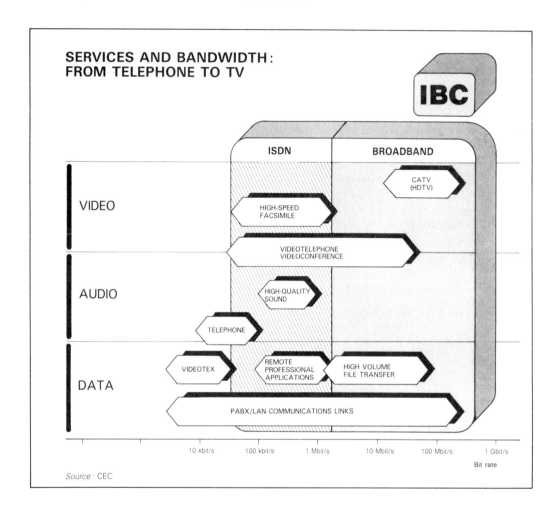

The introduction of computer intelligence into the telecommunications network and the terminals has brought about telematics — the convergence of telecommunications and data processing. The introduction of fibre-optic cable will bring about a further convergence between telematics and the audio-visual sector — TV broadcasting (Figure 6).

Traditionally, telecommunications has meant two-way narrow-band communications — voice grade bandwidth — while TV broadcasting has meant one-way broadband communications — either via open air requiring very broad frequency bands, thus limiting substantially the number of channels available, or via cable TV or master antenna systems based on coaxial cable which can distribute one-way broadband communications (up to 20 or 30 TV programmes) but only over short distances.

The trend in both sectors is now towards two-way broadband communications: fibre-optic cable is beginning to put broadband telecommunications channels into the office and home, while modern cable TV systems will increasingly allow two-way communications, the transmission of messages (e.g. requests for particular programmes) from the subscriber/viewer to the transmitter. The two technologies will clearly merge in the early 1990s.

The extension of the general telecommunications network into a general purpose network able to carry both narrowband and broadband services will bring the widespread introduction of new categories of service: videoconferencing and videophones. It will allow TV distribution via the telecommunications network and call forth new ways of operating by both telecommunications administrations and cable TV operators. TV distribution will be combined more and more with selection and retrieval options. Large flat panel displays will enhance long-distance videoconferences. Computer-aided design techniques will benefit from the presentation of high-resolution images. High-speed data transmission of 2 Mbit/s and more will allow the electronic transmission of bulky documents and of colour images.

Thus a whole new generation of new broadband services will enter Europe's offices and homes during the 1990s. Videoconferencing is already taking off on a large scale in the United States, with annual growth rates of more than 15%.

For the new services to reach their full potential will take well into the next century. GAP, the Group for Analysis and Forecasting, has estimated the eventual potential for videoconferencing at 1 in 10 000 to 1 in 1 000 of total telephones, i.e. some 10 000 to 100 000 videoconferencing participants in the Community. Videoconferencing involves two or more specially equipped studios being linked up in sound and vision, typically to allow a business meeting to take place without the need for travel. The potential for videomeetings was estimated at 1 in 100 to 1 in 10 of telephones, i.e. some 1 million to 10 million subscribers. Videomeetings will involve desktop videophones — with both voice facility and image on the screen, without the additional high-quality features involved in specially equipped studios. The eventual take-up of videophones in households is forecast at 1 in 10 to 1 in 4 of present telephone penetration, i.e. 10 to 25 million videophones for the whole of the Community.

The broadband capability which will become available in the general telecommunications network will thus draw together the two main strands of communications which have hitherto developed separately, two-way narrowband telephone and data and one-way broadband television. The Community's RACE programme aims at providing a framework for this integration process in the 1990s. [1]

The emergence of satellite technology has added two other dimensions: the dimension of flexibility and the international dimension.

---

[1] See Chapter VI, Section 4.

7. Satellites: lifting the limitations of location

Since 1965, when the first geosynchronous communication satellite 'Early Bird' relayed telephone calls and television across the Atlantic for the first time on a commercial basis, satellite communications have seen dramatic advances (Box 11).

Box 11

Satellite communications: the telecommunications system in Europe's sky

Since the first geosynchronous communications satellite 'Early Bird' relayed across the Atlantic 300 voice circuits, or one television channel, between four European countries and the United States, commercial satellite communications have gained a quarter of a century of experience.

The international satellite organization Intelsat now carries two-thirds of intercontinental telephone calls. The new generation Intelsat VI satellites can carry a capacity equivalent to 80 000 voice channels.

The peaceful use of space — for telecommunications, earth resources exploration, navigational aid, weather information, scientific research and experiments — has developed rapidly. Already 110 countries are members of Intelsat, 26 European nations are members of Eutelsat and 48 countries support the Inmarsat global maritime satellite organization.

Hundreds of large Intelsat antennas, thousands of medium-sized earth stations and hundreds of thousands of small low-cost satellite receiving dishes are already spread around the world, relaying different services beamed down by 40 or more commercial satellites.

In Europe, the Eutelsat organization operates the main satellite system — the European communications satellites. Additionally, a number of national and private systems will enter operation over the next few years. The French Telecom 1 telecommunications satellite has been operating since 1984.

The leading role in developing advanced satellite technology and applications in Europe is played by the European Space Agency (ESA).

Communications satellites emit and receive in the 6/4 Ghz and 14/12 Ghz frequency bands. They are placed in orbit at 36 000 km altitude, where they circle the globe at the speed of the earth's rotation and therefore stay fixed with regard to terrestrial location ('geosynchronous orbit'). In order to avoid interference between different satellite beams, the available space-slots have been strictly regulated on a world level by the International Telecommunications Union (ITU).

From the beginning of the satellite communications era, satellites have been used to transmit both point-to-point telecommunications — narrowband voice telephony and broadband television programme transport, Intelsat's main business lines in transatlantic traffic up to now — as well as to broadcast television programmes point-to-multipoint to headends of cable TV networks which distribute the programmes to the final user. The Eutelsat satellite system in Europe is currently being used mainly for broadcasting purposes — distribution of programmes such as Super Channel, Sky Channel, 3SAT, etc. The fifth French channel is now distributed by Telecom 1C, launched in March 1988.

Satellite communication systems may be divided into three distinct elements, namely:

(i)   the uplink, the beaming up of information to the satellite, from a high-powered earth station. This is always considered a fixed point-to-point service;

(ii) the space segment, the transponders on the satellite which re-transmit the information back to earth.

      For 1990 the total available space segment measured by the number of transponders equivalent to 36 MHz transmission capacity is forecast to be 750 for the Intelsat system, more than 1 000 for North American systems, 200 for European systems and more than 400 for the rest of the world. In 1984, the total transponder capacity in Europe was 30 transponders;

(iii) the downlink, which is specified in terms of services, such as a fixed (point-to-point telecommunications) service, a broadcasting (point-to-multipoint TV distribution) service, a mobile service, which beams down to moving receiving stations, such as trucks with roof-top antenna dishes.

In all three areas, there have been substantial developments in satellite technology and performance over recent years, in particular the introduction of digital techniques both to transmission and to processing. Satellites themselves now have more power available for on-board transmission, have increasingly lengthened life times (now up to 10 years), and have increased substantially the efficiency of use of the limited radio spectrum.

The increasing frequency band and higher amplifier power have permitted the use of smaller receiving antennas.

The recent trend has been towards the development of very small satellite antennas (VSATs or 'micro-terminals'). VSATs for receive-only purposes now have dish-sizes of 0.6 metres in diameter; for low data-rate receive/transmit 1.2-1.8 metres, costing less than 5 000 ECU. This compares with diameters of 30 metres for the conventional earth stations integrated in the Intelsat system.

The immediate future of satellite communications will be characterized mainly by two technology trends. Firstly, the entry into service of very high powered satellites suited for directly beaming down television programmes to be received by television receive-only satellite dishes of no more than 35 cm, which can be placed directly on the rooftop of the final subscriber. The first of these high-powered DBS (direct broadcasting satellites) to enter service are to be the French TDF1, the German TV-SAT2, and the UK's BSB satellite.

The second technological trend is the growth of a grey area between the roles of broadcasting and fixed transmission satellites. This area includes aspects such as fixed satellite services providing a point-to-multipoint service — such as the distribution of news data by satellite to a number of news agencies throughout Europe — based on VSAT antennas and looking very much like a broadcast service. Quite generally, there is a growing potential for point-to-multipoint applications linked to the emergence of VSAT earth stations.

Uplink, space segment and downlink are strictly regulated in Europe. The space segment is governed by the virtually exclusive rights of Intelsat and Eutelsat to provide space segment capacity. Uplinks and downlinks are generally under exclusive provision of the telecommunications administrations, with a perceptible trend to liberalize television receive-only antennas and in some instances other small receiving antennas.

In the United States, an open-sky policy for satellite communications has been introduced progressively since the 1970s. As a consequence, the US satellite communications market has seen a rapid expansion. A very large market has been predicted for VSAT services.

The increased flexibility and sophistication of satellite communications and the arrival of very small and low-cost antenna dishes will play a major role for the European market. DBS will be a major element in building a European audio-visual space.[1] VSATs could be a major accelerator in building Europe-wide information services.

---

[1] See Chapter VI, Section 8.

Today Eutelsat, the European Telecommunications Satellite Organization, operates a powerful satellite system in Europe's sky, together with the French system Telecom 1 and other systems which are to be launched before the end of the decade (Box 12).

Box 12

International satellite organizations active in Europe

Satellite communications in Europe are largely provided by the Eutelsat organization and the International Telecommunications Satellite Organization Intelsat. Additionally the International Maritime Satellite Organization Inmarsat is playing a growing role. In 1984, the French telecommunications satellite Telecom I was launched into orbit. Other national and private systems are due to be launched in the near future.

All Community countries are members of Eutelsat, Intelsat and Inmarsat.

Eutelsat, the European Telecommunications Satellite Organization was created by an agreement between the telecommunications administrations which are members of the CEPT, the European Conference of Postal and Telecommunications Administrations. Now 26 European countries are members of Eutelsat, each holding an investment share based on its use of the system. The total investment share of Community countries is 80%.

Eutelsat was established to provide European telecommunications administrations with satellite links to route international telephone traffic within Europe, and the European Broadcasting Union (EBU) with the means to expand its Eurovision system of TV programme exchange.

Subsequent to the launches of the Eutelsat I-F1 and I-F2 satellites, television use has turned out to be by far the more important. Eutelsat is leasing transponders to EBU to carry television programmes within the Eurovision network. In addition Eutelsat leases space-segment capacity to a number of Eutelsat Member States for the transmission of TV programmes to cable TV networks, such as Super Channel and Sky Channel.

The Eutelsat I-F2 satellite launched in 1984 provides space-segment capacity for digital circuits up to 2 Mbit/s via the satellite multiservice system (SMS).

Such circuits can be used for a wide range of intra-European international business services, such as high-speed data transmission, videoconferencing, etc. Transmission capacity for business services is also offered via the French Telecom 1 system which has been made available to Eutelsat under an agreement between Eutelsat and France Télécom.

A user is connected to the SMS either via a community aerial serving a given business area or via a dedicated aerial linked directly to the user's equipment. The SMS earth stations have dish diameters of 3.5 or 5 metres and are provided by the national telecommunications administrations.

Tariffs for the use of the SMS are also fixed in each country by the national telecommunications administrations.

Eutelsat will launch a new generation of satellites (I-F4, I-F5) into orbit in 1988-89.

Intelsat, the International Telecommunications Satellite Organization, was created in 1964. It now counts world-wide 110 nations as its members. The total investment share of Community countries is 25%.

Intelsat provides international communications capacity to telecommunications administrations, which in turn sell this capacity in the form of telephone calls, data and telex circuits, telecom facilities and satellite television channels. Services are provided using large gateways — satellite earth stations with dish diameters of 30 metres, with one or several per country.

Additionally, Intelsat has more recently established a high-quality digital global service. The Intelsat business service (IBS) integrates services such as voice, facsimile, telex, data and videoconferencing. The Intelnet services are confined to data distribution and data collection services.

IBS allows the utilization of small and medium-sized aerial dishes at or close to the end user location which can be owned and operated by the customer if national regulation allows. Intelnet is used mainly as a data broadcasting service, with reception provided by small dish aerials of 60 to 80 cm diameter, so-called 'micro-terminals'.

Intelsat is currently about to launch its next generation of satellites, the Intelsat VI series.

Inmarsat, the International Maritime Satellite Organization was created in 1975. It now counts 45 countries as members. The total investment share of the Community countries is 26%.

Inmarsat's purpose is to provide space-segment capacity 'necessary for improving maritime communications, efficiency and management of ships, maritime public correspondence services and radio-location capabilities'.

Inmarsat operates two dedicated maritime communications satellites (Marecs) and uses additional satellite capacity leased from Intelsat. Coast earth stations consist of high-powered parabolic dishes of 11 to 13 metres in diameter, ship earth stations installed on individual ships consist of aerial dishes of about 0.9 to 1.2 metres.

The main current services are telephony, telex and data. The main new services planned are aeronautical communications — public telephone service with aeroplanes — and possibly land-mobile communications using small 'Standard C' dish antennas which could be located on trucks for low data-rate services and telex.

Inmarsat is planning to put a new generation of satellites into orbit by the early 1990s.

In Europe, satellite communications have grown, over recent years, into a major component of the international telecommunications system which is beginning to cover the Community:

(i) Eutelsat satellites and Telecom I have developed into the backbone of international television in the Community, both by providing national TV networks via the Eurovision system with the broadband capabilities and flexibility needed for programme exchange and joint transmissions, as well as by beaming down new programmes — such as Super Channel, Sky Channel, the fifth French TV channel, 3 SAT and SAT1 — to cable head-ends for onward distribution. They have laid the technical foundations for the growing together of the Community's audio-visual — TV broadcasting — space;

(ii) Eutelsat — with its SMS services — has introduced the first international broadband — 2 Mbit/s — business services in Europe. It has, for the first time, made Community-wide videoconferencing a possibility. It offers the possibility of highly flexible configurations, tailored to specific needs, including the peripheral Member States and their less favoured regions;

(iii) while telecommunications satellites are unlikely to play a major role in international conventional narrowband services on the relatively short distances within the Community and while satellites will be challenged in fixed point-to-point services on the transatlantic routes by the new optical-fibre 'highways' which are being laid, satellites are expanding into the point-multipoint field of 'closed user group' applications where they have unique advantages.

The emergence of low-cost terminal dishes with diameters of less than 1 metre give them a unique potential for the rapid establishment of Europe-wide services both for the business sector and also for special services for the population at large, such as for educational purposes. This exploits to the full the specific advantage of satellites: their high degree of flexibility and their international dimension.

An especially promising area for this type of application is point-to-multipoint data distribution by VSATs (very small aperture terminals). This can cover, for example, the distribution of stock-lists, price-lists or publicity material from the headquarters of a business to all its European branches. This type of operation is at present often expensive and unreliable; the use of VSATs could go a long way towards solving both these problems.

Another important area for the rapid establishment of Europe-wide systems by satellite could be mobile communications, for special user groups such as ships, planes, and also trucks while awaiting the progressive implementation of the Europe-wide digital mobile system which will ultimately provide a full-base for land-mobile communications. [1]

---

[1] See Chapter VI, Section 2.

Inmarsat is providing full mobile communications for international shipping, and is experimenting with voice telephone services for aircraft. Plans have been considered for the introduction of Europe-wide paging and data services for trucks via satellite communications. Such services could be an important step towards introducing a Europe-wide communications system for truck transport in the Community by 1992, with large potential savings by more efficient routeing and Europe-wide fleet management.

The satellite communications systems in Europe's sky will expand substantially before the end of the decade.

A number of satellite communications systems are being planned at present. These are summarized in Table 7. Eutelsat is developing its second generation satellites (Eutelsat II) which could require an investment of about 400 million ECU. In April 1986 Eutelsat signed a contract with Aerospatiale worth 225 million ECU for three Eutelsat II satellites for delivery in mid-1989; options were placed for a further 5 satellites.

TABLE 7

Future satellite systems in Europe

Satellite	Responsible organization	Launch date	Main characteristics and capabilities
Telecom-1	France Télécom (F)	1984	Videoconferencing and corporate communications
Kopernikus	Deutsche Bundespost (D)	1989	Telephone, data, videoconferencing and TV distribution
Italsat	Telespazio (I)	1990	DBS and telecommunications capabilities
Tele-X	Swedish Space Corporation	1989	DBS capability and new data and video services for business community in Denmark, Finland, Norway and Sweden
Olympus	ESA	1989	DBS channels, business services
I-F4, F5 II-F1, etc.	Eutelsat	1988 1990	Business services, telephone and TV distribution
TV-SAT2	BMFT/Deutsche Bundespost (D)	1989	TV broadcasting (high-power DBS)
TDF-1	CNES/TDF (F)	1988	TV broadcasting (high-power DBS)
BSB	British Satellite Broadcast (UK)	1989	TV broadcasting (high-power DBS)
Astra	Société européenne des satellites (L)	1988	TV broadcasting (medium-power DBS)
Atlantic	Atlantic Satellites	1989	DBS channels; eventually transatlantic communications

The Eutelsat II system is designed to provide business services, telephony and TV programme distribution to cable networks and small dish aerials in Europe.

In parallel, a number of European countries have launched or will launch national communications satellite systems such as the French Telecom I — in orbit since 1984 — Germany's DFS-Kopernikus and Italy's Italsat to be launched in 1988 and 1989 respectively.

In addition, a number of private companies in Europe are trying to enter the satellite communications market. In the United States, several companies have applied to provide transatlantic satellite links to Europe.

There are at least four applicants in the United States wishing to provide telecommunications services between the United States and Europe, namely PanAmSat, Orion, Finansat and International Satellite. These applications have been strongly opposed by Intelsat on the basis that the proposed systems will inflict significant economic harm upon Intelsat and would have a considerable impact on Intelsat user charges for international telephone and telegraph services. In the meantime, PanAmSat is the first system to have reached an agreement with Intelsat which permits its operations.

In Europe, there are two groups implementing or planning private communications and television broadcasting satellite systems, the Société européenne des satellites (SES) and Atlantic Satellites Ltd.

The widespread introduction of small dish satellite aerials and their installation on customer premises and individual homes, will take off with the operation of direct broadcasting satellites — DBS — in the Community. DBS satellites beam down programmes directly to homes, instead of passing via cable TV networks as is the case for master antenna systems.

The French TDF1 is due to be in orbit in 1988, while the German TV-SAT2 and the UK BSB satellites are due for 1989 launches.

Satellite launch schedules were delayed by a series of failures in 1986, including the tragic explosion of the manned Space Shuttle in the United States.

However, as these problems are overcome, it is virtually certain that international demand for new satellite communications services will grow further — if current regulatory constraints are lifted. Strict regulation of up-link, space-segment and down-link and receiving antennas have in the past curtailed the growth of satellite services in the Community. Europe will have to consider a more flexible regulatory framework — particularly for the new small dish earth stations — and more effective frequency coordination. These are necessary prerequisites for a more open system, if Europe wants satellite communications to contribute fully to the 1992 Community-wide market.

8. Integrated Broadband Communications: the ultimate convergence of telecommunications and audio-visual communications — the global view

The progressive digitization of the network, the introduction of optical fibres and the trans-national links established by satellites are beginning to form the elements of an all-embracing communications medium, which will bring telecommunications and, ultimately, TV broadcasting to the consumer (Figure 7).

Thus the basic structure is forming in stages for the gradual emergence of a homogeneous digital communications network infrastructure which will serve all of Europe: Integrated Broadband Communications, (IBC). This will be an infrastructure of optical fibres which will progressively replace the copper network, of satellite links and of broadband switching nodes.

Very different players will have to be brought together to realize the economic and social potential of this natural convergence — industry, telecommunications administrations, cable TV operators, satellite organizations. The broadband infrastructure will offer the new potential of video communications and very-high-speed data links, along with substantial improvements in the cost performance and handling of narrow and medium-band services. Provision via one digital medium will be the economic precondition for the successful introduction of the new telecommunications services of the 1990s based on moving images — videophones.

GAP, the EC's Analysis and Forecasting Group has identified the need for joint provision of video communications and TV distribution via a single local network if acceptable tariff levels are to be reached. [1]

The Community's RACE programme is to offer such a framework of cooperation in Europe which can draw together the different strands of development in time. [2] Europe has a chance to establish at this critical stage of development a leading role in world telecommunications — and a Community-wide telecommunications infrastructure which can carry Europe on a firm basis into the information age.

The objective is ambitious. RACE aims at the introduction of IBC taking into account the evolving ISDN and national introduction strategies — progressing to Community-wide services by 1995. RACE requires close trans-national cooperation between the large number of players involved in Europe. It involves comprehensive planning of the introduction of the new broadband services in the Community, and it involves the elaboration of common standards and specifications.

---

[1] Proposals by GAP for the coordinated introduction of broadband services in the Community, 1986.
[2] See Chapter VI, Section 4.

FIGURE 7

STAGES OF SERVICE INTEGRATION

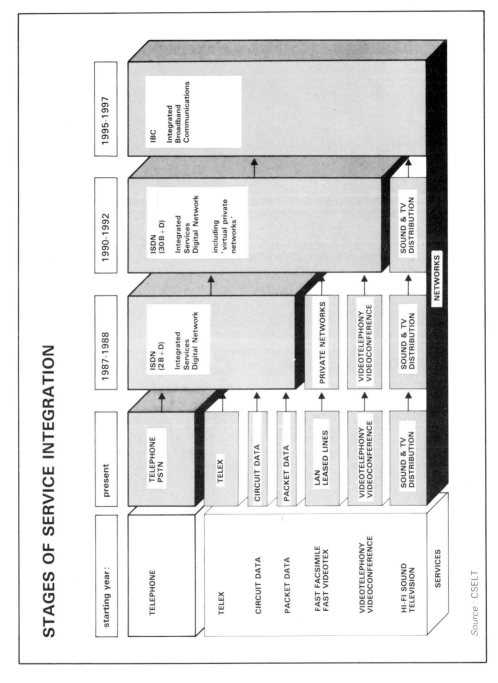

Source: CSELT.

It must above all develop a communications environment in Europe which will allow consumers and service providers to use the new technological opportunities according to their choice.

'The sense in which service providers and customers want to see integration might be called "integration for open access", i.e. the freedom to access and offer any sort of service across general purpose terminal facilities complemented by customized features and a flexible carrier system offering a full range of narrow, medium and broadband transmissions.

They want to be able not only to have a free choice of access but also the ability to combine different services in an *ad hoc* manner, i.e. the *ad-hoc* integration of services to offer new features should be possible.

The physical integration of the transmission into a unique "IBCN" is now seen as less important: several "IBC carriers" could exist simultaneously as a part of an interworking carrier system. Furthermore IBC enhancement of ISDN may, as a transitory measure offer some IBC features till the penetration of broadband carriers has progressed sufficiently. What is seen as important is that coherent and compatible network operations are established so as to permit the dynamic use of the overall transmission capacity to meet the full range of narrow, medium and broadband transmission requirements when and where needed. This implies an increased emphasis on the issues of real-time dynamic network management, maintenance, reliability and security. It also reinforces the emphasis on technological efforts towards the realization of "open systems interconnection" standardization for integrated services and functions.'[1]

The joint development of Integrated Broadband Communications in Europe building on and expanding the evolving ISDN infrastructure will provide an important means to ensure Community-wide network integrity for the telecommunications infrastructure of the 1990s. 'Regulatory reform of the European telecommunications environment must now catch up with the potential created by technological planning and technology development.'[2]

9. The unavoidable need to adapt the regulatory framework to the new environment: the current adjustment process

The progressive merger of the telecommunications and data-processing sectors, digitization, value-added services, the introduction of optical fibre and the new satellite technologies have together had a profound effect on the development of telecommunications

---

[1] Proposal for a Council Regulation on RACE, COM(86) 547, 29 October 1986.
[2] Green Paper, p. 117.

networks and services. They are giving rise to a wealth of new opportunities of immense potential for both users and telecommunications administrations; while at the same time they are making the telecommunications environment vastly more complex:

'(i) Digitization and the associated new transmission techniques — optical fibre and satellites — have dramatically raised research and development costs in the industry. Cooperation and economies of scale and scope become an indispensable requirement for the European telecommunications sector.

(ii) Digitization poses major problems for the future generation of networks in Europe. The new generations — the Integrated Services Digital Network (ISDN), the future digital mobile communications and Integrated Broadband Communications (IBC) — will require a new degree of cooperation between the network operators in Europe over coordinated introduction strategies if Europe-wide communications are to be maintained.

(iii) Agreement on high-level protocols for services and on network interface standards for terminals is needed to ensure proper communications between the highly sophisticated computer-based terminals of the future. (Protocols are the computer languages in which terminals and switches talk to each other to set up calls and prevent transmission losses.) The standardization bodies in the Community, both in telecommunications and in the computer field, face a situation characterized by a new degree of complexity.'[1]

But more fundamentally a decision must be taken about the future use of the new opportunities, both for the telecommunications administrations and for the users:

'(i) The introduction of digital technology has made it possible that many functions that were previously possible only inside the network can now be performed outside the network by increasingly sophisticated terminal equipment including PABXs. The multiplication of possible functions has led to a substantial potential for service differentiation and innovation which is at the heart of the new so-called value-added services.

(ii) Modern telecommunications network infrastructure will be technically more and more able to carry a broad range of services independent of the network infrastructure operator and provided by operators outside the network.'

At the same time, telecommunications administrations will have to decide if they should — and if they want to — go into the new business areas which technology is throwing open to them:

'While the digitization of the network infrastructure has opened new opportunities for other providers, the trend towards integration has led at the same time to substantial economies of scope for integrated service offerings, such as made possible by the Integrated Services Digital Network (ISDN).'[2]

---

[1] Green Paper, pp. 24 and 25.
[2] Green Paper, p. 41.

TABLE 8

The regulatory situation in the Member States in early 1987

	Belgium	Denmark	France	Germany	Greece	Ireland	Italy	Luxem-bourg	Netherlands	Portugal	Spain	United Kingdom
1. Relations with postal services	S[1]	PTT[5]	PTT	PTT[24]	S	S	S/PTT[5]	PTT	PTT[10]	PTT[5]	S[16,23]	S
2. Basic service network:												
(a) Local	GM (PC)	OM[5]	GM	GM	GM (PC)	GM (PC)	GM (PC)	GM	GM[11]	GM (PC)	OM[16]	RC (LIM)
(b) Long distance	GM (PC)	OM	GM	GM	GM (PC)	GM (PC)	GM (PC)	GM	GM[11]	GM (PC)	OM[16]	RC (LIM)
(c) International	GM (PC)	GM	GM	GM	GM (PC)	GM (PC)	GM (PC)	GM	GM[11]	GM (PC+ OM)[5]	OM[16]	RC (LIM)
(d) Mobile	GM (PC)	OM	GM[6]	GM	PL	GM (PC)	GM (PC)	GM	GM[11]	–	OM[16]	RC (LIM)
3. Terminal equipment												
(a) Supply:												
Main telephone set	M	M	L	GM	M	M[21]	M	M	M[12]	M	M[23]	L
PBX	PL	M	L	L	L	L	L	L	M[12]	L	RC (LIB)[19]	L
Telex	PL[2]	M	L	RC (LIM)	L	L	M[2]	L	M[12]	M	L	L
Modem	PL[3]	PL	L	L[20]	L	L	M[3]	PL	L	PL	M[23]	L
Data terminal	L	L	L	L	L	L	L	L	L	L	L	L
Mobile	M[22]	L	L	L	PL	L	L	L	M[13-12]	–	L	L
(b) Maintenance:												
Main telephone set	M	M	L	M	M	M[21]	M	M	M[12]	M	M[23]	L
PBX	PL	M	L	L	L	L	L	L	M[12]	L	L	L
Telex	PL	M	L	M	M	L	M[3]	L	M[12]	L	L	L
Modem	PL	PL	L	L[20]	L	L	M[3]	PL	L	PL	M[23]	L
Data terminal	L	L	L	L	L	L	L	L	L	L	L	L
Mobile	M[22]	L	L	L	L	L	L	L	M[13]	–	M[23]	L
4. Use of leased circuits												
(a) Domestic:												
Shared use/resale	N[4]	N	N[7]	Y[8a]	N	N[4]	N[9]	N	N[14]	N[15]	N	Y[17]
Interconnection with public network	N	N	N[7]	Y[8b]	N	N[4]	N[9]	–	N[14]	N[15]	N	Y[17]
(b) International:												
Shared use/resale	N[4]	N[4]	N[4]	Y[8a]	N[4]	N[4]	N	N	N[4]	N[4]	N[4]	Y[18]
Interconnection with public network	N[4]	N[4]	N[4]	Y[8c]	N[4]	N[4]	N	N[4]	N[4]	N[4]	N[4]	Y[18]

Legend:

PTT   Posts and telecommunications services provided by the same organization

S   Separate organization

M   Monopoly

PL   Partly liberalized (some types liberalized, others not)

L   Liberalized

GM   Government monopoly (government agency)

GM (PC)   Government monopoly (public corporation)

OM   Monopoly of other types (private entity, etc.)

RC (LIM)   Regulated competition with limited entry

RC (LIB)   Regulated competition with liberal entry

FC (LIB)   Free competition with liberalized entry

Y   Generally permitted

N   Generally prohibited

1   RTT and Régie des Postes depend on the same PTT Minister.

2   First telex terminal under monopoly, progressive liberalization announced.

3   On request by the CEC, progressive liberalization announced.

4   Subject to exceptions.

5   Telecommunications services providers exist in addition to PTT, on a monopolistic basis (concessionary basis, regional monopoly, etc.).

6   By end 1987 licensing of additional providers announced for public mobile communications (voice) and several providers for public paging services.

7   By end 1987 steps regarding licensing of private providers of value-added services.

8a   Shared use permitted, resale prohibited.

8b   Voice-band circuits: as far as technically possible, but at one end only (TKO, July 1986).

8c   International fixed connections without restrictions; 'flat-rate' circuits with restrictions.

9   New legislation on VANS is being discussed in Parliament.

10   A larger degree of separation between postal and telecommunications organizations within PTT has been announced for 1989.

11   PTT to be converted to limited liability company by 1989.

12   Government has decided to liberalize all terminal equipment as of January 1989.

13   Cordless telephone/car telephone/public page under monopoly: closed mobile systems, radio telephones on ships, etc. liberalized.

14   Usage for VANS to be liberalized.

15   Currently under consideration in commissions.

16   Telex, telegram, public facsimile (Burofax), etc. are provided by the PTT.

17   Pure resale prohibited until at least 1989.

18   Pure resale prohibited until at least 1989, subject to additional restrictions.

19   Digital PBXs are supplied under monopoly.

20   Complete liberalization has now been implemented after agreement with the European Commission on 30 July 1986 and will take place after conversion of CCITT recommendations into specifications and definition of testing procedures.

21   TE does not hold a monopoly, but is at present exclusively licensed by the Ministry.

22   Liberalized at end of 1987.

23   A new law covering telecommunications was adopted at the end of 1987 ('LOT'), introducing substantial liberalization.

24   In March 1988, the German Government submitted legislation ('Poststrukturgesetz') which aims at restructuring the Bundespost by early 1989 and introducing substantial liberalization.

Note: With reforms already under way in the Member States (see Chapter VII, Section 1), the situation in Europe is changing rapidly.

The telecommunications sector in most Member States of the European Community during the early 1980s was strongly characterized by the heritage of the past: strictly regulated, extensive monopolies for the telecommunications administrations, with organizations adapted to the provision of a very few standardized services to the national area, principally voice telephony. Table 8 surveys the situation in early 1987 in the Member States of the European Community.

This structure was hit by the technologies of the computer, fibre optics and satellites, with their very different point of departure: rapid innovation cycles, high rates of diversification and specialization, a traditionally liberal market environment, and strong private service providers.

Sticking to the status quo is no longer an option. 'All countries are confronted with the option of either extending the application of telecommunications regulation to the sector of data-processing terminals and imposing more and more restrictions (many of which will be difficult to control) on the growing capability of private installations in switching and intelligent functions, such as on digital PABXs or personal computers connected to the network, or defining the telecommunications regulatory framework more narrowly, allowing the full benefits of technical progress to be reaped.'[1]

The world-wide trend points towards the latter solution — the lifting of current constraints. In Europe, the situation is changing rapidly. As set out in more detail later,[2] all European countries have now started to adjust to the new situation. The Green Paper aims to reinforce and accelerate this process, by adding the Community dimension.

---

[1] Green Paper, p. 42.
[2] Chapter VII, Section 1.

IV — The economic dimension: telecommunications expanding into a general infrastructure for the 1992 market

In our society, the telephone has developed into a facility which people rely on for a wide variety of purposes, in all aspects of life. The new technologies will take this further, expanding telecommunications into a general infrastructure for Europe's future economy.

'Three distinct but interlinked growth processes are at work:

(i) improved access to better information raises productivity throughout the economy;

(ii) improvements in communications raise the utility, and consequently the marketability, of both old and new services. This leads to their expansion;

(iii) transition to the new service-driven and information-based economy requires very large public and private investment in new infrastructures, both physical — cable, switches, terminals — and human — the development of value-added telecommunications services.'[1]

Investment in telecommunications has a high short-term multiplier in macroeconomic terms: according to studies, 1 000 million ECU invested brings 1 500 million in extra activity directly. In addition, investment in the network infrastructure has a very high multiplier effect on the terminal market and the market for new telecommunications services, doubling its direct impact.

Telecommunications represents the most significant civil investment in new technologies and services in the Community in the foreseeable future.

---

[1] Green Paper, p. 44.

1. The major lines of development: applications and investment

Figure 8 shows the overall network lines of development in more detail.

The diagram demonstrates that the major trend — the central development path — will be the development of the telephone network towards digitization and the ISDN, making full use of the existing local network, i.e. the copper wires, followed by the progressive introduction of general broadband communications based mainly on optical fibres. The top of Figure 8 shows the projected development path of business communications, with gradual introduction of new services for business users, such as videoconferencing/video-phony.

The third line of development, which will ultimately be the most important, is shown in the bottom part of Figure 8. It concerns the development of TV distribution services, which will gradually broaden to include interactive services and eventually merge with general integrated broadband communications.

An analysis of these paths of development from the viewpoint of investment required in the Community leads to Figure 9. It refers to the Community as a whole. Private investment — the investment needed in terminal equipment — is shown on the vertical axis, network investment on the horizontal axis. The isoquants in the diagram represent the total cumulated investment needed. Figure 9 shows, in overall terms , the role of investment in terminal equipment, as compared with investment in the network.

Investment in telephone equipment to achieve digitization and gradual development towards ISDN over the next 15 to 20 years will be of the order of 300 000 million ECU, with a relatively small margin of uncertainty. The major part of this investment will continue to be accounted for by network equipment, with terminal equipment representing less than 25%.

Broadband business communications, as shown in the top of Figure 9 will develop within a relatively short period of time. The diagram shows on the one hand the large users of PABXs, who will increasingly connect to the network via ISDN primary access and who will use ISDN facilities via their PABXs. They will also be the first users of the new video communications services, in particular videoconferencing.

The main feature here is that user investment in terminal equipment will be crucial for service take-off. It will determine how the first phase of broadband communications develops. Figure 9 also shows major investments by small and medium-sized enterprises, primarily in telematics terminal equipment. There will be growing use of ISDN basic access — with the coming into existence of the ISDN — in this part of the business sector.

84

FIGURE 8

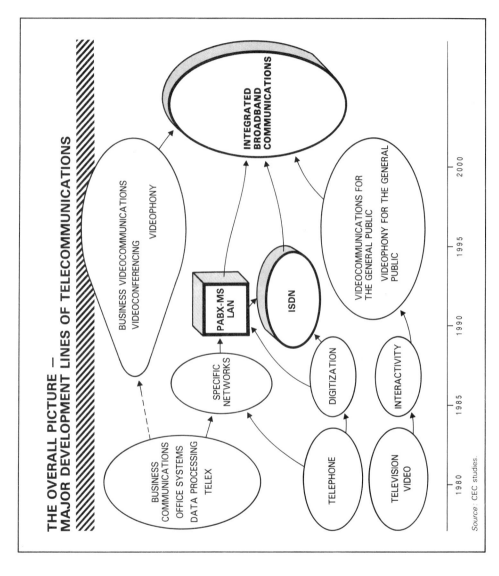

THE OVERALL PICTURE —
MAJOR DEVELOPMENT LINES OF TELECOMMUNICATIONS

BUSINESS VIDEOCOMMUNICATIONS
VIDEOCONFERENCING
VIDEOPHONY

INTEGRATED
BROADBAND
COMMUNICATIONS

PABX-MS
LAN

ISDN

BUSINESS
COMMUNICATIONS
OFFICE SYSTEMS
DATA PROCESSING
TELEX

SPECIFIC
NETWORKS

VIDEOCOMMUNICATIONS FOR
THE GENERAL PUBLIC
VIDEOPHONY FOR THE GENERAL
PUBLIC

DIGITIZATION

INTERACTIVITY

TELEPHONE

TELEVISION
VIDEO

1980   1985   1990   1995   2000

Source : CEC studies.

85

FIGURE 9

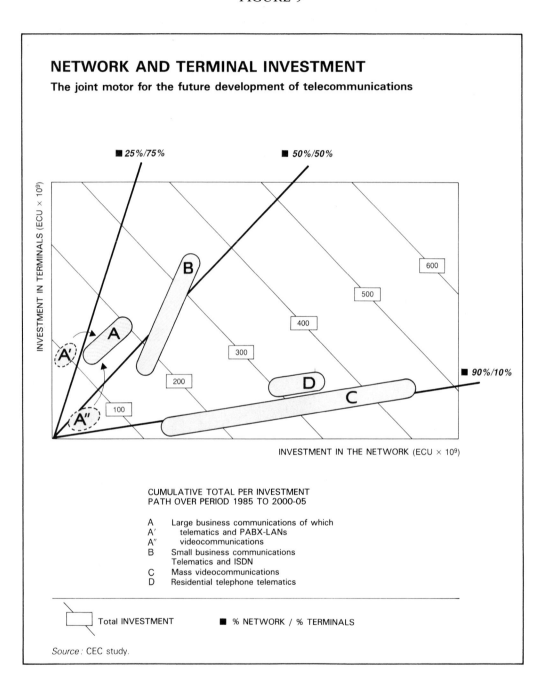

NETWORK AND TERMINAL INVESTMENT

The joint motor for the future development of telecommunications

CUMULATIVE TOTAL PER INVESTMENT
PATH OVER PERIOD 1985 TO 2000-05

A   Large business communications of which
A'   telematics and PABX-LANs
A"   videocommunications
B   Small business communications
     Telematics and ISDN
C   Mass videocommunications
D   Residential telephone telematics

Total INVESTMENT   ■ % NETWORK / % TERMINALS

Source : CEC study.

The cumulative investment in the business sector will be roughly 400 000 million ECU over the next 20 years, with a substantial margin of uncertainty. For small and medium-sized companies half of this will be investment in the terminal equipment, half will fall to the network operator. In the large business sector, more than two-thirds of this investment will go to terminal equipment — integrated business communications systems — making the private investment component the determining factor for the use of advanced communications in this sector.

The bottom of Figure 9 shows, with a very large margin of uncertainty, the gradual changeover of the telecommunications network to include video communications for the user at large. This will imply transition from the present use of copper wire to the use of optical fibre for the 'last kilometre' to the subscriber, with the possibility of both narrowband telecommunications and broadband TV distribution and videophones on the same system — Integrated Broadband Communications. The large margin of uncertainty (see Figure 9) derives from the fact that the total volume of investment needed for the period considered depends on the timing of the large-scale start of the transition, in the second half of the 1990s.

Figure 9 clearly demonstrates that the business sector will play a crucial role in the transition to broadband in the near future. However, the general conversion of the current copper network to optical fibre reaching the private households will be the critical factor in the long term.

The analysis confirms the crucial role of Integrated Broadband Communications — and the RACE programme. [1] The success of transition to broadband will largely depend on smooth interaction between public network investment and private investment in terminal equipment. The long-term general convergence of the network will depend on the social acceptance of the new services by the public at large.

In the short term, the business sector will be the major driving force for the launching of new advanced telematics services. At the same time, businesses will need the new services to operate efficiently in the wider European market.

But the benefits of an efficient economy will work through to the final consumer by reducing the prices of goods in general, and especially services thanks to increased productivity. Telecommunications, in the future, will have to be judged by their overall impact, by the extent to which they generate overall benefits to consumers in a more and more service-based economy.

---

[1] See Chapter VI, Section 4.

2. Telecommunications: the basis of the future service economy

'Demand for data communications capacity is growing among Europe's big industrial companies at a rate of as much as 40% per year. New services, new tariffs, new corporate structures are crowding onto the marketplace. Companies which make consumer goods are using these services to find out more rapidly what their customers want; others are using electronic communications to reduce stocks of parts, to manage cash, to link research centres, to transmit and develop designs, to monitor remote installations and for hundreds of other tasks aimed at securing a competitive edge. In many trading and financial service activities, the availability of the most advanced communication is already essential to commercial success. The same is becoming increasingly true for industry. This applies not only to large companies, which need to move large amounts of data between installations, but to smaller firms for which advanced telecommunications open up markets which were previously out of range.' [1]

The Community's economy has experienced, over the past 25 years, a significant shift in the shares of the major sectors — agriculture, industry, services — in the gross domestic product of the Community. The main thrust of this movement has been a steady decline in the shares of manufactured and agricultural products on the one hand and an expansion of both market and non-market services on the other: financial services, transport, tourism, distribution, consultancy, education, etc.

'At current market prices, the share of manufactured products in gross value-added in the Community (EUR 6) has declined from 33% in 1960 to about 26% in 1983 ... This declining pattern is mirrored by the corresponding share of market services, which expanded from 36% to over 43%. The share of non-market services ... also grew steadily ... from 11% to 15%...'. [2]

'Between 1970 and 1983, the share of employment in the Community (EUR 6) accounted for by market and non-market services rose from 48% to 59%.' [3]

While employment in industry has declined over the past decade, services have been the major job creator, compensating for losses in industry, though unable in Europe — in contrast to developments in the United States — to create enough jobs, under existing conditions, to prevent an overall increase in unemployment.

Telecommunications have been a crucial factor in the service sector's role as a job creator:

---

[1] 'Clearing the lines — a user's view on business communications in Europe', Round Table of European industrialists, October 1986.
[2] 'Annual economic review 1986-87', *European Economy* No 29, July 1986.
[3] 'Annual economic report 1986-87', *European Economy* No 30, November 1986.

'Traditionally, most services, excluding transport and tourism, were produced and consumed locally: through face-to-face contact (e.g. financial services; legal, technical, and economic consulting); or, in the case of informatics, generated through largely local man-machine interactions.

The combined effect of digitization and the phenomenal increase in carrying capacity of modern telecommunications introduces services into the exchange economy at least on a par with goods.' [1]

Indeed, current statistics underestimate by a considerable margin the share of information-based services in the economy: services within manufacturing firms are counted as part of industry. Yet to take an extreme example, up to 80% of the cost of computers (including, for example, telecommunications switches) is made up of software and other services. Even blue-collar workers on assembly lines may simply exercise a service function, e.g. monitoring of tele-guided robots.

World-wide, the share of information-based jobs has risen dramatically over the last two decades (Figure 10). In the Community, by the year 2000 more than 60% of Community employment will be strongly information-related — and will therefore depend on telecommunications.

The rise of services in the economy should not be seen as a 'de-industrialization process'. On the contrary, services and industrial activities penetrate each other to form a new conglomerate. Industry is increasingly buying in services to increase its productivity and expand its marketing and sales. 'For the whole of the Community, from 1975 to 1981, the growth in volume of services bought by industry was between 3.5 and 4% per annum. During the same period, value-added of industry in real terms increased by no more than 2.4% per year' (European Economy).

The difference between the two figures is explained by the fact that the growth in market services is largely due to the increase in consumption of services by industry.

Tele-carried services — particularly value-added services — play a decisive role in this process of linking the economy closer together: production, services, and final consumption (Figure 11).

The opportunity provided by telematics to exchange services — making services 'tradable' — offers a potentially decisive increase in the productivity, in qualitative and quantitative terms, of the whole economy: of local services; of manufacturing due to techniques such as computer integrated manufacturing (CIM); and also of agriculture.

The telecommunications network is now developing into Europe's nervous system. Europe's citizens now spend three times as much on the telephone as on postal services.

---

[1] Green Paper, p. 45.

FIGURE 10

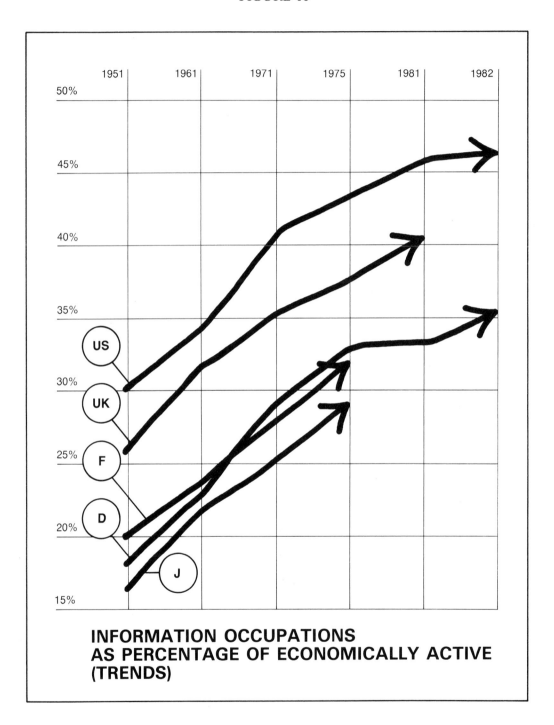

**INFORMATION OCCUPATIONS
AS PERCENTAGE OF ECONOMICALLY ACTIVE
(TRENDS)**

FIGURE 11

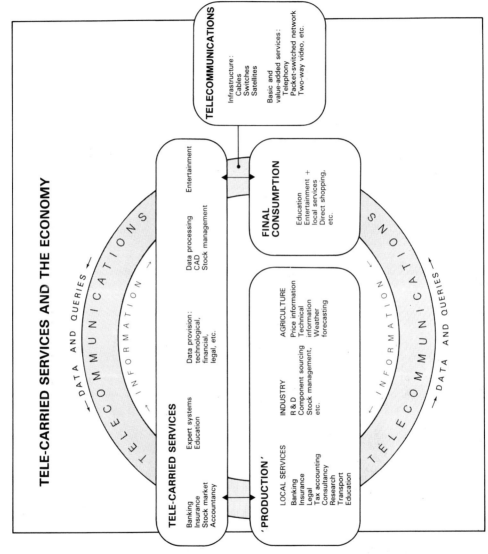

TELE-CARRIED SERVICES AND THE ECONOMY

'Intermediate consumption' — telecommunications as a producer service — accounts for roughly 60% of total telecommunications expenditure, with two-thirds of this consumption by the service sectors, such as banking, insurance etc., and one-third by industry. 'Intermediate consumption' will ultimately be turned by the economy into consumer benefit.

Information and knowledge have become important factors of production. The final beneficiaries of more and better access to information are the consumers. 'If knowledge is to enter continuously into the production and market processes of locally produced goods and services it must be "transported" via an efficient conduit at low cost and high speed. Last, but not least, it must be packaged in ways which maximize its utility. This is the task of a growing part of the services industry, whose productivity, again, depends on the size of the market.' [1]

Services already account for nearly two-thirds of Community output and employment. By the year 2000, two-thirds of the wealth of advanced countries will be generated in strongly information-related activities.

Telecommunications will thus be a determining factor for Europe's future role in the world's expanding services market. It will also exert a crucial influence on another factor which will determine Europe's future position in the world: Europe's position in high technology.

3. Telecommunications: a major factor for the Community's future position in high technology

Investment in telecommunications equipment and related computer-based terminal equipment in the Community over the next 20 years will be between 500 000 to 1 000 000 million ECU — more than the cost of 30 staffed space stations. Roughly 50% of this investment will be spent on telecommunications and terminal equipment which — with the progressive digitization and computerization of telecommunications — will increasingly mean investment in high technology. The rest will be for engineering work, digging up roads, etc., with a substantial direct effect on job creation.

The telecommunications sector is a key component of the general future conglomerate information technology sector. On the one hand, in terms of equipment it already represents more than 25% of the equipment side of the conglomerate: computers, communications, consumer electronics, and components.

If one includes services, telecommunications corresponds to more than 50% of the total new sector of the management and transport of information (Figure 12).

---

[1] Green Paper, p. 46.

FIGURE 12

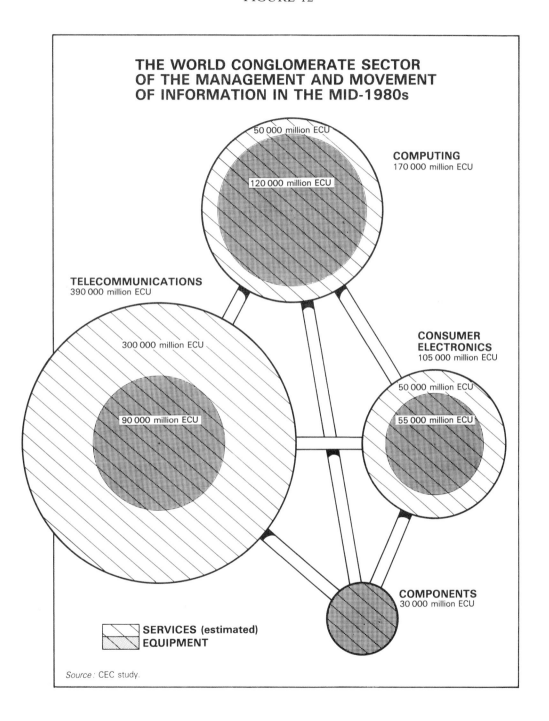

THE WORLD CONGLOMERATE SECTOR
OF THE MANAGEMENT AND MOVEMENT
OF INFORMATION IN THE MID-1980s

50 000 million ECU

COMPUTING
170 000 million ECU

120 000 million ECU

TELECOMMUNICATIONS
390 000 million ECU

300 000 million ECU

CONSUMER
ELECTRONICS
105 000 million ECU

50 000 million ECU

90 000 million ECU

55 000 million ECU

COMPONENTS
30 000 million ECU

SERVICES (estimated)
EQUIPMENT

Source : CEC study.

93

On the other hand, it is one of the main buyers of components and high-performance integrated circuits, the strategic technology on which all other segments of the information technology conglomerate depend. The telecommunications sector is now one of the largest consumers of integrated circuits in the Community. Innovations in network and services — ISDN, Integrated Broadband Communications, digital mobile communications, intelligent terminals — depend more and more on the development of dedicated integrated circuits which will represent an increasingly important element in the added-value of equipment.

But here the position of the European telecommunications sector reveals Europe's fundamental weakness in information technology in general which developed during the 1970s: over 50% of the European telecommunications industry's needs in integrated circuits are imported. A globally strong European communications sector — the only component of the information technology conglomerate which has a strong position in the world market, with a solid export surplus, compared with deficits in all other segments (Figure 13) — depends heavily for an essential input on supplies from external sources, basically from the United States, Japan and the countries of the Pacific rim.

This emphasizes the key role of telecommunications for the Community's future position in high technology. The Community has traditionally been strong in telecommunications. It has developed a weak position in the computer field. With the convergence of telecommunications and data processing Europe's strong telecommunications companies transform into computer companies, but equally the computer giants — notably IBM — enter the telecommunications field.

Europe is now at a crossroads. Either it will be able to expand its strength in the telecommunications sector to the computer sector, or its telecommunications sector will be weakened by its weakness in the data-processing sector.

Europe starts from a strong position in telecommunications. Its industry has excelled in the telecommunications world market (Table 9). The first digital switches were developed

TABLE 9

**European telecommunications companies:
strong suppliers in the world market**

(%)

	Sales to:			
	Europe	N. America	Asia	Other
Alcatel (CGE/ITT)	70	10	13	7
Siemens	71	10	8	11
Ericsson	56	12	13	19
GEC	66	15	10	9
Philips	54	2	31	13
Plessey	74	13	3	10
Italtel	81	0	5	14

Note: European companies are, overall, very strong suppliers in the world market, with between 20 and 45% of their sales outside of the Community.
Source: Estimates based on Arthur D. Little.

94

FIGURE 13

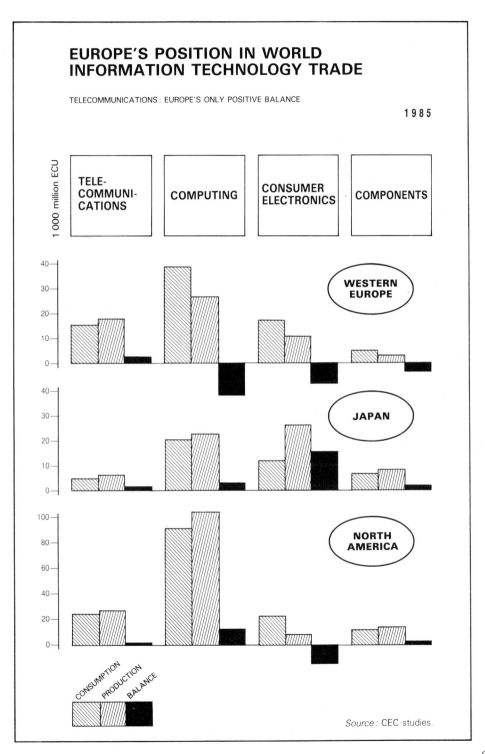

EUROPE'S POSITION IN WORLD
INFORMATION TECHNOLOGY TRADE

TELECOMMUNICATIONS : EUROPE'S ONLY POSITIVE BALANCE

1985

Source : CEC studies.

95

in Europe, by French Alcatel. Europe has a strong starting point in transmission technology. But it will now be tested for its ability to adjust. It will have to enter the booming field of telematics terminals which will be the major growth area. It will have to master computer technology fully, and build its own integrated circuits. It will have to acquire the economies of scale in a larger market which will be the only base for winning in the world-wide competition over the next generation of digital switches and opto-electronics — the ISDN and Integrated Broadband Communications.

Establishing a new framework of industrial cooperation and acquiring a Europe-wide market base are vital to the establishment of a viable position in the world-wide conglomerate information sector which is emerging.

Telecommunications will be Europe's largest civil investment in high technology, along with space technology. Europe's future position in 'high-tech' will strongly influence its overall future economic position because the high-technology sectors are also the sectors of strongest demand.

The high-technology sectors are experiencing an international market in full expansion, with growth rates averaging 7%, in spite of the slow-down of general economic expansion at the world level. Over the last decade, this growth withstood the two oil shocks of 1973 and 1979, without a major decline (Table 10).

TABLE 10

High technology: the high-demand sectors of the economy — a comparison

The high-technology sectors are defined as those sectors of the economy which together account for more than 50% of total research and development. According to evidence from studies, they are in general also the fastest-growing world markets.

Sector	Annual growth rate 1972-82 (%)
High-demand sectors	4.8 - 13.5
Telecommunications, electrical and electronic equipment	3.7 - 15.1
Computing, office equipment and precision instruments	5.7 - 8.9
Chemicals and pharmaceuticals	3.7 - 11.8
Medium-demand sectors	1.9 - 4.8
Rubber and plastics	1.2 - 5.0
Means of transport	1.4 - 7.1
Paper pulp, printing and packing materials	1.8 - 3.7
Food, drink and tobacco	1.7 - 3.8
Industrial machinery	0.2 - 3.6
Low-demand sectors	0.2 - 3.0
Various products	1.3 - 1.8
Textiles, leather and clothing	0.2 - 2.7
Steel and metal ores	−0.7 - 3.7
Metal products	−0.5 - 4.2
Construction materials and non-metallic minerals	0.3 - 1.8
Total manufactured products	1.9 - 6.4

Source: European Economy.

FIGURE 14

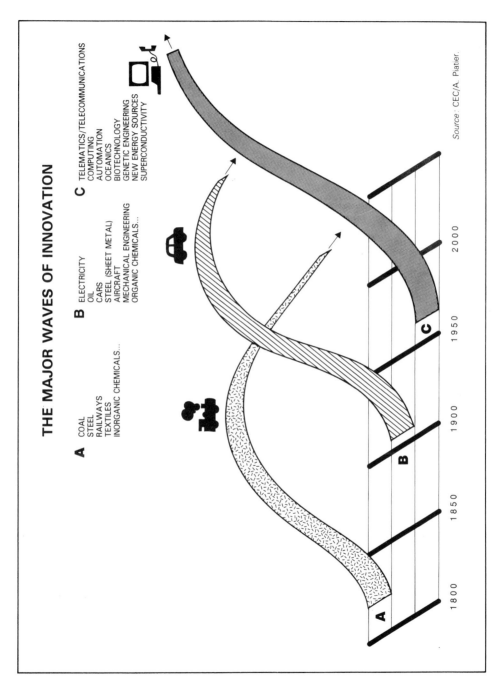

THE MAJOR WAVES OF INNOVATION

A COAL
STEEL
RAILWAYS
TEXTILES
INORGANIC CHEMICALS...

B ELECTRICITY
OIL
CARS
STEEL (SHEET METAL)
AIRCRAFT
MECHANICAL ENGINEERING
ORGANIC CHEMICALS...

C TELEMATICS/TELECOMMUNICATIONS
COMPUTING
AUTOMATION
OCEANICS
BIOTECHNOLOGY
GENETIC ENGINEERING
NEW ENERGY SOURCES
SUPERCONDUCTIVITY

1800   1850   1900   1950   2000

A   B   C

Source : CEC/A. Platier.

The high growth of the high-technology sectors is indicative of the profound restructuring process of the world economy under way. After the first two industrial revolutions during the last two centuries — based on the steam engine first, on the automobile and electricity second — the world seems on the verge of another wave of innovations (Figure 14). The high technology of today will be the backbone of the economies of tomorrow.

Telecommunications will help determine Europe's overall position in high technology. The position in high technology and in the new services will determine to a large extent the wealth of the economy in the future — and with it the standard of living it can offer to its citizens.

4. The pre-conditions for using the potential of telecommunications for the development of the Community's market: strong network operators and a more competitive market environment

The emerging new telecommunications services — and notably the value-added 'tele-carried' services — will have a major impact on the future tradability of services and on the location of economic activities.

By the end of the century, up to 7 % of Community gross domestic product will result from telecommunications and closely related activities, as against around 3 % today. By the early 1990s, telecommunications will have grown into one of the largest industrial sectors.

The new conglomerate sector of the management and transport of information — telecommunications equipment, data processing and telecommunications services — already represents more than 500 000 million ECU for the world as a whole. The world market for telecommunications equipment had reached 90 000 million ECU by 1986, of which 17 500 million was accounted for by the Community market.

The decision on future strategies for telecommunications will therefore substantially shape the future economic structure in the Community. At the same time, the centres of decision-making are shifting. As seen in Section 1 of this Chapter, future investment in telecommunications will be characterized by three factors:

(i)   The very large amount of investment which is likely to take place in the sector. The sheer size of the investment will make telecommunications a determining factor for Europe's future position in high technology.

(ii) The new division of investment. With the growing importance of investment in terminal equipment on users' premises, the private investor is becoming an essential partner for the network operator, if development is to be successful.

(iii) The large degree of uncertainty involved, given the very large amount of investment at stake.

Future telecommunications development will require a close interweaving of public and private investment, of supply and demand, and of economic and social considerations.

Private investment will take place if regulatory conditions allow full use to be made of the investment; social acceptance will not be possible unless users have free choice to buy what they want.

Both these fundamental aspects pose the future economic regulation, under which the sector will develop, as the central problem. It is this question which makes telecommunications a critical crossroads for Europe's future policy on technology and services in general (Box 13).

Box 13

Widening of user choice and the spread of new services: the requirement for a more competitive market

'In general, an open, competitive market for new service providers and terminal manufacturers can make a substantial contribution to the rapid spread of the new services, under the current conditions of rapid development of technology and market opportunities.'[1]

Competition, product diversification and free choice for the user are closely interrelated.

In a recent EC economic research paper, the background is explained as follows:

'(1) Competition, in a world of uncertainty and limited knowledge, is "a process of discovery" (Hayek 1968); we do not know *a priori* what situation is superior, but producers engaged in competition will make experiments (i) to reveal their customers' preferences, (ii) to improve products and (iii) to lower their costs. Those who have better hypotheses will see them corroborated (Popper 1959) in the market; others will imitate them or launch improved hypotheses if their previous tests have failed; competition, just as research, never reaches a stage that could be called "perfect".

(2) While product innovations (including product differentiation) are a means of sensing consumers' preferences, process innovations raise total factor productivity (X-efficiency) by exploiting new knowledge, technical and organizational.'[2]

Given the complexity and multiplicity of the emerging telecommunications services, only the market can efficiently link the producer with the consumer. Economics knows of no other means of fulfilling this purpose and all attempts to replace it by something else have so far failed.

---

[1] Green Paper, p. 52.

[2] Herbert Giersch, 'Internal and external liberalization for faster growth', *Economic papers,* No 54, Commission of the European Communities, February 1987.

Europe will need both strong network operators to develop the infrastructure and finance the major renovation of the network ahead, and a liberalized market environment to allow full use of the network and freedom of choice.

It is this delicate balance which the Community must achieve if it wants to succeed: avoiding heavy economic damage at home by perpetuating outdated structures, and facing on equal terms its main competitors — Japan and the United States — in a rapidly developing world market.

V — The challenge facing the Community

With their new role as a driving force for economic development, telecommunications are coming to the forefront of issues discussed internationally.

Traditionally the international framework for telecommunications has been supplied by the International Telecommunications Union (ITU) (Box 14). The ITU has been successful over many years in ensuring international communications for telephony, telegraph and telex services.

Box 14

The traditional international framework for telecommunications: the International Telecommunications Union (ITU)

The International Telecommunications Union (ITU) has been the traditional framework for international coordination in the telecommunications field.

The ITU is an intergovernmental organization, acting as an agency of the United Nations. The number of member countries currently stands at 159.

The basic text governing its activities is the 'International Telecommunications Convention'.

Structurally, the Union comprises the following:

(i)   The Plenipotentiary Conference;

(ii) The Administrative Conferences;

(iii) The Administrative Council;

(iv) The permanent organs of the Union, which are:

    (a) General Secretariat;

    (b) International Frequency Registration Board (IFRB);

    (c) International Radio Consultative Committee (CCIR);

    (d) International Telegraph and Telephone Consultative Committee (CCITT).

The results of the work of the ITU and its bodies are laid down in three sets of documents:

(i)   The Convention, a sort of constitution of the Union, which specifies the internal organization and sets forth general principles governing telecommunications. It is drawn up at the Plenipotentiary Conference.

(ii) Administrative regulations which supplement the Convention and are framed at World Administrative Conferences convened by the ITU. These regulations contain detailed provisions applying to telecommunications: the Telegraph Regulations, the Telephone Regulations, the Radio Regulations.

(iii) Recommendations of the International Consultative Committees which are produced by telecommunications experts and provide guidance on operational methods and techniques to use.

The Plenipotentiary Conference, the supreme organ of the ITU, is responsible for laying down the basic policy of the organization. It meets once every five years.

The Administrative Conferences are generally convened to consider specific telecommunications matters. They are of two types:

(i)   World Administrative Conferences (WATTC and WARC).

(ii) Regional Administrative Conferences.

The Administrative Council of the ITU is made up of 41 Members of the Union elected by the Plenipotentiary Conference. It meets annually.

The General Secretariat is directed by a Secretary-General.

The Secretary-General is responsible to the Administrative Council for the whole of the administrative and financial side of the Union's work and acts as the legal representative of the Union.

The International Frequency Registration Board (IFRB) acts as custodian of international agreements, coordinating international use of the radio spectrum, to avoid incorrect utilization by the administrations.

The International Telephone and Telegraph Consultative Committee (CCITT) and the International Radio Consultative Committee (CCIR) study and issue recommendations on technical and operating questions relating to radio communications (CCIR) and telegraphy and telephony (CCITT).

The recommendations are published in what are known as the 'CCITT books'.

The work done by CCITT and CCIR in the domain of international standard-ization is extremely important and influential for telecommunications ad-ministrations. Standards are elaborated in the working groups which pre-pare draft recommendations to be examined by the plenary sessions; to adopt a CCITT/CCIR recommendation, unanimous approval is necessary.

In Europe, CCITT/CCIR recommendations are generally reconsidered by CEPT, which either adopts them as its own recommendations or develops them further, mainly excluding some options or adding missing points.

Their new economic importance is now propelling telecommunications into the front line of world-wide technological competition and the future environment for world trade in services which is shaping up in the framework of the GATT, the General Agreement on Tariffs and Trade.

The Community's major competitors in the international telecommunications market are the United States and — increasingly — Japan: this by virtue of their sheer size, but also by the dynamic forces which have been released through the rapid deregulation of their telecommunications markets.

1. A fast-moving international environment: the United States and Japan

The United States' and Europe's telecommunications systems are comparable in size, while Japan is the world's third major telecommunications area (Table 11). The Third

TABLE 11

Telecommunications services and equipment markets in the European Community, the United States and Japan compared

	EC	Japan	USA
Telephone sets connected to the public network (million)	173.0	68.0	225.3
Number of main lines (million)	117.7	44.9	121.2
Total staff in telecommunications services (1 000)	922	311	963[1]
Total income from all telecommunications services (billion ECU)	64.8	31.2	117.5[2]
Total annual gross investment in telecommunications excluding land and buildings (billion ECU)	22.5	7.7	21.6
Telephone main lines per 100 inhabitants	35.8	37.1	50.2
Telephone stations (sets) of all kinds per 100 inhabitants	52.6	56.2	93.3

[1] 1983.
[2] 1986 exchange rate: 1 ECU = USD 0.983.

Source: International Telecommunications Union *Yearbook of common carrier statistics* (1988) and CEC studies. Reference year: 1986.
Note: the ECU/USD rate has varied widely in the course of the 1980s, notably between 1985 and 1986. This should be taken into account in the interpretation of statistics.

World, with some exceptions, is still far behind: with a telephone penetration of 2 telephone lines per one hundred inhabitants, compared with 36 lines in the European Community, 37 in Japan and 50 in the United States. Europe, the United States and Japan together are estimated to account for nearly 70% of the world's current telecommunications equipment market.

The accumulated investments in the telecommunications network — the 'book-value' of telecommunications assets — in Europe and the United States both approximate the 200 000 million ECU mark — they are estimated at 200 000 million ECU for Europe and 180 000 million ECU for the United States. The difference which has developed is in the use of this enormous asset: the annual revenue averaged in Europe 550 ECU per line, in the United States 970 ECU in 1986 (1986 exchange rate). While the European telecommunications sector has only slowly opened itself to the new technologies, the United States set in motion the reform of the sector in the late 1960s (Box 15).

Box 15

The deregulation of telecommunications in the United States

The deregulation of the telecommunications sector in the United States — progressively since the early 1970s and at accelerated speed since 1980 — has had a fundamental impact on the world market. The dramatic transformation of the US market — more than one-third of the world market — which culminated in the dismantling of AT&T and the spinning off of most of the Bell telephone system, has changed irreversibly the context in which world telecommunications is developing.

The regulatory framework of US telecommunications to date is defined in the 1934 Communications Act, which established the Federal Communications Commission (FCC) as the main regulatory agency.

The point of departure in the late 1960s in the United States was a homogeneous network — the Bell system — wholly owned by AT&T. AT&T's manufacturing subsidiary — called at the time Western Electric — produced exclusively for the Bell system, making AT&T a huge vertically integrated complex and the largest privately owned company in the world. Thus, US telecommunications was dominated by a vast private monopoly, closely regulated by the FCC.

The major steps of US deregulation of the telecommunications sector were the following:

1968: 'Carterfone decision'. The FCC ruled that the Bell system should, in principle, allow equipment not produced by AT&T to be connected to its networks.

1971: 'Specialized common carrier decision'. A general licence was granted to specialized common carriers, which allowed them to offer switched telecommunications services, connected directly to the existing network of local telephone exchanges, and a large number of such carriers were formed. This was the first step towards developing competition within the network.

1971: 'Computer Inquiry I'. After a five year investigation of the increasing interdependence of information and telecommunications technologies, the FCC decided that the integrated office automation systems market should become subject to competition. AT&T, as the regulated operator, was to be allowed to supply these types of services only through a subsidiary separate from its regulated activities.

1976: 'Equipment registration programme'. The FCC developed procedures to facilitate the opening up of markets for terminals (simplified certification procedures for terminal equipment).

1980: 'Computer Inquiry II'. In the light of the convergence between information technology and telecommunications, the FCC updated its 1971 decision. It abandoned the earlier distinction between telecommunications and computer services and introduced one between 'basic services' and 'enhanced services', which correspond roughly to 'value-added services'. It deregulated terminal equipment but allowed AT&T to enter deregulated markets through an independent subsidiary: 'AT&T Information Systems'. The separation requirements are known as 'structural safeguards'.

1982: 'Modified final judgment (MFJ)'. The District Court for the District of Columbia ordered the splitting off of the Bell system regional networks which then represented 77% of AT&T's USD 150 000 million capital assets and approximately 50% of its revenue. The new AT&T kept the long-distance services of the Bell system (under the name 'AT&T Communications') and Western Electric and Bell Laboratories (under the name 'AT&T Technologies'). The long-distance network was opened to competition whereas the regional networks remained under monopoly.

1984: 'AT&T divestiture'. On 1 January 1984 the ruling became effective. AT&T divested itself of the 22 Bell Operating Companies (BOCs). These 22 companies then formed themselves into the present structure of seven regional holding companies (RHCs). These RHCs are often referred to by the old name of 'BOCs'.

The MFJ also imposed restrictions on the business lines that both the divested AT&T and the newly formed RHCs could enter. Thus, AT&T was prevented from providing electronic publishing services (for a period of seven years) while the RHCs were prevented from providing inter-exchange services, from offering information services and from manufacturing telecommunications equipment.

Generally, the MFJ imposed 'structural separation requirements' covering provision by the BOCs or AT&T of competitive 'enhanced' services (these services were to be offered through separate subsidiaries).

The MFJ also imposed a requirement on the BOCs to provide 'equal access' arrangements to all long-distance carriers.

Subsequent to the MFJ, a large number of exceptions ('waivers') to the imposed restrictions were conceded by the District Court of Columbia on a case-by-case basis, in order to allow for practical requirements.

The instability of the regulatory regime thus demonstrated finally led to the FCC's 'Computer Inquiry III'. Computer III replaced the concepts of 'structural safeguards' in order to allow the BOCs to offer integrated services. For this purpose it introduced the concepts of comparably efficient interconnection (CEI) and open network architecture (ONA).

In February 1987, the Department of Justice filed with the District Court of Columbia its first triennial report and recommendations on the MFJ which recommended further lifting of restrictions on AT&T and the BOCs. In September 1987, the Court rejected most of the recommendations, but in March 1988 the Court ruled that the BOCs should be allowed to provide information services (e.g. electronic mail) and voice messaging provided the BOCs do not generate the information content of the services.

The present situation of telecommunications supply in the USA can be summed up as follows:

Local basic services

No competition; subject to strict regulation by the State Utility Commissions.

Bell Operating Companies (BOCs).

Long-distance basic services

Competition permitted; 'dominant carriers' (as determined by the FCC) remain subject to strict regulation under the Communications Act. OCCs (Other Common Carriers) are only lightly regulated ('forbearance' by the FCC).

AT&T remains the dominant long-distance carrier, followed by MCI and GTE-Sprint (OCCs).

Long-distance enhanced services

Unregulated; full resale of capacity including voice permitted.

Several hundred resellers in existence.

Local enhanced services

Competition permitted; BOCs will now be allowed to enter this field under the CEI and later, ONA arrangements (Computer III).

The USA represents a market size which is more than five times larger than any of the individual European countries. Bell Operating Companies (RHCs) are of comparable size with the largest of the European telecommunications administrations.

The deregulation process in telecommunications in the United States should be seen in the context of the broader move towards deregulation at work in this country since the late 1970s. It has introduced substantial dynamism into the US telecommunications market. This dynamic strength has led to the determined entry of AT&T and other US manufacturers and service providers into the world market, and particularly into Europe.

The consequences of the convergence between telecommunications and computers was already the subject of an in-depth inquiry by the US Federal Communications Commission — the powerful FCC — at a time when the term 'telematics' was not even coined in Europe: 'Computer Inquiry I' concluded already in 1971 that the integrated office automation system market should be open to competition.

The 'deregulation' process in the United States has been the major event in the telecommunications world-market throughout the 1970s, culminating in the divestiture of AT&T in the early 1980s. It has put Europe into a situation where it must react if it wants to stand up to the dynamics of the future international telecommunications scene which will be a major factor in the future sharing of economic wealth at world level.

For Europe, the impact of the deregulation of the US telecommunications market has been basically two-fold.

First, the economic and industrial forces set free by the deregulatory process in the United States are turning more and more to the international markets. Europe has become one of the major targets.

This can be seen in the evolution of the strategies of the major multinationals — AT&T and IBM, and increasingly also the Bell Operating Companies, spun-off from AT&T in

1984 as part of the AT&T divestiture process. It can be seen in the increased competition on the transatlantic routes, where the competitors of AT&T — MCI and GTE Sprint — and new entrants compete for the dense Europe/US traffic (Box 16). It can be seen in the new tone of urgency which has made telecommunications a major topic in the protectionist trade legislation which, in the wake of the persistent trade deficit, has been tabled in the US Congress since 1985.

Box 16

A new era: competition for the provision of international telecommunications services

For many years AT&T was the sole US provider of international telephone services, with international data services provided by ITT World Communications, RCA Global Communications and Western Union International. In the course of the US deregulatory process, other US service providers, such as MCI, US Sprint and Graphnet have expanded into the international voice or data markets.

In 1985 and 1986 the US Federal Communications Commission, the FCC, granted permission for the establishment of eight international satellite services, separate from Intelsat, subject to certain conditions. Currently, the United States is in the process of consulting with Intelsat on one proposed system (PanAmSat), as foreseen according to Article XIV of the Intelsat Convention, which calls for there to be 'no significant economic harm' to Intelsat. There has been no consultation initiated yet for any other system.

At the same time, the FCC granted applications for licences to two US companies to install and operate private optical submarine cable facilities in which bulk transmission capacity is to be sold on a non-common carrier basis.

The situation has become still more complex owing to the FCC decision in 1986 to extend 'recognized private operating agency (RPOA)' status — the status reserved by the International Telecommunications Union for telecommunications administrations — to enhanced service providers to assist these providers in obtaining operating agreements with foreign administrations and to purchase 'indefeasible rights of users (IRUs)' — traffic rights — in overseas cables. [1]

---

[1] Green Paper, p. 156.

Second, the deregulation process in the United States by itself inevitably influences the discussion on future regulation in Europe. There are two elements of the US deregulation which must be carefully separated. They have been present throughout the long evolution from the Carterfone decision through 'Computer Inquiry I and II', the AT&T 'divestiture' and the decision on 'Computer Inquiry III'.

The first element has as its origin the general phenomenon of the merger of the regulated telecommunications and the non-regulated computer sector — and a subsequent need for redefinition of the boundary lines of the monopoly. The second element — US legislation under the Sherman anti-trust act and US judicial traditions — is specific to the US situation and therefore of limited value for comparison with the European situation.

It is the first element which is of most relevance for Europe, in so far as Europe and the United States face the same transformation in telecommunications, i.e. the convergence of telecommunications and data processing. Like the United States, Europe must think about developing a dynamic market.

Japan has liberalized its telecommunications system dramatically since 1985 — partly due to US pressure to open its market but much more due to the general Japanese consensus that a dynamic telecommunications market is needed to propel Japan into a position of leadership in the future world information economy (Box 17).

Box 17

The deregulation of telecommunications in Japan

Since the early 1950s, domestic telecommunications services in Japan have been provided by the Nippon Telegraph and Telephone Corporation (NTT), whilst all of the international services were provided by Kokusai Denshin Denwa Company Ltd (KDD).

In 1985, Japan started to deregulate its telecommunications industry.

Two new laws were introduced intended to bring about a process of deregulation and liberalization within the Japanese telecommunications industry: the telecommunications business law and the Nippon Denshin Denwa Kabushiki Kaisha law (NTT law). The two new laws came into effect on 1 April 1985.

The new laws have:
(i)   authorized a liberalized use of telecommunications facilities;
(ii) ended the domestic telecommunications monopoly of NTT;
(iii) restructured NTT as a private corporation ready to participate in a competitive market-place; and
(iv) provided a framework for allowing competition with KDD in the international market-place.

In the light of the Computer II definition problems in the USA, the Japanese Government has attempted to avoid the US 'basic' versus 'enhanced' ('value-added') distinction of Computer II which it saw as unworkable. Instead they opted for a distinction between 'facilities providers' (Type I) and 'service providers' (Type II).

These two classifications are described as follows:

(i) Type I operators: Type I operators are regulated operators who own and operate their own transmission facilities. Type I operators remain subject to prior approval by the MPT, the Japanese Ministry of Posts and Telecommunications.

Both NTT and KDD are established by the new law as Type I operators.

In the meantime, the MPT has authorized five additional new facility-based competitors.

Three of these new Type I operators plan terrestrial networks (one using microwave transmission, the second, optical fibre laid along the roads and the third, optical fibre alongside the railway lines), whilst the other two intend to build networks based on satellite technology.

(ii) Type II operators: Type II operators are all other telecommunications operators and are less regulated. In effect these are operators providing enhanced (or value-added) services who do not own transmission facilities. There are currently several hundred Type II operators in Japan.

The telecommunications business law does not restrict Type II services to non-voice only, but there may be a *de facto* limitation to data services.

Whilst KDD remains as the dominant international telecommunications operator, the MPT is likely to issue further licences for international operations. At present two consortia have been formed:

(i) a consortium called International Telecommunications of Japan (ITJ) constituted by the largest Japanese trading houses (Mitsubishi, Mitsui and Sumitomo) and others (and assisted by KDD itself); and

(ii) a consortium called International Digital Communications including C Itoh, Toyota Motors, Pacific Telesis, Fujitsu, NEC, and in which Cable & Wireless also has a major share.

In order to ensure that the dominant operators do not use their position to influence other parts of the market unfairly, the MPT issued guidelines in August 1986 restricting the involvement of NTT in international ventures to less than 10% of capital share (and similarly KDD's involvement in national ventures).

The privatization of NTT is being carried out in tranches. The rapid increase of the value of NTT shares floated on the Tokyo stock market has made NTT the world's biggest company in terms of market value.

In spring 1987, Japan concluded a special arrangement with the United States on the operation of international value-added services. Japan can be expected to exert major pressure on both the telecommunications equipment and international services markets in the future.

In parallel, Japan's MITI, the powerful Ministry of International Trade and Industry, and the MPT, the Ministry of Posts and Telecommunications, have encouraged NTT, the Nippon Telegraph and Telephone Corporation and now the world's largest company in market value, to follow the ambitious plan towards implementation of the INS, the information network system which has turned into a huge long-term investment effort for the accelerated general digitization of the NTT network and the rapid introduction of ISDN — with the expected spin-off of a strong position in the future digital terminal markets.

Based on its newly gained dynamics, by a determined policy towards liberalization in its home market, Japan is currently rapidly penetrating the world telecommunications market.

The European Community traditionally has a strong position on the world telecommunications market, [1] with a total surplus of 1 000 million ECU in 1987. But since the early 1980s this position has been eroded. Europe maintains a strong position in telecommunications in the Third World but has a growing deficit with both the United States and Japan.

Broadly speaking, the US and Japanese exports are of the same order of magnitude as those of the Community. The differences are on the import side. In 1987, the Community exported to the United States a total value of telecommunications equipment — including telecommunications components — of 417 million ECU, and to Japan only 40 million ECU. Yet it imported from the United States 910 million ECU worth of equipment, and from Japan 984 million ECU worth (Figure 15). [2]

Since 1986, Japan has overtaken the United States as the country with which the Community has the largest deficit in telecommunications equipment trade. All Member States are in deficit, with the list being led by Germany first and the United Kingdom second.

The fact that all Member States are in deficit — though the regulatory systems still show very different degrees of openness — also demonstrates that regulation cannot be used to protect a country's industry against competition on the world market. There is no alternative to exposing the industry to competition if it is to maintain itself on the world market. But Europe must build a more dynamic home market if it wants to compete.

---

[1] See Chapter IV, Section 3.

[2] The trade aggregate used to calculate these trade flows also includes components used for telecommunications.

FIGURE 15

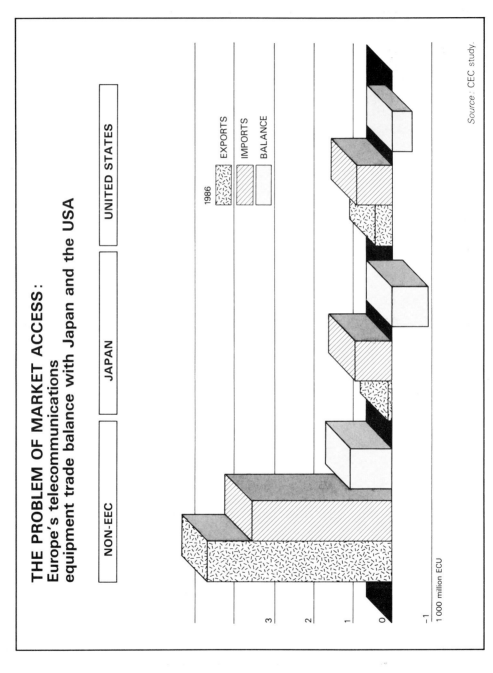

Source: CEC study.

There are signs that, based on their strong dynamic markets, the United States and Japan are poised to share out between them the lucrative new international telecommunications market, without European participation. In 1986, the United States and Japan concluded an arrangement on future market development of integrated circuits, the centrepiece of the new information technology. [1] In spring 1987 the United States and Japan concluded an agreement on the future operation of international value-added services.

In both cases, the European Community made it clear that Europe must participate when its interests are at stake. But the international competition will become tougher, as the discussion on the future international environment for telecommunications proceeds.

Other new entrants are waiting in the wings: Taiwan, Korea, Hong Kong, Singapore. According to statistics published by the US Department of Commerce, by 1984 the EC share of US telecommunications equipment imports had already dropped to 3.6%, compared to a share of US imports from Japan of 51%, from Taiwan of 11.3% and Hong Kong of 7.3%.

Only united will Europe have a strong voice in the future shaping of the world market.

2. The legacy of the past: the cost of 'non-Europe' in more detail

Nevertheless, strategies in Europe during the early 1980s continued to be influenced by the model of the past which had developed during the build-up of the telephone network of the 1970s. [2] The traditional model in Europe is of a national champion, with planning centred principally on the national market — and with access to other networks and markets as an additional feature only.

Digitization — and the associated new transmission techniques, optical fibre and satellite [3] — have dramatically pushed up the R&D costs of the industry. In one of the traditional sectors of European strength — public switching systems — the cost structures were completely reversed by the 1980s. In 1970 software accounted for roughly 20% of the total R&D cost and hardware for 80%. By 1990 this ratio will be reversed — 80% for software and 20% for hardware. Currently, the software to operate a public switching system comprises some 1 million programmed instructions. It is estimated that by the early 1990s, with the growing complexity of switches, this figure will have risen to 3 million.

A digital switching system now costs up to 1 000 million ECU in research and development, with a life-cycle of hardly 10 years and with permanent expensive updating of the software which operates the system required. This compares to a total development cost of 15 to 20 million ECU for an electromechanical switching system in the early 1970s,

---

[1] See Chapter IV, Section 3.
[2] See Chapter II.
[3] See Chapter III.

with an expected life-cycle of 20 to 30 years and no major changes to the system during operation. This means that the new digital systems need to secure 8% of the world market in order to break even. No national telecommunications market in the Community — the traditional base of national manufacturers — corresponds to more than 6% of the market.

But in spite of these fundamental changes in basic costs, the European industrial scene went into the 1980s without a reorientation towards the European market. The simple continuation of the national champion model of the past led to the costly development of eight digital switching systems in Europe, against two in Japan and three in the United States (out of which one, the ITT system — System 12 — was also largely developed in Europe). The price to be paid was a fragile market base for some of these systems and duplication of research and development.

Less obvious but probably even more serious was the cost of 'non-Europe' in the field of the emerging new services. The lack of coordination during service introduction and the costly requirement of establishing compatibility *ex post* between national networks led to substantial delays in the introduction of new services.

One major example was the difficulties encountered during the introduction of public packet-switching networks in Europe — an ideal carrier for many value-added services (Box 18). The lack of a European-wide public homogeneous medium to carry value-added services, and the difficulties which plagued international packet-switching services in Europe throughout the early 1980s — despite a very promising start — have been a major contributing factor to the current weakness of Europe in the field of international value-added services — where the high value-added nature of its economy should give Europe, in principle, an ideal starting point in this area.

Box 18

The cost of 'non-Europe': the example of packet-switching services in Europe

In the late 1970s a new type of public telecommunications network started developing in Europe: packet-switched public data networks (PSPDNs).

Packet-switched networks transmit data via the network in bursts ('packets'), with the routeing of the packets determined according to the most economic use of free network capacity. They permit far more efficient, and therefore less expensive, data transmission than was ever possible with conventional techniques of data transmission.

This advantage comes into its own over long distances: costs for PSPDNs are nearly independent of distance, since the additional cost of transmitting over long distances is negligible as PSPDNs make extremely efficient use of trunk transmission capacity.

A technology, therefore, with exceptional promise for trans-border communications in Europe. Packet-switched services will also be offered at a future stage within the Integrated Services Digital Network, the ISDN.

Packet-switched data services are ideally suited for the interconnection of, and ready access to, different data bases and computer centres throughout Europe, which can clearly play an important role as a catalyst in overall economic and scientific activities. They are well suited to act as a basis for value-added services.

During the 1970s, Europe took an early lead in the development of packet-switching technologies and standards. France introduced its Transpac service which has developed, since then, into Europe's largest packet-switching service. The basic packet-switching X.25 standard was introduced in the CCITT on a European initiative.

The same period saw a determined European effort in the field. The Commission decided, within the framework of its information market programme,[1] to sponsor the development and implementation of Euronet, a true trans-European packet-switched network with switching or access nodes in each country and a single European network management centre, providing a universal and homogeneous packet-switched service between the different European subscriber institutions and organizations, and charging distance-independent tariffs throughout Europe. Euronet entered into service in 1980.

However, in parallel, from the late 1970s onwards, each Member State started to implement its own national PSPDN, in the tradition of the focus on national network development. The development of these national PSPDNs followed different time schedules, commercial policies and priorities, leading to different implementations and to difficulties in the provision of truly harmonized, high quality, international packet-switched services.

By 1984, most Member States had implemented national PSPDNs and were offering commercial packet-switched services. Euronet was replaced by international services between national networks, provided through several interconnections, either directly or via transit networks but encountering substantial problems of incompatibility.

By 1986, major users described the situation as follows:

'Packet switching is the ideal solution for rapidly growing low-speed "burst" data traffic. All European countries are providing packet-switching services via national data networks which comply with the agreed X.25 interface, but development policies have varied widely, as have national tariffs. Volume charges in Italy are three times the level of those in Belgium and the UK for example. Trans-European tariffs are significantly higher than those in the USA... Charges for trans-European services are between half and four times as much (as domestic charges) in the case of packet-switching volume charges. There is a danger that excessive long-distance communications charges are creating a significant handicap to the efficient development of the European internal market'. [2]

It is only during the last two years that, within the framework of European telecommunications policy and the objective of the common development of Europe-wide services, substantial progress has been made, in close cooperation with the CEPT, in order to redress the situation.

[1] See Chapter VI, Section 8.
[2] 'Clearing the lines — A user's view on business communications in Europe', Round Table of European Industrialists, 1986.

Another major cause for the delay in the development of a European value-added services market was the introduction of incompatible videotex services in the Community — the potential of which for carrying value-added services to a wide public is being so clearly demonstrated by the success of the Minitel in France. [1] As late as 1987, Europe-wide videotex services were still not possible (Box 19).

Box 19

The cost of 'non-Europe': videotex in Europe

The development of videotex in Europe is another example of the setback to service development which has resulted from incompatibility of systems in Europe.

Originally conceived as a data transmission and retrieval service using home television sets, videotex has taken on the aspect of a genuine telematic service.

The success of the French Télétel/Minitel services has demonstrated the potential of videotex for the public at large. Over 4 000 private providers now offer services via the 3 million Minitel terminals installed by the end of 1987.

No unified approach took place at the international level at the time of early system development. Consequently, continuing evolution, influenced by differences in separate and contrasting national approaches, has led to today's situation where the single label 'videotex' covers a wide range of private and public services with generally incompatible standards for information transmission and presentation.

[1] See Chapter III, Section 5.

The CCITT recommendation T.101 defines three families of videotex, corresponding to:

(i) Data syntax I: Captain, the Japanese system;

(ii) Data syntax II: European videotex services defined by the CEPT;

(iii) Data syntax III: NAPLPS, the North American service.

Within Europe, Data syntax II actually comprises four different 'profiles':

(i) Profile I: Bildschirmtext, Germany;

(ii) Profile II: Télétel, France, the Minitel service;

(iii) Profile III: Prestel, UK;

(iv) Profile IV: Prestel Plus, Sweden.

The different European systems are quite incompatible with each other in practice. Interconnection between any two European systems, where at all possible, therefore requires complex gateways.

Videotex terminals now in use in the different European countries can be essentially classified according to the following families:

(i) Television-based devices with videotex adapter, modem and keyboard; price range 450 ECU to 1 150 ECU.

(ii) Specialized terminals developed for videotex, such as the French Minitel; price about 115 ECU.

(iii) Mid-range devices with colour display and some basic features; price from 680 ECU for Profile 3 to 150 ECU for Profile 1 terminals.

(iv) High-performance devices with editing facilities and possible compatibility with several presentation standards; price from 1 700 ECU to 2 250 ECU.

(v) Business terminals with microcomputer-based full editing facilities and videotex capability; price 2 250 ECU to 5 700 ECU.

(vi) Adapters for personal or microcomputers; price 115 ECU to 1 150 ECU.

Two opposing trends in technology development can be identified:

(i) Large-scale production of low-cost videotex dedicated terminals, the Minitel approach.

(ii) Multiservice terminals capable of handling sophisticated applications (text processing, telesoftware, etc.) and presentation techniques (geometric, graphical, etc.) and also encompassing features of the CEPT A4 videotex terminal reference model.

At present, there are contrasting trends in the Member States.

The spread of videotex in Europe has been hampered by the different standards adopted by the national services. Unfortunately, some of the worst aspects of the current situation seem to perpetuate themselves. Differences between France, Germany, the UK and other Member States can hold back the development of videotex in Europe. There is some risk that the situation will facilitate penetration of the North American standard, at least at the customer level.

Within the framework of its telecommunications policy, the Community is making substantial efforts to develop Europe-wide videotex services. The Ovide system[1] is a leading project for Europe-wide applications of videotex.

The recent decision by the German Bundespost to allow connection of Minitel terminals to its network may be a first encouraging sign that Europe-wide videotex services will develop.

---

[1] See Chapter VI, Section 6.

In the field of mobile services, the lack of European cooperation showed up in a dramatic way. By 1986, the Group for Analysis and Forecasting, the GAP — charged by the Community and SOG-T[1] with a study of the situation — found that five different incompatible systems had been implemented in the Member States. 'Mobile communications break down when frontiers within the Community are crossed. A car driver crossing the Community would currently need five different mobile telephone systems to be able to communicate in all areas where mobile services are currently provided.

As a consequence, markets for mobile terminals are fragmented. Three different frequency bands are used in the Community for two-way public mobile telephone services and three different frequency bands are used for one-way paging services. Economic low-cost solutions cannot be obtained under these circumstances'[2] (Box 20).

---

[1] See Chapter V, Section 5.
[2] Proposal for a Council Recommendation and Directive on the coordinated introduction of public pan-European digital mobile communications in the Community, Communication by the Commission, COM(87) 35, p. 6.

Box 20

Mobile communications: a case in point

At present, public mobile communications are limited to telephony, with a relatively small but rapidly growing number of users; as more sophisticated portable and hand-held terminals are developed, data communications and other services will be introduced, making communications on the move essential for a broad range of business and private users.

The development of Europe-wide mobile services has been held back in the past by the incompatibility between the five different systems established in the Member States of the European Community. By 1986, these systems were:

1. TACS   United Kingdom/Ireland
2. NMT 450   Denmark/Spain
   NMT 900   Denmark
3. C-450   Germany
4. ITAL-450   Italy/Portugal (planned)
5. Radiocom 2000   France

Prices for mobile telephones were between 1 800 ECU in the Nordic (NMT) system shared between the Scandinavian countries, and up to 6 500 ECU in the national systems in the Community.

The recent success of mobile communications in the United Kingdom where an active market policy has been followed since 1985 — with the licensing of two operators, Cellnet and Vodafone — has demonstrated the need of European users for mobile communications. By the end of 1987, France also licensed a second operator (Compagnie générale des eaux), in addition to France Télécom. With the anticipation of the new common digital mobile system,[1] mobile communications are expected, in a Europe-wide market context, to be booming in all European countries. Cars with telephones could become as familiar as cars with radios on the Community's roads within the next 10 years.

_____

[1] See Chapter VI, Section 2.

As a result, by 1986 there were no more than 150 000 subscribers to public car telephone systems in the whole of the European Community. By this time, this figure had been surpassed by far by the Scandinavian countries alone, which had established a common system.

It is only with the launching by the Community and CEPT, the European Conference of Postal and Telecommunications Administrations, of the new common digital mobile system that Europe-wide services in mobile communications — with a major potential for the future development of telecommunications — will be possible. [1]

Thus, by the early 1980s it became clear that the traditional loose coordination mechanisms between the European telecommunications administrations which had served well in the past to establish international telephone services, had become insufficient to cope with the complexity of the new digital age. The Community and the CEPT started to act together to redress the situation. This led to the telecommunications action programme in 1984, as a first step, and to the 1987 Green Paper as a second. [2]

With a view to 1992, the telecommunications administrations will also have to act together to address another more fundamental problem of European telecommunications: the cost of crossing frontiers. Throughout the early 1980s substantial tariff barriers persisted for intra-Community telecommunications services. In its report of April 1984, the European Parliament found that 'an international leased telegraph circuit between Brussels and Milan is twice the cost of a similar circuit between Brussels and Marseilles — the same distance — and the Belgian administration's charges for leased telegraph lines to Athens are higher than the charges for a circuit to Moscow'.

Table 12 shows the situation which existed by 1988 in the Community. Table 13 compares charges for intra-Community calls. The different accounting methods and different charging led to differences of more than 100% for the same lines between different Member States in some cases.

TABLE 12

International telephone calls in the Community:
the cost of crossing borders (ECU)

	Most expensive domestic long-distance call	Intra-European Community	
		Average call	Most expensive call
B	0.62	2.22	2.76
D	1.67	1.67	1.67
DK	0.31	1.31	1.39
E	0.98	3.15	3.27
F	1.39	1.85	1.85
GR	1.05	2.73	3.49
IRL	1.30	2.88	2.94
I	1.54	2.92	3.42
L	0.12	1.41	2.32
NL	0.25	1.75	2.32
P	1.01	2.88	3.38
UK	0.73	1.94	2.42

NB: Calls are for 3 minutes; where there is a difference, peak rates have been used; incl. tax (VAT).
Source: CEC studies. Reference date: December 1987/January 1988. 1987 exchange rates used.

---

[1] See Chapter VI, Section 2.
[2] See Chapter V, Section 5.

TABLE 13

Comparison of intra-EC telephone tariffs

The following table shows the cost of a 3 minute call during business hours, measured in ECU, including tax (VAT) and not taking account of special border tariffs

Destination country \ Originating country	B	D	DK	E	F	GR	IRL	I	L	NL	P	UK
B	–	1.67	1.17	3.27	1.85	2.55	2.94	2.98	0.87	1.42	2.89	1.83
D	1.90	–	1.17	3.27	1.85	2.55	2.94	2.60	1.30	1.42	2.89	1.83
DK	2.76	1.67	–	3.27	1.85	2.79	2.94	2.98	1.30	1.42	2.89	1.83
E	2.76	1.67	1.39	–	1.85	2.79	2.94	2.98	2.32	2.32	2.25	2.09
F	1.77	1.67	1.39	2.78	–	2.55	2.94	2.60	1.30	1.42	2.89	1.83
GR	2.76	1.67	1.39	3.27	1.85	–	2.94	2.60	1.30	2.32	3.38	2.42
IRL	2.76	1.67	1.39	3.27	1.85	3.49	–	3.42	1.30	1.88	2.89	1.64
I	2.76	1.67	1.39	3.27	1.85	1.98	2.94	–	1.30	1.88	2.89	2.09
L	1.24	1.67	1.17	3.27	1.85	2.55	2.94	2.60	–	1.42	2.89	1.83
NL	1.24	1.67	1.17	3.27	1.85	2.55	2.94	2.98	0.87	–	2.89	1.83
P	2.76	1.67	1.39	2.44	1.85	3.49	2.94	3.42	2.32	2.32	–	2.09
UK	1.77	1.67	1.39	3.27	1.85	2.79	2.31	2.98	1.30	1.42	2.89	–

Source: CEC studies. Reference date: December 1987 / January 1988. 1987 exchange rates used.

3. The challenge: promoting social and regional cohesion

The transformation of Europe into an information- and communications-based society will inevitably pose major problems to the Community.

The major challenges are three-fold:

(i)   Technical change will result in substantial shifts in employment opportunities. Old jobs will disappear, many new jobs will be created.

(ii) Europe will have to determine how it will define the future position of the individual in an environment which will be substantially richer in information and communication than before.

(iii) The Community will have to maintain — or build-up — cohesion between its Member States throughout the difficult process of adjustment. Europe must avoid a Europe of two speeds in telecommunications — future information-rich and information-poor regions within the Community — because such a gap would translate into an economic and social gap within Europe.

Digitization will bring substantial gains in productivity both in production of equipment and maintenance of the network. While this will increase the productivity of the economy — the only solid basis for economic growth and increasing job opportunities in the long term, without increasing inflation — it confronts the telecommunications industry in Europe with a sometimes difficult short-term challenge.

FIGURE 16

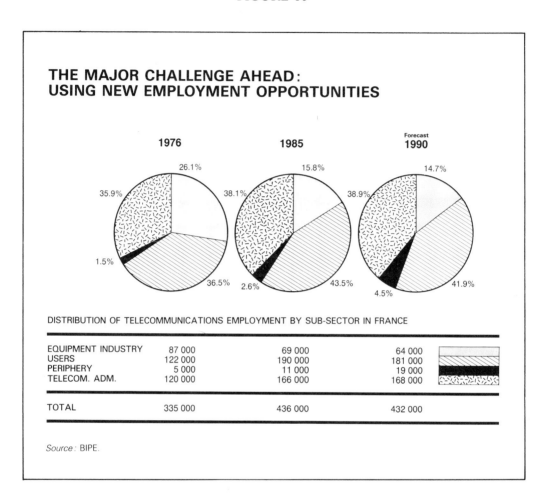

THE MAJOR CHALLENGE AHEAD: USING NEW EMPLOYMENT OPPORTUNITIES

DISTRIBUTION OF TELECOMMUNICATIONS EMPLOYMENT BY SUB-SECTOR IN FRANCE

	1976	1985	1990	
EQUIPMENT INDUSTRY	87 000	69 000	64 000	
USERS	122 000	190 000	181 000	
PERIPHERY	5 000	11 000	19 000	
TELECOM. ADM.	120 000	166 000	168 000	
TOTAL	335 000	436 000	432 000	

Source : BIPE.

For an electromechanical switching system — the size of which is measured by the number of lines which can be connected and switched — the number of work hours needed to manufacture the equivalent of one line was 10 hours; for a digital switching system — the major part of which is made up of software — it can be as low as one third of an hour. As a result, telecommunications in Europe has experienced throughout the 1980s annual productivity gains as high as 6 to 7% per annum, while facing at the same time slackening demand in some of the traditional markets in some countries, such as gradual saturation in the public switching market.

Jobs are shifted by this process to new sites of demand: the rising sector of telematics products and services — the interweaving of the new telecommunications with the work process and the home.

This process has led in one Member State — France, which was the early leader in digitization in Europe — to a thinning out of jobs in manufacturing between 1976 and 1985 from 87 000 to 70 000, with figures forecast to stabilize for the rest of the decade. It has led to an increase in telecommunications jobs on the users' side and in peripheral equipment from 127 000 up to 201 000, with a total expansion of approximately 100 000 jobs in the sector (Figure 16).

This concerns employment in the telecommunications sector. But the impact of telecommunications on overall employment reaches much further. [1] As a basic infrastructure for the future service sectors and for the productivity of the economy as a whole, telecommunications will have a substantial influence on overall job creation potential in Europe.

In the whole of the European Community the telecommunications administrations employ nearly 1 million people. The telecommunications equipment industry employs a further 350 000 people. Some of them will be faced by profound changes in the nature of their jobs resulting from the introduction of computer-controlled exchanges. The overall balance will be determined largely by the regulatory environment which will prevail. Loosening of regulation will allow new activities. New activities will mean new solidly based jobs.

It will be first of all in the employees' interest to create a stable environment in Europe for this sector. 'The reinforcement of the potential for growth and the resulting employment performance necessarily go hand in hand with structural adjustment. But this structural adjustment will be that much smoother if it unfolds against a background of dynamic growth in which the social dimension of the adjustment can be more easily taken into consideration.' [2]

Creating a stable environment will equally depend on developing a consensus in Europe on the second major challenge: how European society will view the future position of the individual in the new information environment.

The new digital technology allows substantially more flexible treatment of data, substantially more diversification of services and substantially broader choice for the user.

The right of choice of access to information and the enhanced exchange and free-flow of information which advanced telecommunications allow are closely related to the fundamental rights which underlie the basic political and cultural consensus of the Community. Freedom of expression is guaranteed by Article 10 of the European Convention on Human Rights. This Convention is not only binding upon its 21 Member States but has also been recognized by the Commission, the Council, the European Parliament [3] and the European Court of Justice as a basis for the development of civil rights within the European Community. [4]

---

[1] See Chapter IV.
[2] 'Annual economic report, 1986-87', *European Economy,* No 30, November 1986, p. 61.
[3] OJ C 103, 1977.
[4] ECJ, 13 December 1979, Case 44/79.

The Commission has emphasized the importance of Article 10 of the Convention of Human Rights for the development of a common market of information and ideas.

'Adequate telecommunications infrastructures and services are a *sine qua non* for the free expression and free flow of information in the Community in the future. The provision of telecommunications network infrastructure and telecommunications services will provide the conduit within which information can flow. The provision of information services and a free market for information content are indispensable requirements for putting telecommunications network infrastructures and telecommunications services to best use.'[1]

While the new telecommunications services will allow a substantially broader choice of information, they will require, in Europe, new common positions with regard to the best ways to protect the individual against abuse of personal data, and to guarantee security and secrecy of communications.

The new technology will allow both more possibilities of abuse but also better ways of protection. The new intelligence of the digital network allows new forms of protection to be built into the network (Box 21).

Box 21

Data protection and telecommunications: meeting social concerns

The enhanced possibilities of advanced telecommunications networks give rise to new problems about the protection of personal data of those who communicate, such as registration of calls, etc.

Data protection is a shorthand formula for the protection of an individual's right and fundamental freedoms, and in particular his/her rights to privacy, with regard to automatic processing of personal data relating to him/her.[1]

The merger of telecommunications and information processing has created new problems of data protection regarding the free flow of information. At this point in time, all Member States have recognized the need for appropriate legal instruments to solve these problems and have taken regulatory measures or are in the process of preparing such measures.

---

[1] See Article 1 of the Convention for the Protection of Individuals with Regard to Automatic Processing of Personal Data, 17 December 1980.

---

[1] Green Paper, p. 139.

The Council of Europe's Convention for the protection of individuals with regard to the automatic processing of personal data, which has been signed by most Community Member States, provides guidelines for the protection of individual's rights to the privacy and security of personal data relating to themselves. [1]

The enhanced processing capabilities of digital networks open not only new possibilities for abuse but also new possibilities for protection of the private sphere. The Integrated Services Digital Network, the ISDN, may serve as an example. It could make the registration of calls easier and rules of conduct for handling call data must be established. But it will also allow enhanced protection of the individual against malicious calls, e.g. by providing the possibility for automatic rejection of unwanted calls.

Technological development will have to take special account of the need to protect the privacy of the individual. Security of communications has been included as an important topic in the development of Integrated Broadband Communications in the RACE programme.

Since 1973, the European Parliament has emphasized on several occasions that the right to privacy should not only be protected by national law, but that harmonizing legislation should be introduced at Community level. [2]

The work programme for a common information market foresees a Council Decision on ratification of the Council of Europe Convention, or a Directive based on Commission Recommendation 81/679/EEC and the Resolution of the European Parliament of 9 March 1982.

---

[1] Green Paper, p. 142.
[2] OJ C 140, 5.6.1979, p. 34.

The major challenge for Europe is to find a common answer to this new challenge. Divergence on basic social values with regard to information and communications could fundamentally impede the future development of European society. It could introduce substantial barriers in the future working of the Europe-wide market.

The third major challenge will be any trend towards the emergence of an information-rich centre and an information-poor periphery in the Community.

The danger exists.

Indices based on both telephone penetration and use of data terminals clearly indicate a low degree of communications equipment in the less favoured peripheral regions of the Community relative to the economically rich parts of Europe (Figure 17).

FIGURE 17

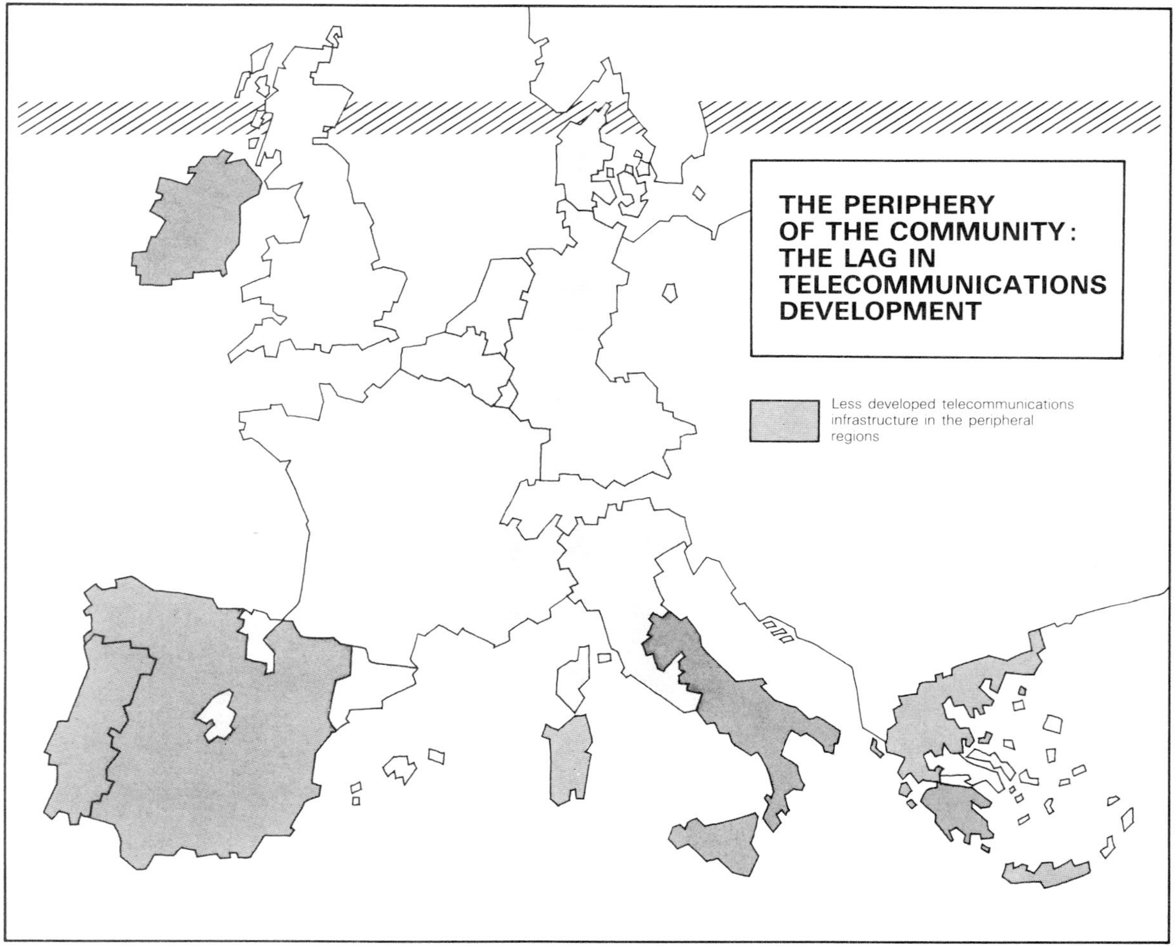

THE PERIPHERY
OF THE COMMUNITY:
THE LAG IN
TELECOMMUNICATIONS
DEVELOPMENT

Less developed telecommunications
infrastructure in the peripheral
regions

The challenge for the Community will be to prevent those regions lacking developed telecommunications from turning into the future information-poor regions of the Community.

A fundamental pre-condition for a Community-wide market in 1992 is the full integration of the less favoured regions of the Community into the economic mainstream of Europe. The Community cannot tolerate the perpetuation of the current gap if a united Europe is to develop. This has made the promotion of cohesion one of the main topics of current Community policy.

4. Europe starts to move: the new trends in the Member States

A strategy for European telecommunications will have to be based primarily on developing the European market. The potential of the EC's market is vast — providing it is realized. At present, Europe does not consume telecommunications products to anything like the same extent as in the United States and Japan. During the early 1980s, telecommunications equipment purchases *per capita* were USD 32 in the Community compared to USD 80 in the United States and USD 46 in Japan. However, the very fact of this relatively low consumption points to the unrealized potential of the European market which, after enlargement to include Spain and Portugal, now comprises 320 million inhabitants.

As has been shown,[1] it is estimated that total public and private investment in the Community in telecommunications over the next 20 years could be 500 000 to 1 000 000 million ECU — more than the total gross investment of the Community for a whole year. It is this potential which Europe will have to tap. Europe must find its own response to current structural change.

Since the early 1980s and accelerating towards the middle of the decade, this general conviction started to become apparent with the European users, European governments and at board level in European companies.

The change in the economic base of the industry and the need for economies of scale led to a frantic rush for new industrial alliances which started to break up the 'national champion' model. While during the early phase of this process the aim was often for short-term gains by linking up with US and Japanese partners — during 1985/86 European/US and European/Japanese agreements still outnumbered agreements between European companies by 3:1 — increasingly a European trans-national restructuring process has been developing. The experience of cooperation between European companies in R&D within the ESPRIT[2] and RACE programmes — more than 100 European companies

---

[1] See Chapter IV, Section 1.
[2] See Chapter VI, Section 8.

cooperating during the RACE definition phase during 1986 [1] — has created a new willingness to work together within Europe.

By 1987, new Europe-wide groups had formed or expanded, or negotiations were under way: French Alcatel took over American ITT's European telecommunications manufacturing operations and became the world's second largest telecommunications group. Siemens took over US GTE's European operations and expanded substantially its European base. Ericsson of Sweden strengthened its alliances with Community countries, thus reinforcing the ties in telecommunications between the EFTA countries and the Community — in addition to the traditional close links which exist between EC telecommunications administrations and the administrations of the EFTA in the framework of the CEPT, the European Conference of Postal and Telecommunications Administrations. The merger between the telecommunications divisions of UK GEC and Plessey and the talks between Italian Italtel and Telettra — though later suspended — indicated the determination at board level to create a stronger industry base (Table 14).

TABLE 14

**Shaping new alliances: the new position of Europe's industry
in the telecommunications world market**

	Country/Region	Telecom sales (USD 1 000 million)	as % of total worldwide sales of company
AT&T	USA	10.2	30% [1]
Alcatel (CGE/ITT)	EC	7.8	61%
Siemens	EC	6.2	22%
NEC	Japan	5.0	31%
Northern Telecom	Canada	4.8	98%
Motorola	USA	3.5	57%
Ericsson	EFTA	3.3	64%
IBM	USA	2.4	4%
Fujitsu	Japan	2.0	16%
GPT (GEC/Plessey)	EC	2.0	100%
Philips	EC	1.7	7%
Bosch	EC	1.5	11%
Hitachi	Japan	1.4	4%
GTE	USA	1.1	7%
Italtel	EC	1.0	95%

Reference year: 1987; *Source:* Eurostratégies-BIPE.

Note: The sales figures represent company structures as at July 1988. Radiocommunications equipment and cable are included. Sales figures depend on the definition of telecommunications equipment adopted. Turnover in areas other than telecommunications equipment is excluded from these figures; the second column of figures indicates what proportion of total company sales are accounted for by telecommunications equipment.

European companies play an important role and enjoy a strong position in the world telecommunications market. Four of them rank among the top ten manufacturers in terms of sales. Alcatel, formed in 1987 through the acquisition of ITT's telecommunications operations by CGE, is now the second largest telecommunications manufacturer in the world, while Siemens is the third largest.

[1] Most of AT&T turnover is in long-distance telecommunications services in the United States.

[1] See Chapter VI, Section 4.

TABLE 14 (*cont'd*)

Company shares of the European telecommunications equipment market
(Community and EFTA countries)

	Share of total (%)
Alcatel (CGE/ITT)	31
Siemens	19
GEC/Plessey	15
Ericsson	9
Philips	5
IBM	5
GTE	3
Italtel	3
Other companies	12
	100

Source: Estimates based on Arthur D. Little.

The European telecommunications sector is highly competitive. The top seven European firms together account for over 80% of sales of telecommunications equipment in Europe.

Alongside the start of the restructuring process of the supply side of telecommunications in Europe, there developed the general conviction that the regulatory framework had to adjust to the new conditions. The United Kingdom was first with the basic regulatory reform of its telecommunications sector starting in 1982. But the other Member States of the Community took up the issue soon after. [1] By the mid-1980s, the debate had developed fully in all Member States.

With the growing consciousness of the new economic and social dimension of telecommunications and the progressive break-up of the national model of the past, there also developed a consciousness of the new dimension needed for European telecommunications: the need for policy formulation at Community level, in order to create a single Europe-wide market.

5. The Community joins forces: the drafting of a Community telecommunications policy

European telecommunications policy progressed only slowly during the early phases of the development of the European Community. From the early 1970s onwards the Commission had urged the opening of public procurement in the sector, as a major prerequisite for the future development of the sector. The Member States did not react at the time. Telecommunications was one of the three sectors excluded from the application of the 1976 EC Directive on the opening of public procurement supply contracts. [2]

---

[1] See Chapter VII, Section 1.
[2] Directive 77/62/EEC, OJ L 13, 15.1.1977.

A first sign of the new consciousness of the technological revolution which was in the offing — the first steps in the merger of telecommunications, data processing and the audio-visual sector — was the reaction to the Commission's communication of 1979, 'European society faced with the challenge of new information technology: a Community response',[1] one year after the publication of the famous Nora-Minc report on the emergence of 'telematics'.[2] But it was only from 1983 onwards, with the creation within the Commission of the Task Force on Information Technology and Telecommunications, that the consensus that had built up on the future importance of information technology and telecommunications for the Community was translated into an active policy approach.

From 1983 onwards, policy formulation progressed rapidly:

(a) By early 1984 the foundations of the ESPRIT programme, the European Strategic Programme for Research and Development in Information Technology, were laid.[3] At the same time, a policy framework was established for the first time, and for telecommunications the Senior Officials Group on Telecommunications (SOG-T) was created and started to play a key role (Box 22).

Box 22

The making of European telecommunications policy

The main participants in the formulation of EC telecommunications policy are the EC Commission, the Council of Ministers, the European Parliament and the Economic and Social Committee.

A number of committees and organizations also play an important role in policy formation:

(i) the Senior Officials Group on Telecommunications (SOG-T), attended by representatives of the Member States, advising the Commission on all aspects of telecommunications policies; the GAP ('Analysis and Forecasting Group') is an important subcommittee of the SOG-T;

(ii) the Senior Officials Group on Information Technology Standards (SOGITS);

(iii) the Senior Officials Advisory Group for the Information Market.

---

[1] COM(79) 650.

[2] Nora, Simon and Minc, Alain: *L'informatisation de la société,* La documentation française, Paris, 1978.

[3] See Chapter VI, Section 8.

Within the framework of the RACE and ESPRIT programmes [1] special committees have been created to represent Member States and user and industry interests.

In addition, a range of European initiatives have been taken at different levels which play an important role, such as the ESPRIT Round Table of industrial companies, the Standards Promotion Action Group (SPAG), Ectel, the European Telecommunications and Professional Electronics Association, and the recent creation of EWOS, the European Workshop for Open Systems.

A wide-ranging system of consultation has been established in the framework of the discussions on the Green Paper with the participation of more than 45 organizations: users, telecommunications administrations; the European telecommunications, data-processing and services industries; and the trade unions in the field. [2]

Regarding formal contacts with other organizations on telecommunications issues, particularly on standards, the most important interlocutors for the Commission are the CEPT, the European Conference of Postal and Telecommunications Administrations, and the CEN-Cenélec, the European Committees for Standardization and for Electrotechnical Standardization, by virtue of the cooperation agreements concluded by the Commission with those two organizations. [3]

---

[1] See Chapter VI.
[2] See Chapter VIII.
[3] See Chapter VI, Section 3.

(b) In May 1984, the Commission, on the basis of the work of SOG-T, submitted its proposed lines of action, setting out a consistent programme in telecommunications. [1]

(c) By July 1984 the first cooperation agreement was signed between the Commission and the CEPT (Box 23). A similar agreement was signed soon after with the CEN-Cenelec.

---

[1] COM(84) 277.

Box 23

The European Conference of Postal and Telecommunications Administrations (CEPT): mechanisms and cooperation with the Community

The CEPT is the Community's major partner in the development of telecommunications policy.

The CEPT was founded in 1959. It is open to all European postal and telecommunications administrations. It now comprises 26 European countries: all the Member States of the European Community and of the European Free Trade Association (EFTA), together with Turkey, Yugoslavia and six smaller countries.

The Plenary Assembly is the supreme body of CEPT. It deals with questions concerning the structure and management of the organization and is competent in all questions related to posts and telecommunications. The Plenary Assembly meets periodically, generally every two years, for an ordinary session.

In the course of plenary sessions, the Conference nominates the administration to organize the following ordinary session. This administration is known as the managing administration. It guarantees the Conference's continuing work in between sessions.

Two different commissions deal with posts and telecommunications. They have special responsibility for questions concerning service provision, technical aspects and tariffs.

The committees of the Telecommunications Commission are as follows:

(i)   Coordination Committee on Harmonization (CCH);

(ii)   Commercial Action Committee (CAC);

(iii)   Coordination Committee for Satellite Telecommunications (CCTS);

(iv)   Liaison Committee for Transatlantic Telecommunications (CLTA).

A Memorandum of Understanding establishing a framework for cooperation between the Community and CEPT was signed in July 1984.

In line with the CEPT/Commission agreement,[1] working programmes of CEPT regarding standardization have been agreed since 1985 with the Commission. The CEPT has reached a similar agreement with EFTA.

---

[1] See Chapter VI, Section 3.

The CEPT decided — at the request of the Commission — on the working out of a 'family' of specifications which could be made binding on its members. These are known as NETs (normes européennes des télécommunications — European telecommunications standards). To reach this goal, a Memorandum of Understanding has been prepared to bind the signatory countries to compulsory acceptance of the specifications to be used, in particular for the type approval of telecommunications terminals.

By 1987, 15 countries had signed this memorandum, namely the 12 EC Member States, Sweden, Finland and Norway.

This memorandum has resulted in the creation of a new body, the Technical Recommendations Applications Committee (TRAC), with the task of adopting the NETs under a qualified majority system. [1]

A similar memorandum has been established by the Commission with CEN-Cenelec.

In addition, an understanding has been reached between the CEPT and CEN-Cenelec, the European Committees for Standardization and Electrotechnical Standardization, to coordinate the work of the three bodies.

---

[1] See Chapter VI, Section 3.

(d) From Autumn 1984 onwards the Council started, following proposals by the Commission, to take a series of decisions on telecommunications, at accelerating speed. By the end of 1987, 12 directives, decisions, regulations and recommendations had been adopted (Box 24).

Box 24

Legal instruments under the EEC Treaty: a short summary

The legal instruments available under the Treaty of Rome are the following:

(i) The direct application of the Treaty rules, such as Community competition rules (e.g. Articles 85, 86 and 90). Such provisions entitle legal or national persons in the Member States to rights which they can invoke before national courts and the European Court of Justice. The Commission can also obtain the enforcement of such provisions before the European Court of Justice.

(ii) EC Directives: a Directive is binding on the Member States as to the aim to be reached but leaves the Member States the choice of form and methods for attaining within the national legal system the objectives laid down at Community level.

Directives are in general issued by the Council, on proposals from the Commission. However, under Article 90 (3) the Commission can issue Directives (or Decisions) to 'ensure the application of the provisions of this Article' concerning public undertakings and undertakings to which Member States grant special or exclusive rights.

(iii) EEC Regulations: a Regulation is a legal measure which has general application, is binding in its entirety and is directly applicable in all Member States. It is issued either by the Council or, in certain cases, by the Commission.

(iv) EEC Decisions: a Decision is an individual measure addressed either to a Member State or a natural or legal person. It is binding in its entirety only upon those to whom it is addressed. It is issued either by the Council or in certain cases by the Commission.

(v) EEC Recommendations: a Recommendation has the object of recommending a particular course of conduct to the addressees without legally binding them thereby. It is issued either by the Council or by the Commission.

Since 1984, all of these instruments have been applied in the telecommunications field.

(e) In 1986, the Commission's Task Force for Information Technologies and Telecommunications was merged with other Commission departments and transformed into the Directorate-General for Telecommunications, Information Industries and Innovation to broaden its base.

(f) At the same time, the Commission's Directorate-General for Competition stepped up its campaign to open the telecommunications market. On 29 March 1985 the European Court adopted its ruling on the 'British Telecom case' which turned out to be a cornerstone for future case-law on telecommunications in the Community. [1]

(g) On 30 June 1987, the Commission published its Green Paper on telecommunications, launching a broad debate on the adjustment and liberalization of the telecommunications sector in Europe.

(h) On 30 June 1988, the Council adopted a resolution approving the basic objectives of the Green Paper.

---

[1] See Chapter VI, Section 7.

VI — Telecommunications actions under way: laying the foundations for a strong European telecommunications infrastructure for the 1992 market

1. An overview: a consistent concept for the development of advanced telecommunications in Europe — the action lines

The Commission put forward its telecommunications action programme in 1984.[1] This was approved by the Council the same year (Box 25).

Box 25

Telecommunications action programme

The Council at its meeting of 17 December 1984 agreed the following action programme:[1]

'(a) the creation of a Community market for telecommunications equipment and terminals via:

(i) a standardization policy aimed at the effective implementation in the Community of common standards derived from international standards;

(ii) the progressive application of procedures for the mutual recognition of type approval for terminals;

(iii) the opening of access to public telecommunications contracts, the first phase of which was initiated by the Council's Recommendation of 12 November 1984.

(b) improving the development of advanced telecommunications services and networks:

---

[1] Minutes of the 979th meeting of the Council, 17 December 1984.

---

[1] Communication from the Commission to the Council on telecommunications, COM(84) 277, 18 May 1984.

> (i) by opening discussions, based on available studies, on:
>   - the implementation of infrastructure projects of common interest;
>   - launching a development programme for the technology required in the long term for the implementation of future wide-band networks;
>
> (ii) by defining and progressively setting up a video-communications system to link the various political authorities in the Community;
>
> (c) improved access for less favoured regions of the Community, through the appropriate use of Community financial instruments, to the benefit of the development of advanced services and networks;
>
> (d) coordination of negotiating positions within the international organizations dealing with telecommunications, based on discussions carried out jointly with the Working Party of Senior Officials on Telecommunications.'

Over the last four years, the Commission has advanced proposals along five main lines, in order to implement this action programme:

'(i) Coordination of future development of telecommunications in the Community and shared infrastructure projects. The main focus here is on the principal future stages of network development: the Integrated Services Digital Network (ISDN), digital mobile communications, and the future introduction of broadband communications.

(ii) Creation of a Community-wide market for terminals and equipment. Promotion of Europe-wide open standards, in order to give equal opportunity to all market participants.

(iii) The launch of a programme of pre-competitive and 'pre-normative' R&D, covering the technologies required for Integrated Broadband Communications (the RACE programme).

(iv) Promoting the introduction and development of advanced services and networks in the less favoured peripheral regions of the Community.

(v) Building up common European positions in relation to international discussions in this area.'[1]

On this basis, in close cooperation with the SOG-T, substantial progress has been made. Box 26 shows the Decisions, Regulations, Directives and Recommendations adopted up to June 1988. These decisions by the Council were reached within a very short time span.

---

[1] Green Paper, p. 98.

Box 26

**Council decisions taken since 1984 in the field
of telecommunications**

Council Recommendation of 12 November 1984 concerning the implementation of a common approach in the field of telecommunications (84/549/EEC).

Council Recommendation of 12 November 1984 concerning the first phase of opening up access to public telecommunications contracts (84/550/EEC).

Council Decision of 25 July 1985 on a definition phase for an R&D programme in advanced communications technologies for Europe (RACE) (85/372/EEC).

Council Resolution of 9 June 1986 on the use of videoconference and videophone techniques for intergovernmental applications (86/C 160/01).

Council Directive of 24 July 1986 on the initial stage of the mutual recognition of type approval for telecommunications terminal equipment (86/361/EEC).

Council Regulation of 27 October 1986 instituting a Community programme for the development of certain less favoured regions of the Community by improving access to advanced telecommunications services (STAR programme) ((EEC) No 3300/86).

Council Directive of 3 November 1986 on the adoption of common technical specifications of the MAC/packet family of standards for direct satellite television broadcasting (86/529/EEC).

Council Decision of 22 December 1986 on standardization in the field of information technology and telecommunications (87/95/EEC).

Council Recommendation of 22 December 1986 on the coordinated introduction of the Integrated Services Digital Network (ISDN) in the European Community (86/659/EEC).

Council Recommendation of 25 June 1987 on the coordinated introduction of public pan-European digital mobile communications in the European Community (87/371/EEC) and Council Directive of 25 June 1987 on the frequency bands to be made available for the coordinated introduction of public pan-European digital mobile communications in the European Community (87/372/EEC).

Council Decision of 5 October 1987 introducing a communications network Community programme on trade electronic data interchange systems (TEDIS) (87/499/EEC).

Council Decision of 14 December 1987 on a Community programme in the field of telecommunications technologies-research and development in advanced communications technologies in Europe (RACE programme) (88/28/EEC).

A detailed review of progress can be found in the Commission's May 1988 communication on telecommunications: 'Progress report on the implementation of a Community telecommunications policy', COM(88) 240 I/II, 31.5.1988. The Green Paper lists three factors which have permitted progress to be made:

'(i)   implementation within the context of a consistent action programme fully backed by the Council and the SOG-T;

(ii)   creation of a framework of cooperation with the telecommunications administrations and industry, in particular with the CEPT and CEN-Cenelec;

(iii) full alignment with the main broad goals of the Community: completion of the internal market; general policy on standardization; research and technological development (R&TD) policy; economic and social cohesion; competition policy.'

2. Coordinating the future development of telecommunications in the Community: the Integrated Services Digital Network; digital mobile communications; trade electronic data interchange

The Integrated Services Digital Network (ISDN)

The coordinated introduction of ISDN is a major step forward for network development in the Community. By adapting the increasingly available digital narrowband infrastructure ISDN will allow voice, data, text and simple video communications on the existing network. As set out in Chapter III, ISDN creates the potential for an open digital network infrastructure in the Community, and lays the basis for the Community-wide introduction of new services.

Digitization is already bringing major benefits to telephone operating companies, industry and users. The services offered by ISDN represent an even greater step forward:

(i)   for the users, there is the prospect of a fast, flexible and reliable system that can be tailored to meet the full range of telecommunications needs, from the corporate user to the small business and the home;

(ii)   for the operating companies, there are the prospects of increased revenue from new services and a growing use of the network, coupled with reduced costs in the local network, improved operations and maintenance efficiency, the merging of voice and non-voice services and the gradual disappearance of dedicated networks;

(iii) for the industry there is the promise of increased market volume for equipment for the provision of new services.

Unlike RACE which reaches further into the future, ISDN does not require substantial R&D at Community level. Rather it is based on the ongoing digitization of the telephone network.

Community telecommunications policy took a decisive step forward with the agreement at Community level on the coordinated introduction of ISDN covering the agreed interfaces, time schedule and set of services to be provided in all Member States. The Recommendation on Community-wide introduction of ISDN was approved by the Council on 22 December 1986.

Joint planning at Community level was only initiated after some national administrations had already advanced considerably on the elaboration of different ISDN versions. On these definitional problems, the recommendation lays down timetables for agreement on the various elements, notably with the CEPT, and a requirement for annual progress reports to the European Parliament (Box 27).

Box 27

Council Recommendation 86/659/EEC: the Integrated Services Digital Network (ISDN)

The main features of ISDN, and the reason for wanting to introduce it, were explained in Chapter III, Section 4.

In December 1986 the Council issued a Recommendation for coordinated introduction of ISDN. [1]

Standards

Community action on ISDN standardization is focused on the need to introduce standards as early as possible in the evolutionary stages of ISDN, in order to counteract the development of non-standard solutions in individual Member States. Thus the Recommendation insists on common implementation of standard physical interfaces at the CCITT 'S' and 'T' reference points.

Tariffs

The Recommendation also addresses the question of tariffs, noting that tariffs should become less dependent on distance than at present, and that a relationship of ISDN tariffs with conventional telephony tariffs should be established in a way that will promote the rapid take-up of digital services in Europe. The recommendation calls for the Community's financial instruments to contribute to the extra investments required for ISDN.

Services

A basic set of common services, to be provided in all Member States starting from 1988, is also defined as follows:

---

1. Services to be provided in all Member States starting from 1988:
   (i) 'Bearer services':
        Circuit switched transparent at 64 Kbit/s.
   (ii) 'Teleservices':
        Digital telephony 3.1 kHz at 64 Kbit/s;
        Facsimile at 64 Kbit/s (Group IV);
        Teletex at 64 Kbit/s;
        Mixed-mode teletex/facsimile at 64 Kbit/s.
   (iii) 'Supplementary services':
        Call-waiting;
        Calling line identification;
        Closed-user group (may be implemented later by some countries);
        Direct-dialling-in.
2. Services which might be implemented during the period 1988 to 1993:
   (i) 'Bearer services':
        Packet bearer service on D channel.
   (ii) 'Teleservices':
        Hi-fi quality telephony (7 kHz at 64 Kbit/s);
        Audioconference at 64 Kbit/s;
        Alphageometric videotex at 64 Kbit/s;
        Image transmission and computer communication at 64 Kbit/s.
   (iii) 'Supplementary services':
        Advice of charge;
        Completion of call meeting busy;
        Conference call;
        Call diversion;
        Freephone;
        Malicious call identification;
        Three party call;
        Called user identification.

Time schedule

The Recommendation defines two penetration objectives for ISDN: 'The administrations should plan to provide by 1993 ISDN access for a number equivalent to 5% of 1983 subscriber main lines (i.e. 5 million ISDN lines by the end of 1992). The territorial coverage should be sufficient to permit 80% of customers to have the option of the ISDN access.'[1]

---

[1] Council Recommendation on the coordinated introduction of the Integrated Services Digital Network (ISDN) in the European Community (86/659/EEC), OJ L 382, 31.12.1986, p. 36.

The Recommendation sets forth essential elements for providing an open ISDN environment:

(i) specification of interfaces between the network and terminals;

(ii) specification of a number of end-to-end services to be provided with universal availability;

(iii) general tariff principles to ensure open use of the network infrastructure.

Digital mobile communications (car telephones)

In the past, car telephones have been one of the worst examples of lack of Community-wide compatibility and the cost of 'non-Europe'. [1] As a technology, mobile communications have a clear vocation for trans-border availability — the inherited European patchwork of different systems, which makes a mobile telephone useless as soon as one crosses a border, cries out for a common European policy.

The imminent changeover to a second generation of mobile communications technology — digital cellular communications — presents a unique opportunity for the introduction of a pan-European system in the Community.

The new system will be based on digital rather than the current analogue technology, allowing low-cost solutions to technical problems and compatibility with the Integrated Services Digital Network.

The European Conference of Postal and Telecommunications Administrations (CEPT) has made a vigorous start on using the transition to second-generation technology, expected at the end of this decade, as a chance to develop a common European system of digital cellular mobile communications. A special working group — the 'groupe spécial mobile' (GSM) — has been set up by the CEPT for this purpose (Box 28).

Box 28

Council Directive 87/372/EEC: developing pan-European mobile communications

The lack of coordination in current car telephone systems, leading to delayed introduction of service, five different incompatible systems in the Member States and high prices has been explained in Chapter V, Section 2.

---

[1] See Chapter V, Section 2.

In June 1987 the Council adopted, on a Commission proposal:

(i) a Recommendation for the coordinated introduction of public pan-European digital mobile communications [1] and

(ii) a Directive on the frequency bands to be made available for the purpose. [2]

The Directive instructs the Member States to reserve progressively the whole of the 890-915 and 935-960 MHz frequency bands for the future pan-European digital mobile service. Availability of frequency bands is the major guarantee for the emergence of the new pan-European system.

The Recommendation calls for the start of the service at the latest from 1991 onwards.

The future pan-European digital mobile communications system will:

(i) use the 890-915 and 935-960 MHz frequency bands;

(ii) permit a greater traffic flow and therefore substantially quicker connections;

(iii) provide the user with higher voice-transmission quality;

(iv) allow for hand-held terminals which users can carry outside the car;

(v) facilitate the introduction of new services related to ISDN.

Services to be available from 1991:

(i) Bearer services:

Non-transparent bearer service for speech;

Transparent bearer service for data transmission;

(ii) Basic services:

Hand-over;

National/international roaming;

(iii) Teleservices:

Telephony at 3.1 kHz;

(iv) Supplementary services:

Calling line identification;

Advice of call duration;

Speech encryption.

The tariffs will take into account the current trend towards less distance dependence.

The introduction date will be 1991 at the latest. Major urban areas should be covered by 1993 at the latest. The main links between these areas should be covered by 1995 at the latest.

Given the economies of scale of the larger unified 1992 European market, prices for the future mobile telephones are expected to fall substantially. In the early 1990s they are forecast to be in the range of 450 to 1 600 ECU, i.e. the most expensive equipment in 1995 will be lower in price than the cheapest mobile telephone in 1988.

As a consequence of the new technology, the number of users of the public car telephone system in the Community is expected to increase dramatically. It will pass from 150 000 in 1985 based on current incompatible technologies in the Community up to 2.5 million in 1996 based on the introduction of the Community-wide system. The rapid take-off of the mobile telephone in the UK since 1985 has demonstrated the great market demand for the new services.

---

1 Council Recommendation of 25 June 1987 on the coordinated introduction of public pan-European cellular digital land-based mobile communications in the Community (87/371/EEC), OJ L 196, 17.7.1987, p. 81.
2 Council Directive of 25 June 1987 on the frequency bands to be reserved for the coordinated introduction of public pan-European cellular digital land-based mobile communications in the Community (87/372/EEC), OJ L 196, 17.7.1987, p. 85.

The telecommunications administrations have already agreed, within the CEPT, to reserve the frequencies 905-915 MHz and 950-960 MHz for the initial introduction of the future pan-European mobile communications services. In the long term, both the 890-915 MHz and 935-960 MHz bands should be available.

But time is short. Outside these reserved frequency bands, saturation of available frequencies for current systems will be reached in several Member States, particularly in large cities, by 1990-91. Pressure will therefore increase to release the bandwidths reserved for the future pan-European system for use by current national or regional systems.

This would jeopardize any real prospect for the introduction of pan-European mobile communications. The saturation problems expected in the next few years make 1991 the latest date for the availability of a pan-European second generation system. Industry must therefore be ready to provide the technical equipment for such a system by 1991.

The Community has moved fast to achieve the consensus and set up the timetable required to meet this deadline. The Directive and Recommendation of June 1987 are designed to ensure an orderly and rapid transition from the current incompatible systems to true pan-European mobile communications.

It is recognized that the 1991 starting date for the pan-European system calls for adherence to a tight time schedule.

143

The Commission has announced that it intends to raise Community-wide awareness in both the business and the private sectors by sponsoring information on the development of services and standards. Given the tight schedule for the full specification of services and standards the Commission proposes to support the work of the telecommunications administrations within the CEPT, in the framework of its agreement with this organization. [1]

With regard to the specifications for terminals — mobile, portable or hand-held — the Commission has announced that it will give high priority to this issue in the framework of the implementation of the Directive on the first phase of the establishment of mutual recognition of type approval for telecommunications terminal equipment and the related elaboration of NETs (normes européennes des télécommunications — European telecommunications standards) for this type of equipment, in order to permit international roaming and to promote the European market for terminals.

The new pan-European mobile communications system and services should put business and private users in contact on the move throughout the Community in the 1992 market.

Trade electronic data interchange

Trade electronic data interchange has developed rapidly into a high-priority action for the European Community. [2]

For centuries paper documents have formed the basis of commercial transactions in Europe as elsewhere. From invitations to tender to final payments, numerous documents are exchanged between trading partners.

Today, in most cases, these commercial documents are processed electronically then put in envelopes and sent by post. Prepared at the speed of light, they are dispatched over one million times more slowly.

In addition to the slowness of delivery by post this way of doing business has other, equally serious disadvantages such as the re-encoding of data, transcription errors, data duplication, lost time, delays in processing data and low productivity. Together these mean increased costs.

In intra-Community trade, the costs related to paperwork are estimated to lie between 3.5% and 15% of the value of the merchandise. On a volume of total Community trade of nearly 400 000 million ECU, the financial repercussions of any reduction in paperwork are therefore enormous. Even saving 1% of the total value of merchandise by reducing paperwork would correspond to a saving of 4 000 million ECU for the European economy (Box 29).

---

[1] See Chapter VI, Section 3.
[2] See Chapter III, Section 5.

Developing the electronic tissue for Community trade in 1992: Trade Electronic Data Interchange Systems (TEDIS)

In October 1987, the Council adopted the initial phase of a programme on trade electronic data interchange.[1]

The objectives are:

(i) to avoid a proliferation of closed trade EDI systems and the widespread incompatibility which this would entail in the 1992 market;

(ii) to promote the creation and establishment of trade EDI systems which meet the needs of the users, in particular small and medium-sized enterprises;

(iii) to increase the awareness of the European telematics equipment and services industry in order to meet users' requirements in this area;

(iv) to support the common use of international and European standards, where these exist, and in particular the recommendations of the UN ECE (Economic Commission for Europe) with regard to international trade procedures.

To these ends the programme proposes horizontal actions — actions concerning common interests of all trading sectors such as standardization, tariffs, multilingualism, confidentiality, security, etc. necessary for the development of EDI — as well as vertical actions — the sectoral pilot projects. The current preparatory phase is concentrating on developing work on standardization, on promotional activities and other conditions for EDI at Community level, and the development of a strategy for a full programme phase. Its budget is 5.3 million ECU in 1987/88.

---

[1] Council Decision of 5 October 1987 introducing a communications network Community programme on trade electronic data interchange systems (Tedis) (87/499/EEC), OJ L 285, 8.10.1987.

To avoid progressing from a paper mountain to an electronic tower of Babel, it is imperative that international standards are used. Optimal connections between all trading partners can only be achieved if everyone respects ISO (International Standards Organization) standards, the European standards of the CEN and the recommendations of the United Nations with regard to international trade procedures.

Standardized electronic data interchange (EDI) has therefore developed as one of the most promising lines of value-added services based on cooperative ventures mainly established by industry associations. It can afford great savings for European business. This would provide a significant boost to the competitiveness of European economies, at a time when EDI is developing fast elsewhere, notably in the USA.

Moving towards the 'electronic highways of 1992'

Following the action programme, the European Community is committed to the development of advanced telecommunications services and networks by the implementation of infrastructure projects of common interest. The current establishment of high-speed optical fibre and satellite links between Member States on a bilateral basis has the potential to develop into a common high-speed digital infrastructure for the Community. The Commission has carried out a series of studies in this area to accelerate current plans in the Member States in order to ensure that the intra-Community digital infrastructure is in place in time for the 1992 market (Box 30).

Box 30

The 'electronic highways' of the 1992 market

According to the action lines, the European Commission is committed to the development of advanced telecommunications services and networks via the implementation of infrastructure projects of common interest. One such project, designed to harmonize the traditionally nationally-orientated network planning in the Community, concerns the joint European development of the transnational part of the future Europe-wide broadband infrastructure.

In 1985, the Commission contracted a study with an international consortium of consultancies specialized in the field, with the support of all EC telecommunications administrations, as well as the participation of other CEPT countries, such as Sweden and Switzerland.

The expert team gathered data concerning the network planning in the field. They evaluated the technological developments and worked out the anticipated volume in international digital telecommunications traffic in the years to come.

The following details were established:
(i)   It is feasible to provide, from 1988 onwards, a Community-wide digital transmission infrastructure, able to carry the traffic of all foreseeable narrowband services, including first applications of 2 Mbit/s.
(ii) This infrastructure will to a large extent be covered by bilateral links already planned between Member States, including their neighbouring countries, and by the national trunk lines being installed.
(iii) By connecting this infrastructure with the international gateways in the national networks it should be possible to commence digital telephony, including the expected ISDN traffic, by 1990.
(iv) This infrastructure will, however, only provide for a small volume of broadband services within the Community.
(v)   In order to allow the Community-wide introduction of higher capacity broadband communications in the future, expansion of existing plans is recommended. This could be done with very limited additional expenditure.

These links could have the capacity to handle the entire anticipated narrow-band and broadband traffic generated by large-scale business users, tele-ports and the locally emerging broadband 'islands'.

In their study, the experts recommended further that the international infra-structure should be based on monomode optical-fibre systems, with the added use of satellite links. This corresponds to the overall trend in the network planning.

GAP, the Group for Analysis and Forecasting, considered these proposals in the general context of Community-wide introduction of broadband services and the RACE programme. The result of this screening process was the confirmation of the RACE programme and the proposal to launch a field trial for the Europe-wide introduction of broadband services.

The Commission issued its conclusions in June 1988.[1] It proposes:

— to make a firm commitment towards developing the emerging national and bilateral high-speed links into Europe-wide 'electronic highways', necessary as the basis for advanced Europe-wide broadband service introduction, implemented within the Community in an open manner, in conformity with the principles expressed in the Green Paper;

— to compare national projects and plans and identify routes of pan-European significance, in order to advise on those national and international links in the Community which should receive a formal 'declaration of European interest', once the respective Council Decision proposed in COM (87) 724 concerning the promotion of large scale infrastructure projects of European interest has been taken. On this basis, such a declaration could be allocated to projects, in the framework of the Community's general commitment to promote large scale infrastructure projects;

— in parallel, the telecommunications administrations should intensify their cooperation on the preparation of Community-wide market intro-duction of broadband services. Intensified cooperation within the framework of CEPT or the new forms of cooperation which have been developed with the memorandum signed by telecommunication admin-istrations for the joint implementation of digital mobile communications in Europe may serve as examples, as far as compatible with Community competition rules and taking full account of the objective of the creation of an open Community-wide market for telecommunications services for all market participants, particularly for value-added services. Information on agreements envisaged should be communicated to the Commis-sion.

A market study carried out for the Commission in 1987 by an international consortium of market research companies with more than 4 000 enter-prises in Europe showed that a pro-active market approach could lead to the use by 1996 of videoconferencing by 16% of enterprises with more than 50 employees, of videophony by 21%, and of high-speed data by 17%.

---

[1] COM(88) 341, 'Developing the high-speed telecommunications links ("electronic high-ways") for the Community's 1992 market', 21 June 1988.

3. The creation of a Community-wide market for telecommunications services and equipment: promoting Europe-wide interconnectivity and standards

How standards make new services possible

The emergence of the digital network and of computer-based terminals has made standard-setting in telecommunications highly complex. The specifications of the ISDN alone fill several thousand pages. Agreement on sophisticated interface standards is required to ensure future communications.

Standardization therefore has become a cornerstone of Community policy aimed at:

'(i) ensuring the future integrity of the telecommunications infrastructure in the Community;

(ii) ensuring a future open competitive market;

(iii) promoting future inter-operability of telecommunications services.'[1]

The complex issue of international technical standardization is one of the principal obstacles to be overcome before the full range of new telecommunications services becomes generally available.

Pieces of equipment such as the telephone, personal computer and television can increasingly be combined into integrated information systems due to the convergence of digital information processing, telecommunications and audio-visual technology. But without standardization this is as complicated as trying to combine a food-mixer, a cooker and a freezer into a single kitchen 'workstation'.

Standards — linking up the future market

Differing standards fragment the market. Europe-wide standards will be a major link in the future Europe-wide market.

National telecommunications industries have tended to focus on the needs of national markets and specifications. Besides restricting choice this tends to limit European telecommunications equipment and services to markets which are increasingly too small to provide an adequate return on investment, particularly in view of the high costs of R&D.

---

[1] Green Paper, p. 99.

Standards mean cheaper products. Only standardization allows large markets and large production runs. The European telecommunications industry must therefore be able to operate in this wider European market, by selling standardized equipment on a bigger scale and thereby moving to a position where it is better able to meet competition from the USA and Japan in global markets.

As the infrastructure of new digital networks is developed and advanced new services used by complex customer terminals (often multi-functional) come into operation, it is essential to achieve a harmonized approach with a high degree of end-to-end communications capability. As the Commission points out, this can only be achieved if very precise technical standards are developed and widely used.

Standards — promoting new services and products

Standards provide for inter-operability of equipment, investment certainty, larger production runs and lower costs on the one hand; they must not stifle innovation on the other. The Community's standardization policy in information technologies and telecommunications must be seen in the context of the new general approach to standardization, as developed by the Community since 1984.[1]

According to this approach, Community standardization policy concentrates harmonization on essential aspects and acts to promote the drawing-up of advanced standards and technical specifications through European standardization bodies. The Commission is to ensure that common standards become binding on all Member States through Directives and that they are used in calls for tender for public contracts. According to Directive 83/189/EEC Member States must notify the Commission in advance of all draft regulations concerning technical specifications that they intend to introduce. A legislative standstill may be imposed if the proposed regulation might create barriers to trade.

A similar obligation exists regarding the advance notification of drafts of national standards by the national standards bodies.

As the Commission has pointed out in its White Paper concerning the internal market:[2]

'While a strategy based purely on mutual recognition would remove barriers to trade and lead to the creation of a genuine common trading market, it might well prove inadequate for the purposes of the building up of an expanding market based on the competitiveness which a continental-scale uniform market can generate. On the other hand, experience

---

[1] See the other publications in this series of *European Perspectives* covering different aspects of the 1992 objective.
[2] 'White Paper concerning the completion of the internal market', Communication from the Commission to the Council, COM(85) 310, 14 June 1985.

has shown that the alternative of relying on a strategy based totally on harmonization would be over-regulatory, would take a long time to implement, would be inflexible and would stifle innovation.

What is needed is a strategy that combines the best of both approaches but, above all, allows for progress to be made more quickly than in the past.'

Cooperation with CEN-Cenelec and CEPT

Within this general framework, Community standardization policy in information technologies and telecommunications since 1984 has been developed to take account of the specifics of the sector:

(i) interworking between telecommunications systems;

(ii) importance of international standardization in this field (in particular CCITT and ISO);

(iii) the requirement for open systems (OSI — open systems interconnection) and ISDN standards.

Major steps have been the conclusion of cooperation agreements with the CEPT and CEN-Cenelec in 1984 and 1985 respectively. Under these agreements the two organizations produce standards and specifications for the Community (Box 31).

Box 31

Telecommunications standards: developing the European 'information socket'

Lack of resources for the international standards process has been one of the major contributing factors in the past leading to incompatible national or proprietary specifications.

The Community has approached telecommunications standards through a number of measures. These have taken the form of:

(i) Directives, decisions and regulations (all legally enforceable) covering the initial stage of the mutual recognition of type approval for telecommunications terminal equipment, the adoption of common standards for direct satellite TV broadcasting, and the elaboration of information technology standards.

(ii) Agreements (such as recommendations) demonstrating the political will of the EC countries to move ahead voluntarily together, to set the scene for the joint development of advanced telecommunications technologies, such as the coordinated introduction of ISDN and digital mobile communications.

The Commission has concluded cooperation agreements with the CEPT and CEN-Cenelec and has helped to step up the work of these two European organizations responsible respectively for telecommunications and information technology recommendations and standards. The CEPT has responded with a major reorganization, including the formation of a high-level Technical Recommendations Applications Committee (TRAC), and a significant increase in its activities.

According to the agreements, the Commission together with its advisory bodies transmits priorities for the standardization work of the CEPT in telecommunications and defines mandates for CEN-Cenelec to develop ENs (European standards) and ENVs (European pre-standards) in information technology. Both organizations take full account in their work of international standardization.

In 1986, the Community adopted a directive on mutual recognition of conformance tests for terminals which allows industry to market its equipment after only one set of tests in an approved laboratory — instead of 12. This new move coordinated with the EFTA countries will accelerate the development of a free terminal equipment market.

Under the Directive, NETs (European telecommunications standards) will be used in the type approval process. The NETs will be produced, on request by the Commission, by the CEPT, under a memorandum signed by most of the CEPT telecommunications administrations.

The first two of these NETs have already been adopted in 1988. They cover major current European user concerns: X.21 and X.25 specifications (NET1 and NET2) covering access to the public circuit and packet-switched data networks; NET3 will concern basic access to ISDN (the ISDN 'S-interface'), covering the 144 Kbit/s standard access to the future Integrated Services Digital Network.

Seventeen other NETs are currently in development, covering *inter alia* the future digital mobile system, fast facsimile (Group IV) terminals, modems, and primary (2 Mbit/s) access to ISDN.

At the same time, CEN-Cenelec is processing a number of ENVs in the information technology field, covering in particular OSI standards, electronic message handling and character sets. A European pre-standard (ENV) has been established for the physical design of the ISDN socket.

The NET on ISDN basic access combined with this ENV will provide the Community with one single Community-wide 'information socket' for the 1990s.

In the Green Paper, the Commission announced proposals for full mutual recognition of type approval for terminals between Member States and called for the creation of a European Telecommunications Standards Institute (ETSI) to speed up further the production of standards and specifications. The Institute will operate on a full-time basis, drawing on a wide range of experience and skills to produce effective and timely standards. [1]

In parallel, Community efforts for the rapid definition and introduction of OSI standards have been strengthened through the creation of EWOS ('European Workshop for Open Systems'), in which all the major organizations with an interest in OSI standards are represented.

It has been estimated that Europe-wide standards could generate annual savings of 5 to 10 % in the equipment market alone, corresponding to some 1 000 million ECU per annum, or approximately 50 % of the 2 000 million which the European telecommunications industry was spending annually on research and development in the early 1980s.

---

[1] See Chapter VII, Section 6.

Community telecommunications standards policy has focused on two key areas:

(i) use of open standards in telecommunications administrations' procurement, central to the real opening of the procurement process;

(ii) use of open standards in type approval of terminal equipment. Type approval procedures determine the connection of terminal equipment to the network. They are therefore essential for the implementation of an open Community-wide market.

Terminal equipment

The Community has therefore a special interest in harmonizing terminal equipment standards and the process of approving the terminals for attachment to public networks.

This currently operates on the basis of each country requiring testing for conformance with its appropriate national standards in one of its own testing laboratories. For European manufacturers this has meant undergoing lengthy and expensive testing and approval procedures in each country before launching a product in the potential Community market. The Community has therefore acted to introduce mutual recognition of conformance testing.

It is also promoting the development of recognized conformance testing centres in Europe via the CTS programme (Conformance Testing System).

4. Facilitating the introduction of Integrated Broadband Communications for the 1990s: the RACE programme

The RACE programme has developed into the key Community programme for promoting the future coherence of the network and ensuring a powerful Europe-wide communications infrastructure for the Community of the 1990s. RACE — Research and Development in Advanced Communications Technologies for Europe — is a central programme planned in the context of the Community's R&D framework programme for the period 1987 to 1991.[1] Together with the ESPRIT programme it forms one of the main Community programmes for promoting Europe's industrial competitiveness.

The objective of RACE is defined as 'Community-wide introduction of Integrated Broadband Communications (IBC) by 1995, taking into account the evolving ISDN and national introduction strategies'.

Based on the Europe-wide trend towards a digital infrastructure carrying both telecommunications and audio-visual (TV) services,[2] the programme is:

(i) to achieve the necessary Europe-wide agreement on fully-defined future broadband services, interfaces and network concepts;

(ii) to mobilize, on the basis of Europe-wide collaboration between telecommunications firms and network operators, the enormous R&D resources necessary. Cheaper technology is required in order to extend broadband communications to the private household sector.

The programme was worked out with the broad participation of industry and the telecommunications operators. From July 1985 to December 1986, a definition phase was carried out to cover the initial work needed to improve the definition of the functional requirements of IBC, together with exploratory research and development in key areas of agreed urgency.

---

[1] See Chapter VI, Section 8.
[2] See Chapter III.

The definition phase comprised two parts:

(i) Development of an IBC reference model, covering the network itself, the kinds of terminal equipment attached to the network and applications/services provided by their interworking, together with economic trends assessments.

(ii) Long lead-time R&D relating to the technology involved. Certain topics had been identified as being crucial to the development of IBC, but due to the existence of a number of technological options, research had to be done at this stage to identify the path to be adopted for the full-scale R&D effort. These included: broadband switching and coding, micro- and opto-electronics and software requirements.

The fundamental technologies of the broadband networks of the 1990s already, for the most part, exist. What is required is extensive R&D to bring these technologies to an implementable form, including the specification and definition of network architectures, standards, protocols and interfaces.

The work on the IBC network reference model during the definition phase was carried out by the CEPT working group on broadband communications, the GSLB ('groupe spécial large bande'). The development of the IBC terminal reference model was conducted by a consortium of 30 Ectel companies and research laboratories including all major participants in the telecommunications field in Europe: AEG; APT; ACEC; Alcatel; ATEA; Barco; BTM; CGCT; CSELT; Fatme; GEC; Hellenic Aerospace; Industry Intermetal; Italtel; Jeumont-Schneider; Nixdorf; Philips; Plessey; SAT; SEL; SESA; SGS; Siemens; STC; Telenorma; Telettra; Thomson CSF; Thomson Brandt; Thorn EMI. The analysis of user requirements was carried out by the Group for Analysis and Forecasting (GAP).

In total, transnational consortia involving 109 industrial companies, universities, and telecommunications administrations' research laboratories participated in the definition phase. The total Community contribution was 20 million ECU matched by another 20 million by the participating companies.

On the basis of the successful completion of the definition phase, the main RACE programme was developed covering the period 1987-91. It was adopted by the Council of Ministers on 22 December 1987. The total allocation from the Community budget for this period is 550 million ECU. This implies a total project volume of 1 100 million ECU (Box 32).

Box 32

The RACE programme: Integrated Broadband Communications for the Europe of the 1990s

The RACE programme — Research and Development in Advanced Communications Technologies for Europe — is a strategic, market-responsive R&D programme. It is closely related to ESPRIT, the information technology programme.

The RACE main phase is divided into three segments:

(i) Systems

(ii) Technology

(iii) Integration

Part I — IBC development and implementation strategies

Further development of the IBC reference model

- Network reference model
- Customer premises reference model
- Applications and services reference model
- Mobile communications integration

Systems analysis and functional specification

- Network architecture
- High layer functions in integrated network
- IBC termination
- Channel definition, code conversion and redundancy reduction
- Switching requirements
- Signalling techniques
- Customer access systems
- Network management and operation
- Human-machine interfaces
- Security and privacy
- Requirements of mobile communications
- Hardware and software simulation and testing

Implementation and planning support

- Common tool environment for telecommunications design, development, testing, and maintenance
- Joint definition of common test facilities
- Development of IBC simulations for functional integration
- Joint definition of software development environments
- Standards and conventions for portability and re-usability

Part II — IBC technologies

Supporting IBC technologies

- Specific integrated circuits for IBC
- Integrated opto-electronic devices for IBC
- Broadband switching techniques
- Design tools for complex systems
- Low-cost optical components
- High bit-rate links

Communications software technologies

- Software infrastructure
- Requirements definition tools

Basic technologies for IBC users

- Audio/video processing — redundancy reduction
- Broadband in the customer premises network
- Image sensors
- Communications display technology
- Digital image recording techniques
- HDTV components

Subsystems and techniques

- Customer access realization
- Broadband switching modules
- Broadband links
- Human factors/terminal engineering
- Systems organization

Part III — Functional integration

Customer facilities

- Fixed terminal functions
- Customer premises network functions
- Mobile termination

User access

- Customer access functions
- Local switching functions

- Cable-TV head-end functions
- Local exchange functions

Network functions

- Trunk exchange functions
- Transmission functions
- Operating and maintenance functions

By 1992, RACE will have created the foundation for a set of standards for Integrated Broadband Communications in Europe. These will then provide a framework for the development of Integrated Broadband Communications through the 1990s.

The RACE programme comprises a total volume of 1 100 million ECU, 50% from the Community budget and 50% from industry. The first series of trans-European projects under the programme was launched in January 1988. The major European telecommunications companies are part of the RACE industrial consortium. On the telecommunications administrations side, the newly created European Telecommunications Standards Institute will play an important role.

By coordinating research activity on IBC, RACE is ensuring that scarce resources are not wasted through needless duplication. In establishing a common framework for IBC from the start, RACE has the potential to achieve a level of network cohesiveness that has never before been possible. Cost savings will therefore be achieved through a virtual elimination of the elaborate interface equipment that would otherwise be necessary. The integration of different services into IBC should lift production volumes and so help ensure that economies of scale are realized by Europe's manufacturers.

Broadband networks make available rates of data transfer of an even higher order of magnitude than those offered by ISDN. The nature of some broadband services is already apparent — they are extensions and combinations of existing services such as cable television, videoconferencing, high-speed data transfer for such applications as CAD (computer-aided design) and general computer mainframe-computer mainframe transfer. [1]

For the consumer, IBC means greater flexibility in the choice of equipment and the quality and selection of services. Broadband is associated with high speed and high quality. For commerce and industry, IBC will offer easier and quicker communications. Videoconferencing, CAD, mobile telecommunications, electronic mail: RACE seeks to provide all such services via similar digital communications networks for the whole of Europe using an infrastructure of optical fibres, satellite links and broadband switching nodes.

---

[1] See Chapter III, Section 8.

5. The STAR programme — promoting the introduction and development of advanced services and networks in the less favoured peripheral regions of the Community

The less developed peripheral regions of the Community — broadly speaking, the western and southern belts of Europe — are at present prevented from participating fully in the European economy both by physical transport costs and by an often sub-standard telecommunications infrastructure. As the knowledge-content of economic output increases, this last factor represents a larger danger of isolation than mere geography ever did. [1]

On the other hand, proper telecommunications can suppress geographic distance like no other technology before. They can also, at a very low cost, supply missing inputs in economic regions characterized by an uneven scientific, technological and services infrastructure. An accelerated programme of investment in digitized, and later broadband, technologies, as foreseen by the STAR programme, could turn the potential danger to the development of the periphery posed by the informatics society into a unique opportunity to overcome the handicap of geographic isolation.

STAR starts from the recognition that the telecommunications infrastructure of the peripheral Member States and their less developed regions lags badly behind the rest of the Community, while at the same time the availability of telecommunications services will be a growing factor in the location of new industries and the viability of existing ones (Box 33).

Box 33

The STAR programme: Special Telecommunications Action for Regional Development — ensuring Community cohesion in telecommunications

STAR is a five-year programme (1987-91) aimed at making use of advanced telecommunications services to promote the economic development of the less favoured regions of the European Community. STAR is financed by the Community's Regional Development Fund.

---

[1] See Chapter V, Section 3.

The STAR programme is active in seven Member States: France, Greece, Ireland, Italy, Spain, Portugal and the United Kingdom. For some countries, only certain designated regions are eligible for assistance, e.g. the Mezzogiorno in Italy; Corsica and the Overseas Departments in France; Northern Ireland in the United Kingdom.

The programme follows two fundamental lines of action:

(i) helping to set up the kind of telecommunications infrastructure necessary to provide advanced services to business users in the less favoured regions;

(ii) supporting measures designed to stimulate demand and encourage use of the telecommunications infrastructure in the less favoured regions.

Three major areas of physical infrastructure come within the scope of the STAR programme:

(i) Establishment of the necessary links between the less favoured regions and the new advanced networks which are being set up across the Community, in order to allow the full integration of the peripheral regions into the new communications structures.

(ii) Acceleration of digitization, a precondition of ISDN, and thus compression of the time lag which otherwise would occur between the introduction of digital services in central areas and outlying regions.

(iii) Establishment of data networks in advance of ISDN to give a quicker response to needs and requirements which are already evident.

STAR was established by Council Regulation in October 1986.[1]

The programme became fully operational with the Commission's approval of the individual national plans in November 1987.

The Community is contributing 780 million ECU to the programme with a matching contribution from the Member States. Since the Community is financing 60% of the total, the overall size of the programme is around 1 300 million ECU.

---

[1] Council Regulation (EEC) No 3300/86 of 27 October 1986 instituting a Community programme for the development of certain less favoured regions of the Community by improving access to advanced telecommunications services (STAR programme).

STAR plays a role at all critical junctures: from the initial capital investment ... through the establishment of telecommunications services ... to facilitating use of these services as a catalyst for economic development.

Because the objective is economic growth, STAR is specifically conceived for business users — with special emphasis on small- and medium-sized enterprises (SMEs). The Community recognizes the key role of the SMEs in the economic fabric of Europe, and it recognizes that enterprises of this dimension have particular needs which must be identified and catered for.

Besides investments in infrastructure, STAR funding also aims at promoting the supply and encouraging the use of advanced telecommunications services in the regions as rapidly as possible. Six broad categories of activity are now being implemented:

(i)   preparing local or regional programmes for telecommunications use;

(ii) designing and implementing information campaigns;

(iii) encouraging SMEs to use advanced services;

(iv) establishing telecommunications services;

(v)   implementing 'teleworking' projects, i.e. working on a terminal at a remote site;

(vi) providing specialized regional information services.

Besides the STAR programme, the Community contributes substantially to investment in telecommunications in the periphery of the Community. In 1987 loans for telecommunications investment by the European Investment Bank of the Community totalled 369 million ECU. In that year, the European Regional Development Fund invested 199 million ECU in the framework of its normal operations in telecommunications.

Under the general reform of the Community's finances, as agreed by the European Council in February 1988 in Brussels, a major increase in the 'structural instruments', in particular the Regional Development Fund, is planned.

6. The Community institutions as pioneers for advanced applications: videoconferencing; INSIS programme; Caddia programme

Videoconferencing

Meetings absorb an increasing amount of time and money for business and administration in Europe. Besides the direct cost of travel and hotel accommodation, loss of time, reduced efficiency and fatigue, there are additional overheads.

Although some face-to-face meetings will always be necessary or preferred, the development of the new telecommunications systems, combining technical and infrastructural facilities for holding conferences or working meetings without requiring participants to spend so much time away from their usual workplaces, will improve the situation considerably. This is where videoconferencing has a particularly promising future.

The Community is itself a leading client for international videoconferencing facilities, since progress in Community affairs — indeed, the management of the Community as a whole — depends largely on Europeans talking to each other. Brussels and Luxembourg host numerous meetings involving European and national officials every day.

As a potential leading-edge user itself, the Community has therefore taken a number of steps to promote videoconferencing facilities, pioneering the application of this new technology across frontiers to open up new services and market opportunities (Box 34).

Box 34

Linking up Europe's capitals: videoconferencing

Since February 1984 the EC has begun to link the capitals of the Member States and the three locations of the Community institutions — Brussels, Luxembourg and Strasbourg — by videocommunications, putting videoconferencing at the service of political decision-making in Europe.

This trans-Community network of videoconference studios is operated mostly via the Eutelsat SMS satellite system. Multi-point videoconference technology will become available in the near future.

In 1985 the Community set up two studios, in the European Parliament in Luxembourg and in the Commission's Berlaymont building in Brussels, as a short-term follow-up to the INSIS videoconference activities. EC officials use these studios whenever possible for their meetings, not only between Brussels and Luxembourg but also between Brussels and studios in the capitals of the Member States. The Permanent Representations (EC embassies) of the Member States also use the Brussels studio. The possibility of simultaneous interpretation compatible with videoconferencing is being examined.

The Commission has brought together representatives of the telecommunications administrations and the other organizations concerned. The telecommunications administrations are also organizing demonstrations of cross-border videoconference services to demonstrate and raise awareness of their feasibility among professional users. Given that many users are high-level policy-makers dealing with sensitive matters, a high degree of confidentiality is required. A common encryption system will be defined.

'Videomeetings' — communications between individuals sitting in front of a terminal comprising a screen and a camera in their own office, rather than in specially equipped studios — are also to be included in the project.

The Commission has taken advantage of the work being done in other frameworks, in particular by the European videoconference experiment (EVE) undertaken by the CEPT.

Videoconferencing is starting to be widely used by multinational companies in the United States and Japan. The pioneering use by the Community of this new telecommunications technology today will rapidly become commonplace tomorrow in Europe for business and administrative meetings throughout the Community, and will help make European organizational structures more efficient.

INSIS: the Interinstitutional Integrated Services Information System

Community institutions and Member State administrations themselves form a major user group for the new telematics services.

The INSIS programme aims to improve communications between the Member States and Community institutions by promoting the coordinated and harmonized exploitation of new techniques.

INSIS is following two main lines of action:

(i) horizontal programmes, aimed at preparing the technical and industrial environment and at promoting consensus;

(ii) pilot projects, aimed at creating experimental systems to assess the technical problems and the impact on working life of introducing new technology into the complex environment of Community administrations.

An idea of the potential of the Community institutions as a pioneer in the field can be gained from a look at the Commission's own information distribution and processing resources:

(i)   The Commission's modern Brussels PABX is one of the largest in Europe, with 12 000 extensions and nearly 900 outside lines.

(ii) The telex exchange, which is fully automated, handles 2 000 to 3 000 messages a day.

(iii) For data processing, the Commission has four large mainframes, 20 medium-range computers, around 1 500 terminals, 800 word processors and 100 facsimile terminals, as well as a rapidly growing number of PCs.

On this basis, the Commission is, within the INSIS programme, rapidly developing its resources along four lines:

(i)   electronic transmission of written text (documents) and electronic messaging to reduce delivery delays between Member State administrations and Community institutions;

(ii) facilities to give easier and more coherent access to information of interest to the Community, most of which is held in a variety of computer data bases;

(iii) establishment of videoconferencing facilities to reduce travel costs and save time;

(iv) horizontal integration of informatics services to facilitate access to services and facilities for non-computer professionals (Box 35).

Box 35

Using telecommunications to make the work of Community institutions more efficient: the Interinstitutional Integrated Services Information System (INSIS)

Three projects are at present in an advanced stage of development: INSEM (Interinstitutional Electronic Mail System), videoconferencing techniques, and Ovide (Organisation de vidéotex pour les députés européens).

INSEM

Electronic mail is defined as 'a service enabling documents to be routed in electronic form from a sender to one or more recipients and delivered to the latter in accordance with the conditions specified by the sender'. The new techniques are intended to provide a service which is functionally equivalent to those currently offered by the postal and internal mail services, but with the speed of electronic transmission.

In view of the size and the heterogeneity of the target populations to be served by Insem and in view of the multivendor policy pursued by the Community institutions, adherence to common standards is essential.

The MHS (Message Handling System) model has emerged as the most suitable message transmission standard. For document handling, the project will use the International Standards Organization's (ISO) ODA (Office Documentation Architecture) standard.

The project is in its first phase, during which it is transmitting messages based on teletex protocols until commercial products embody the standards mentioned. In the medium term, teletex will also be included in Insem as a medium for exchanging documents with national administrations.

Videoconferencing

INSIS's videoconferencing activities are supporting the videoconference project explained previously.

The technical problems of point-to-point videoconferencing have been resolved and at its present stage the INSIS pilot project is primarily concerned with evaluating consumer response to and acceptance of the current facilities.

Ovide

Members of the European Parliament (MEPs) have specialized information needs. Initially, Ovide is attempting to provide for day-to-day information needs such as meetings calendars in the major languages. The aims of the initial pilot system were to determine the MEPs' needs and to assess the acceptability and use of Ovide by them as well as to study the problems involved with a data base of high-turnover information.

Ovide's second phase, which will be implemented in 1988, seeks to extend the service to all MEPs, including access from wherever in the Community their constituencies are located.

Given Europe's uncoordinated introduction of videotex services,[1] Ovide has met serious technical obstacles which are only gradually being overcome.

Access to Community information

INSIS will more and more provide access to Community information. Among these information services, two are particularly important: Cronos for the diffusion of Eurostat's data — the Community's Statistical Office which assembles statistics from all Member States in the economic, social and cultural fields; and Ecdin, the Commission's information system on environmental data.

---

[1] See Chapter V, Section 2.

Caddia: Cooperation in automation of data and documentation for imports/exports and agriculture

Administrative paperwork constitutes a heavy load on the future functioning of the European market. Here the European Commission has pioneered a specific action plan, launched in 1985, aimed at replacing paper documentation relating to Community procedures, with the more efficient and cost-effective electronic data interchange (Box 36).

164

Box 36

Automating Community data and document interchange in preparation for the 1992 market: the Caddia programme

Caddia defines three fundamental objectives:

(i) Automation, by the Member States and the Commission, of the data interchange and processing required for management of the Community's customs union, the Community's measures in the commercial field, its management and financial control of agricultural markets, and its procedures for collection and dissemination of statistical data on Community trade.

(ii) Coordination of related actions by the national administrations to ensure technical compatibility.

(iii) Aligning Community developments with those currently underway in the industrial and commercial sectors of world trade — in particular those developments in the UN ECE (Economic Commission for Europe) concerned with setting standards for paperless trading.

Caddia will facilitate most the Community's activities in the following fields:

(i) the Statistical Office;

(ii) agriculture;

(iii) customs union and indirect taxation.

Customs sector: the Coordinated Development (CD) project

The purpose of the CD project is to revise and harmonize customs procedures of the Community with third countries and to implement their coordinated computerization by means of links between customs systems and other administrative and commercial systems.

The 1992 objective reinforces the need for new data on trade necessary both for the functioning of the Community's internal market and for trade between the Community and other countries.

Major actions currently under way concern computer systems for third-country import/exports, management of the new integrated customs tariff (Taric) with its interface for dissemination to Member States, and systems for computer-to-computer trade data interchange (Edifact).

These are being progressively introduced through pilot projects which are currently becoming operational.

Agriculture

The Caddia programme has enabled the introduction of computerized data-processing systems for the Commission's management of agricultural markets and the European Agricultural Guidance and Guarantee Fund (EAGGF) — fundamental for the day-to-day operations of the Community.

(i) Market management: AMIS (Agricultural Management Information System) processes communications on market prices, import/export licences, stock levels and production balances, and calculates monetary compensatory amounts, import levies, export refunds and production aids, all central for the information of farmers and the functioning of the Community's agricultural system.

(ii) EAGGF: AGREX is an accounting system for expenditure under the guarantee and guidance sections of the EAGGF. The management of agricultural markets currently represents nearly 70% of the Community's total budget of more than 40 000 million ECU. To reduce costs and time-lags, AGREX procedures for the management and use of funds are currently being revised with the aim of setting up an electronic fund transfer system.

Statistics

The information systems of the EC Statistical Office have been improved to allow Member States to receive and transmit information about external trade and other sectors such as agriculture via the public telecommunications network.

Transport

Transport is also closely associated with Caddia because of the converging interests of the CD trade interface project and the European research project on computerization of data interchange for the transport of goods.

The transport sector also has specific requirements in the field of mobile communications which can now be satisfied as a result of the introduction of the common European mobile telephone system by 1991.

7. The first steps to opening the market: applications of Community competition policy to the telecommunications sector to date

'Rapid technological change and the related growing number of new opportunities have led to a rising number of cases relating to Community competition rules being brought before the Commission.' [1]

---

[1] Green Paper, p. 121.

While the general applications of the Treaty to telecommunications must be seen against the broader background of the Treaty and case-law developed by the Court of Justice, a number of specific cases and decisions are summarized below.

Telecommunications have been treated by the Commission under competition law basically according to two considerations:

(i) A State monopoly's or a public undertaking's (including telecommunications administrations) anti-competitive behaviour may be due to domestic laws or government instructions. In such cases action has been taken under Articles 37 and 90(1) and (3) against the infringing Member States.

(ii) Enterprises in the telecommunications or information technology fields may be involved in anti-competitive arrangements or behaviour. This may concern public network operators (telecommunications administrations) or 'undertakings' within the meaning of Articles 85 and/or 86 when they are not simply implementing laws or government instructions but are performing independent entrepreneurial activities. [1]

The 'British Telecom' case: opening new ground for value-added services

The 'British Telecom' case can be considered a cornerstone of the Community case-law which has developed over recent years in telecommunications. With its ruling on the case, the European Court gave a clear indication on how the Court is likely to look at the liberalization of the telecommunications market.

The case originated from a complaint lodged by a private UK message-forwarding agency against the UK telecommunications authorities. It concerned prohibitions imposed by the UK Post Office and, after the Telecommunications Act 1981, by British Telecom as to the transit of telexes between third countries, e.g. between continental Europe and North America, and as to the forwarding in telex or telefax form of messages received via computer connections.

A Commission Decision of 10 December 1982[2] under Article 90(3) condemned such prohibitions as abuse of a dominant position. The Italian Government challenged the Decision before the European Court of Justice.[3]

---

[1] See also Box 42 for explanation of Treaty Articles.
[2] OJ L 360, 21.12.1982, p. 36; Twelfth Competition Report (1982), point 94.
[3] Case 41/83.

In its judgment of 20 March 1985, the Court dismissed in its entirety the action brought by the Italian Republic. The judgment [1] clarified several fundamental points concerning the application of the Treaty and Community law to telecommunications administrations, finding notably that:

(i) 'When it took action against private message-forwarding agencies, BT was acting not as an official body but as an undertaking. The management of public telecommunications equipment and the placing of such equipment at the disposal of private users on payment of a fee amounted by its very nature to a business activity. The same reasoning must apply to the contested schemes, which merely laid down charges and conditions for the services provided by BT to users of the British telecommunications network';

(ii) 'The Court also rejected the submission to the effect that the application of Article 86 to the case in point infringed Article 222 because it encroached on Member States' rights to create or preserve national monopolies for particular economic activities. It noted that, whilst BT has a statutory monopoly with regard to the management of the telecommunications network and to making it available to users, it held no monopoly over the provision of ancillary services such as the retransmission of messages on behalf of third parties';

(iii) 'The employment of new apparatus and methods which accelerated the transmission of messages constituted technical progress in conformity with the public interest and could not be regarded as an abuse';

(iv) 'Nor were the measures at issue covered by Article 90(2)';

(v) 'The applicant had failed to demonstrate that the Commission's censure of BT's schemes had put the performance of the particular tasks entrusted to BT in jeopardy from the economic point of view. Whilst the speed of message transmission made possible by technological advances undoubtedly led to some decrease in revenue for BT, the presence of private agencies attracted to the British public network a certain volume of international messages and the revenue which went with it. Taken as a whole, the results were therefore in no way unfavourable to BT.' [2]

The British Telecom judgment clearly confirmed the Commission's view that the competition rules of the Treaty apply to telecommunications administrations. The operation of telex forwarding agencies as allowed for by the judgment is a special form of value-added service. The ruling by the Court can therefore be interpreted as a clear signal by the Court to allow more competition in this market.

It also made clear that the Court would favour a narrow interpretation of monopoly rights and would strongly disfavour the extension of a service monopoly, as new technologies arise.

---

[1] Reported in Fifteenth Competition Report (1985), points 95 to 101.
[2] Ibid., also cited in the Green Paper, pp. 123 and 124.

'The Court's judgment in this case must be seen as a cornerstone for the future interpretation of the Treaty with regard to telecommunications.'[1]

The terminal equipment cases: the right to connect new terminals to the network

The growing diversification of terminal equipment and the new uses made possible as a result have given rise to a growing number of cases under the competition rules since the early 1980s.

These cases have concerned the illegality of extending monopolies in the terminal equipment sector.

Cases which arose in Germany:

The 'cordless telephone' case was reported as follows:[2]

'The Commission challenged the German Federal Republic's plans to extend the Bundespost's monopoly to cordless telephones.

The German Government wished to give the Bundespost the exclusive right to supply almost all equipment connected to the public telephone network. The only equipment excluded was that to be connected to private automatic branch exchanges (PABXs) supplied by independent firms. The Commission considered that even such a partial monopoly fell within the second subparagraph of Article 37(1) EEC, since equipment imported from other Member States could thereby not be freely sold in Germany even if it met the country's technical standards. After the Commission's intervention, the German Government dropped its plans to extend the Bundespost's monopoly to cordless telephones.'

The modem case was reported as follows:

'The Commission also challenged the extension of the Bundespost's monopoly to modems. Here too, the German Government took the view that such equipment was an integral part of the telephone network and therefore could be supplied only by the Bundespost. The only exceptions were modems used to connect private digital equipment otherwise than via the public telephone network.

---

[1] Green Paper, p. 124.
[2] Fifteenth Competition Report (1985).

The Commission considered that such an extension of the Bundespost's monopoly fell within the second paragraph of Article 37(1) and that the tying of the provision of telephone network services to the purchase of modems was also an abuse of the Bundespost's dominant position as network operator contrary to Article 86. To terminate the infringements of Articles 37 and 86, the Commission informed the German Government that it was contemplating issuing a decision under Article 90(3).'[1]

In June 1986, the Bundespost agreed on measures to allow the sale and connection of modems provided by other suppliers.

Action against Italy

A similar complaint was made about the monopoly of the importation and sale of modems and first telex terminals in Italy.

Here, modems and first telex terminals to be connected to the public network were to be supplied and installed only by the SIP (Società italiana per l'esercizio telefonico) and the DCST (Direzione centrale servizi telegrafici). This arrangement affected imports of modems and telex terminals from other Member States as the manufacturers of such equipment in other countries could not reach Italian users directly.

After intervention by the Commission, the Italian Government announced that it would open up the provision of modems and telex terminals.

Action against the Netherlands and Denmark

The Commission enquired about the exclusive rights to import and sell terminal equipment in these two countries. The Dutch Government announced shortly afterwards that it would reform the provisions.

The cases taken up under Community competition rules during the early 1980s have contributed substantially to accelerating the trend in Europe towards free unrestricted connection of new terminal equipment to the network. They prepared the base for the global approach to the opening of the terminal market, proposed in the Green Paper.[2]

The IBM undertaking on SNA interfaces: the disclosure of interface specifications

Systems Network Architecture (SNA) is the proprietary network standard used by IBM for interconnecting computer systems and networks.

---

[1] Cited in Green Paper, p. 125.
[2] See Chapter VII, Section 2.

On 1 August 1984, the Commission accepted a unilateral undertaking from IBM to provide other manufacturers with the technical interface information needed to permit competitive products to be used with IBM's most powerful range of computers, the System/370. The Commission thereupon suspended its proceedings under Article 86 of the Treaty which it had initiated against IBM in December 1980.

In the course of the proceedings, towards the end of 1983, some major European computer manufacturers expressed concern that IBM's interface disclosure practice was also having an adverse effect on the European market for data communications products (the interconnection and interaction of data-processing systems). Accordingly, the SNA issue was included in the informal discussions on interface disclosure.

The significance of the undertaking finally agreed, with regard to telecommunications, was that the Commission made it clear that it would review private participants in the market as strictly as the telecommunications administrations, in order to avoid the abuse of dominant market positions.

The importance of open standards as a precondition of fair competition was also emphasized. In the undertaking, IBM stated that 'IBM has actively participated in international standards efforts in support of open systems interconnection (OSI) and will continue its active support of OSI as the standard for interconnecting systems, products and networks of different manufacturers.'[1]

International Air Couriers and other cases: telecommunications administrations are commercial undertakings subject to competition rules

The International Air Couriers case[2] — value-added services in the postal field — related to freedom of international air couriers activities, under Articles 90 and 86 of the EEC Treaty. The Commission took the opportunity presented by this case to point out:

'That it regards the Member States' postal and telecommunications authorities as commercial undertakings since they supply goods and services for payment and that any extension by one or more of these undertakings of their dominant positions may constitute an abuse under Article 86 of the EEC Treaty.'

The Telemarketing v Compagnie luxembourgeoise de télédiffusion ruling under Articles 177 and 86 of the EEC Treaty (European Court preliminary ruling of 3 October 1985 in Case 311/84) further strengthened the Community's legal base to push for market opening in the terminal field and the field of value-added services. It related to the abusive

[1] Bull. EC 10-1984, point 3.4.1.
[2] Bull. EC 1-1985, point 2.1.10 (Germany); Bull. EC 12-1985, point 2.1.79 (France).

extension of a dominant position to a neighbouring but separate market — which is closely analogous to the telecommunications administrations' action in the terminal and value-added fields.

In the SWIFT (Society for Worldwide Interbank Financial Telecommunications) and SITA (Airlines Worldwide Telecommunications Network) cases[1] relating to the pricing of international leased lines, the relevance of Community competition rules to the field of telecommunications services was directly demonstrated.

National courts may apply the prohibitions contained in Articles 85(1) and 86. For a number of years, and especially in the past three, the Commission has tried to move the domestic courts to enforce the EEC competition rules more systematically. The Brussels court summary injunction of 31 July 1986 based on the Telemarketing ruling, relating to the attempt by the Belgian telecommunications administration to expand its monopoly to PABXs with 50 to 150 extensions, is an example of this approach.

The British Telecom ruling, the terminal cases and the cases on value-added services have confirmed the application of Community competition rules to the telecommunications sector. They have prepared the ground for the more global approach proposed by the Commission in the Green Paper.

8. Community telecommunications policy in the general context of the move towards the 1992 market: the R&D framework programme; information market policy; the move towards television without frontiers

'Telecommunications policy is closely related to the major new policy goals of the Community defined in the Single European Act: completing the internal market (the 1992 goal), realizing a European Research and Technology Community and strengthening European cohesion.'[2]

Policy goals of the Community whose relationships with telecommunications policy merit special attention are:

(i)   research and technological development (R&TD) policy;

(ii) the establishment of a Community-wide information market;

(iii) the establishment of a Community-wide audio-visual (TV broadcasting) space.

---

[1] See Chapter III, Section 5.
[2] Green Paper, p. 136.

The Community-wide development of telecommunications infrastructure and of advanced services will be indispensable for the attainment of the internal market objective.

R&TD policy

The Community's overall R&TD policy is laid down by the new framework programme for research and development, finally adopted on 28 September 1987 by the Council.

This was adopted under the procedures of the Single European Act which had entered into force on 1 July 1987 and which established the European Technology Community as one of its major goals.

The budget finally approved by the Council for the framework programme was 5 400 million ECU (Box 37).

Box 37

Framework programme of Community activities in the field of research and technological development (1987-91)[1]

	(million ECU)
1. Quality of life	375
1.1. Health	80
1.2. Radiation protection	34
1.3. Environment	261
2. Towards a large market and an information and communications society	2 275
2.1. Information technologies	1 600
2.2. Telecommunications	550
2.3. New services of common interest (including transport)[2]	125
3. Modernization of industrial sectors	845
3.1. Science and technology for manufacturing industry	400
3.2. Science and technology of advanced materials	220
3.3. Raw materials and recycling	45
3.4. Technical standards, measurement methods and reference materials	180
4. Exploitation and optimum use of biological resources	280
4.1. Biotechnology	120
4.2. Agro-industrial technologies	105
4.3. Competitiveness of agriculture and management of agricultural resources	55

---

5. Energy	1 173
5.1. Fission: nuclear safety	440
5.2. Controlled thermonuclear fusion	611
5.3. Non-nuclear energies and rational use of energy	122
6. Science and technology for development	80
7. Exploitation of the sea-bed and use of marine resources	80
7.1. Marine science and technology	50
7.2. Fisheries	30
8. Improvement of European science and technology cooperation	288
8.1. Stimulation, enhancement and use of human resources	180
8.2. Use of major installations	30
8.3. Forecasting and assessment and other back-up measures (including statistics)	23
8.4. Dissemination and utilization of science and technology research results	55
Total	**5 396**

[1] Council Decision 87/516/EEC of 28 September 1987 concerning the framework programme for Community activities in the field of research and technological development (1987 to 1991, OJ L 302, 24.10.1987, p. 1).

[2] Under this point more than 50 million ECU are allocated to the pilot phases of the information technology application programmes — AIM, DELTA, DRIVE.
Information technology (the ESPRIT II programme), telecommunications (the RACE programme) and the pilot phases of the information technology application programmes account for about 40% of the Community's expenditure on research and development, as set out in the framework programme.

The framework programme fully recognizes the central importance of telecommunications and information technology for overall R&TD development. It foresees the allocation of 40% of total R&D expenditure to R&D in telecommunications and information technology in particular:

(i) Implementation of the main phase of the RACE programme. [1]

(ii) Second phase of the ESPRIT programme, the European Strategic Programme for Research and Development in Information Technology. In the current first phase, more than 200 projects on advanced information technology are being carried out on a shared-cost basis, by transnational consortia of industrial enterprises, research laboratories and universities.

(iii) Applications of telecommunications and information technology. This concerns the pilot phases for the programmes AIM (Advanced Informatics in Medicine in Europe), DELTA (Developing European Learning through Technological Advance) and DRIVE (Dedicated Road Infrastructure for Vehicle safety in Europe).

[1] See Chapter VI, Section 4.

The IT (information technology) application programmes aim at developing the potential of telecommunications and information technologies for broad areas of social needs: education, road traffic and medicine. They aim to adjust technology to evolving social needs on the one hand; and allow the satisfaction of evolving social requirements by technology on the other (Box 38).

Box 38

The information technology application programmes: bridging the gap between technology and social concerns

AIM (Advanced Informatics in Medicine in Europe)
AIM is described in COM(87) 352 final, 24 July 1987: 'Proposal for a Council Regulation on Community action in the field of information technology and telecommunications applied to health care — Pilot phase'.

The purpose of AIM is:

(i) the improvement of the effectiveness of public and private actions by means of the development of a common conceptual framework for cooperation at the planning and management level in Europe;

(ii) the strengthening of Europe's position in MBI (medical and bio-informatics) and health care by means of cooperation in pre-normative and pre-competitive technology exploration concentrating selectively on reinforcing and complementing the technology base of MBI and its services; and

(iii) the creation of an environment favourable to rapid progress in the introduction and appropriate application of MBI in health care by means of the development of specific proposals addressing the policy, regulatory, legal and organizational framework of MBI applications including the training and manpower-related factors.

DELTA (Developing European Learning through Technological Advance)

DELTA is described in COM(87) 353 final, 24 July 1987: 'Proposal for a Council Regulation on Community action in the field of learning technology — Pilot phase'.

The purpose of DELTA is:

(i) interdisciplinary concertation on present and future learning support requirements;

(ii) cooperative development of advanced learning technology;

(iii) testing and validation of advanced learning technology concepts based on systems integration and communications; promotion of interoperability of learning technology equipment, software and services; and

(iv) creation of favourable conditions for advanced learning throughout Europe.

DRIVE (Dedicated Road Infrastructure for Vehicle safety in Europe)

DRIVE is described in COM(87) 351 final, 24 July 1987: 'Proposal for a Council Regulation on a Community programme in the field of information technology and telecommunications applied to road transport'.

The purpose of DRIVE is:

(i) an operational real-time multilingual road information and navigation system in Europe by 1990, and

(ii) an operational fail-safe anti-collision system for impact speeds exceeding 30 kph by 1995.

The Community also participates in a number of Eureka projects in the information technology and telecommunications fields, as well as the COST programme (European cooperation on scientific and technological research).

Information market policy

RACE, ESPRIT and the IT application programmes form a broad technological 'upstream' base on which the new European information environment develops. 'Downstream' the Community's information market policy promotes the use of Europe-wide information services.

Historically, the European information market has been fragmented and underdeveloped. The Community has in the past undertaken a series of measures to change this state of affairs. It developed the Euronet/DIANE network — the first transnational packet-switched data network in Europe — in order to support on-line services for data base access. The Euronet network operated successfully during 1980-84.[1] The Diane services offered by a multiplicity of public and private providers of on-line information data bases continue to develop.

The Community has supported the development of European data bases in key areas. It has also spearheaded the use of satellite communications for Community-wide document transmission and distribution.

In July 1987, the Commission proposed — on the basis of the review of the changes in the European information market — an overall policy and plan for the development of the information market (Box 39).

---

[1] See Chapter V, Section 2.

The Community's policy for establishing Europe's information market: information services for the European citizen at home and at work

In July 1987 the Commission proposed an overall policy and plan for the development of the information market. [1]

This defines a series of priority initiatives:

(i)   The setting up of a European information market observatory;

(ii)   The elimination of technical, administrative and legal barriers to setting up an information market;

(iii) The improvement of the conditions for transmitting and accessing information services;

(iv)   Actions intended to increase the synergy between the public and private sectors;

(v)   The launching of pilot projects;

(vi)   Action in favour of libraries;

(vii) Facilitating user access to existing information services.

Advanced information services represent a rapidly growing market in Europe:

(i)   The 93 000 libraries in the Community, with a total budget of about 10 000 million ECU, are increasingly playing an intermediating and advisory role in data-base searching, and represent an important potential market;

(ii)   Desktop publishing of catalogues and technical documents may have a turnover of 5 000 million ECU by 1990;

(iii) Electronic mail and electronic data transfer are growing rapidly, and may reach a turnover of 6 000 million ECU by 1990;

(iv)   Electronic information services will grow from 1 000 million ECU to over 10 000 million ECU in the coming 10 years, meaning annual growth of 20 to 30%.

There are already 100 000 people employed in the electronic information sector in Europe — a figure that is growing rapidly.

But Europe is only introducing on-line data bases at half the rate of the USA, and each one is only used half as much. This is explained by the many technical, legal and linguistic barriers which fragment the Community market and prevent the achievement of the necessary economies of scale. The Commission has proposed a strategy to overcome these three obstacles.

For the technical obstacles, 'The Commission will develop actions which will support standardization in the area of data base access... They will bear on the following matters:

(i)   harmonization of procedures for connection to networks and computer hosts;

(ii)   automatic identification by networks of the configuration parameters of terminal equipment;

(iii)   harmonization of documentary search software commands;

(iv)   harmonization of formats for data transfer by diskette and by downloading and harmonization of down-loading command;

(v)   definition of a logical standard for structuring sound, image and text data, independent of the medium;

(vi)   establishment of a protocol for transmitting requests for primary documents between bibliographic data base hosts and electronic primary document delivery services;

(vii)   harmonization of certain criteria for the description of data bases in order to facilitate the user's choice;

(viii) harmonization of the names and codes of fields which are common to data bases of the same type in a given information area, so as to facilitate searching by occasional users, the automatic transfer of a search strategy from one base to another and down-loading, adaptation of the principles used for indexing and cataloguing electronic products and services;

(ix)   active promotion of existing standards.'

Concerning the legal obstacles, the Commission will make proposals by 1989 concerning:

(i)   intellectual property (a Green Paper will be published on copyright);

(ii)   authentication of electronic transactions;

(iii)   electronic fraud;

(iv)   liability in information services.

For the linguistic obstacles, the Commission proposes 'Community support for a number of pilot or demonstration projects, which would... incorporate the necessary multilingual aspects.'

---

[1] Communication from the Commission together with a draft Decision concerning the establishment at Community level of a policy and a plan of priority actions for the development of an information services market, COM(87) 360, 24 July 1987.

The plan will on the one hand support the development of a Europe-wide information market — and thus the putting to best use of the Community's evolving telecommunications infrastructure. It will on the other hand depend on the development of an open environment for telecommunications, to allow further development of private initiatives in the sector.

TV broadcasting

The development of a European audio-visual space is another major target of Community policy for 1992.[1]

As set out in Chapter III, developments in cable TV networks and satellite-based broadcasting are converging with the mainstream technological development of the telecommunications network infrastructure.

Since 1984, the Community has started to develop its audio-visual policy on a consistent basis.

The policy has developed along three main lines:

(i) Harmonization of technical standards and technological developments. This is closely related to the telecommunications sector.

(ii) Creating the common market for broadcasting, especially by satellite and cable. In 1984, the Commission transmitted to the Council a Green Paper on television in the Community.[2]

In April 1986, the Commission, on the basis of broad consultation, submitted the proposal for a Directive which is currently before the Council.[3] The Directive aims to permit broadcasts which comply with its requirements to be received and re-transmitted freely in all Member States.

The main requirements concern European programme promotion, advertising, protection of minors and copyright.

(iii) Promotion of the European audio-visual industry, in particular by the launching of the preparatory phase of the MEDIA programme to encourage the development of the European TV programme industry.

The Commission has emphasized in the White Paper on the completion of the internal market the high priority which it attributes to the development of a Community-wide TV broadcasting space and the free flow of broadcasting.

---

[1] See the other publications in this series covering different aspects of the 1992 objective.

[2] 'Television without frontiers', COM(84) 300, 14 June 1984.

[3] Proposal for a Council Directive on the coordination of certain provisions laid down by law, regulation, or administrative action by Member States concerning the pursuit of broadcasting activities, COM(86) 146, 28 April 1986.

A major pre-condition for reaching this objective will be to avoid repetition of the PAL/Secam split which has plagued Europe since the introduction of colour television.

Based on the new developments in telecommunications — in both satellite communications and terrestrial broadband (cable TV) distribution, [1] the technology in the TV field will be revolutionized over the coming years.

The first satellites suitable for direct satellite TV broadcasting (DBS) — are due to be operational from 1988-89 onwards (TDF1, TV-SAT2, BSB, Tele-X, Olympus). [2] The TV programmes broadcast by these satellites will be received by individual and community antennas (MATV — master antenna television systems) and the corresponding satellites could broadcast some 10 new channels from 1988-89 onwards to the whole of Europe. Local cable networks are rapidly developing in various European countries. They can distribute a wide range of products including cable-originated programmes or programmes transmitted by satellite. Major innovations are also expected in the medium term in the field of TV reception, with the prospect of the development of high-definition television yielding a picture quality which was previously unattainable.

The introduction of the new technologies makes the introduction of new technical standards necessary (Box 40). It gives at the same time the opportunity to overcome the heritage of the PAL/Secam split — another example of the cost of 'non-Europe' in the past.

Box 40

New television technology: from direct broadcast satellites to high-definition television

The television technology now being developed will provide a far greater choice of programmes, with very high sound and picture quality, across Europe in the 1990s. If TV is a window on the world, the view will be much wider and clearer than ever before — and the implications, from cultural to commercial, are far-reaching.

Satellite broadcasting

High-powered direct broadcast satellites (DBS) will soon be broadcasting to many European viewers. By 1990 there will be at least five of them in orbit: TDF1 (France), TV-SAT2 (Federal Republic of Germany), Olympus (European Broadcasting Union/Italy), BSB (United Kingdom) and Tele-X (Scandinavia). Each

---

[1] See Chapter III, Sections 6, 7 and 8.
[2] See Chapter III, Section 7.

will carry up to four TV channels receivable in most of western and central Europe, and over an even broader area if larger receiving dishes are used.

DBS will use a new TV transmission system: developed by the European Broadcasting Union (EBU), the family of MAC-packet standards improves picture quality and brings TV sound into the hi-fi league, with up to eight channels of compact-disc quality digital sound; so multilingual broadcasting becomes a real possibility and spare channels can also be used for teletext. Anyone who plugs a low-cost converter into their existing TV set will be able to receive MAC DBS broadcasts via a 35 cm rooftop dish, because the system was designed to build on consumers' existing investments in video.

High-definition television

First generation MAC DBS broadcasts will add a new dimension with digital sound; the next generation promises an equivalent quantum leap in picture quality: a wide-screen, cinema-style viewing experience. This is high-definition television (HDTV), when wall-mounted flat screens and projection TVs will ultimately replace today's televisions, which are still based on the 50-year-old concept of a glass vacuum tube in a box.

The range of consumer equipment will include more advanced versions of products already available, such as VCRs and camcorders, and the studio version of the technology will provide such good quality that cinema films may well be shot in HDTV, with the added benefit that electronic effects currently available on video systems will be easily and cheaply available to the cinema industry.

MAC standards: the evolutionary approach to HDTV

The Community is rich in the creative and information skills required to provide the best television in the world. Yet failure to evolve a concerted European approach towards technological and regulatory issues could hand these new opportunities over to be exploited world-wide by the European TV industry's overseas competitors. One of the key issues is technical standardization.

Up to now, different technical standards have been used for broadcasting in different Community countries — Secam in France and Greece, various versions of PAL elsewhere — so that viewers cannot receive cross-frontier broadcasts without dual standard TV sets or, if they are on a cable network, conversion equipment. A dozen different sets are therefore needed to pick up all the TV channels in Europe, limiting the viewer's choice and pushing up manufacturers' costs in a highly competitive world market. Now, a Commission initiative has led to the acceptance by European governments (in November 1986) of the MAC family of DBS TV transmission standards for the future.

This consensus means that the European television market should overcome the differences that have so damaged the competitive prospects of European manufacturers in the pre-satellite generation of TV.

At the same time Europe must aim at safeguarding the major investment which Europe's consumers have made in their television equipment. The introduction of the next generation of television — HDTV (high-definition television) — should allow future use of current sets in the new environment, until users decide to upgrade (Box 41).

Box 41

Community cooperation on a high-definition television standard: avoiding a re-run of the PAL/Secam split

While it might seem that individual European TV-makers have enjoyed protection of their national markets by using incompatible standards, the Japanese have been developing TV manufacturing into a global industry with much greater economies of scale. The large revenues generated have financed Japanese development of new products, contributing significantly to the Far Eastern dominance of the European and American consumer electronics markets; these resources have also funded Japanese research in other areas of information technology, such as computers and memory chips.

The Japan Broadcasting Corporation (NHK) has been developing an alternative 1125-line 60 MHz HDTV production system since the late 1960s. The system uses 27 MHz of bandwidth, equivalent to five ordinary TV channels, so it is not practical to broadcast it in that form because it would take up too much radio spectrum. Over the last five years, NHK has developed the MUSE transmission system which fits the standard 8.1 MHz DBS channel. It uses similar techniques to MAC, with a wide-screen picture and digital sound.

The essential feature of the Japanese HDTV/MUSE package is its incompatibility with all existing television systems. NHK decided to break with the past totally. By contrast, the European MAC approach has been based on compatibility with existing systems, permitting a low-cost evolution through improved television to HDTV. Community manufacturers and broadcasters chose this route because it shows greater respect for consumers' existing equipment investment, allowing the customer to choose when he or she wants to upgrade, rather than using obsolescence to dictate this decision.

Now, in the framework of European cooperation, European TV companies are developing the high-quality HDTV system needed to evolve towards a new generation of television. European HDTV is designed to meet international requirements, not just those of a particular region, and European consumer electronics companies are producing the answer to those requirements, after committing some 200 million ECU in R&D over three years.

The deadline for an international decision on HDTV is 1990. Through Community cooperation, that deadline will be met.

The future of European television is therefore increasingly being decided at Community level. Satellites, after all, do not recognize national boundaries. And the Commission's initiatives in regulation and standardization — decided in close consultation with broadcasters, manufacturers, researchers and national authorities — are designed to ensure coordinated, Community-wide acceptance of the changes which will allow the European television industry to meet new competitive challenges on an international scale. The aim is to benefit the viewer, by providing more choice and cheaper equipment, and to ensure the future of a consumer electronics industry of major importance to the Community.

A common technological base in Europe is a pre-condition for Europe's users to benefit fully from the major aim of Community telecommunications policy as expressed in the Green Paper: a more open telecommunications environment, with more choice for the user.

VII — The Green Paper: a Community-wide market in a more competitive environment

In June 1987, the Commission of the European Communities issued the Green Paper on telecommunications. [1]

The Green Paper was addressed by the Commission more explicitly to: 'the Council of Ministers; the European Parliament and the Economic and Social Committee; the telecommunications administrations and recognized private operating agencies; the European telecommunications, data-processing, and services industry; the users; and the trade unions and other organizations representing social interests in the area.'

The Commission's aim in issuing this Green Paper was to launch a Europe-wide debate on the future regulatory conditions of telecommunications with a view to the overriding objective of the 1992 market.

The Green Paper is permeated by three basic messages:

(i)   Failure to adapt the system of regulation of the telecommunications sector in Europe to the new technological and market conditions would risk immense damage to the long-term economic strength of the Community as a whole — and to the fulfilment of the requirements of the European citizen who is entitled to freedom of choice in his or her way of life: communications will be an increasingly important aspect of life in the future.

(ii) Existing structures have grown up over a long period and have been successful in bringing telephone services within the reach of everybody in Europe. The objective of general public service must be reconciled with the objective of broader choice for the user.

(iii) Regulatory changes in telecommunications must therefore take account of the views of all parties concerned. The Green Paper process itself — conceived as a broad consultative process — testifies to this conviction.

The Green Paper thus builds on — and complements — the Community's telecommunications actions under way, as set out in the previous chapter, by addressing the future regulatory environment of telecommunications.

---

[1] 'Towards a dynamic European economy — Green Paper on the development of the common market for telecommunications services and equipment', COM(87) 290, 30 June 1987.

In the Green Paper, the Commission proposes more competition in a Europe-wide market, in order to develop the full potential of telecommunications in a fast-moving environment. Europe needs more opening of the telecommunications sector to competition, in order to achieve a single Community-wide market by 1992. At the same time, only a unified Europe-wide market can offer the economies of scale needed by the more liberal environment developing in all Member States of the European Community, at the national level.

1. The current adjustment: constructing together with the Member States an open Community-wide market

In the light of developments in technology and market conditions and the transformations in the United States and Japan, all Member States of the European Community are now reshaping or reconsidering the regulation of their telecommunications sectors. Table 15 illustrates, in a simplified form, the profound changes which have taken place or are under way in the Member States.

TABLE 15

All the Member States are reviewing the regulatory conditions of their national telecommunications sector: changes in the provision of telecommunications in the European Community

Country	1977	1988 (changes since 1977 and future orientations)
Belgium	RTT (Régie des télégraphes et des téléphones), reporting to the Secretary of State of the Ministry of Posts and Telecommunications	Possibility of transforming RTT into an entity with a much greater degree of autonomy is under discussion ('four wise men' committee)
Denmark	P&T, government department, reporting to Minister for Public Works KTAS, JTAS (50% State-owned) and PKT (owned by local authorities), telephone only	Following the report of the Bernstein Committee (1985), some restructuring took place in 1986. Statens Teletjenste runs national trunk network and international services
France	DGT (Direction générale des télécommunications), department of Ministry of Posts and Telecommunications FCR (France câble et radio), State-owned Company	● Setting up of Cogécom (Compagnie générale des communications), holding company of all the PTT subsidiaries (société Transpac, Télésystèmes, FCR, Entreprise générale des télécommunications) ● Communications law of 30 September 1986; an informal draft law on competition in telecommunications was circulated by end of 1987 ● 1987: opening of mobile radio service provision to competition. DGT renamed 'France Télécom'

186

Country	1977	1988 (changes since 1977 and future orientations)
Federal Republic of Germany	DBP, Deutsche Bundespost, a federal administration	Government commission reported on future regulation of telecommunications in September 1987. Legislative proposals for substantial liberalization tabled in March 1988 ('Poststrukturgesetz'). The structural part of the reform envisages the establishment of a public enterprise called 'Deutsche Bundespost Telecom'
Greece	OTE, publicly-owned but financially autonomous corporation, founded in 1949	Discussion in progress
Ireland	P&T, headed by Minister for Posts and Telegraphs	Telecom Eireann (TE), State-owned public corporation set up in 1984. The regulatory authority lies with the Department of Communications
Italy	ASST (azienda di Stato per i servizi telefonici), DCST (direzione centrale servizi telegrafici), DCSR (direzione centrale servizi radioelettrici), directly controlled by Ministry of Posts and Telecommunications. SIP, Italcable, Telespazio: concessionary companies, subsidiaries of the State-controlled STET group	• Increase of SIP privatization • Bill on the institutional reorganization of the sector proposed • Bill on the liberalization of maintenance has been approved (March 1987) • Bill on rules for telematic services is under discussion
Luxembourg	P&T, government administration	Government is considering whether to introduce a new law on telecommunications to redefine boundaries between the monopoly and the competitive sectors
Netherlands	PTT, State organization under responsibility of the Ministry of Traffic and Civil Works	Government decision to convert PTT from a State organization to a limited liability company (government-owned), starting from 1989, following reports from Swarttouw and Steenbergen Committees
Portugal	CTT for services outside Lisbon and Oporto, TLP for Lisbon and Oporto; both State-owned but financially autonomous. CPRM for intercontinental services	CTT & TLP boards merged in 1978: operationally still independent. Two commissions have been appointed to report on a new telecommunications law, and on reorganization of the sector (reports were presented in June 1987)
Spain	CYT, Government Department for telegram/telex services. CTNE, set up by ITT in 1924 but large State share since 1945, for telephone/data transmission	CTNE re-named Telefonica and granted greater autonomy. A new comprehensive law on telecommunications adopted in December 1987 (LOT)
United Kingdom	Post Office, State-owned corporation reporting to the Secretary of State for Industry	• British Telecommunications plc, 49% government-owned private company. Mercury Communications Limited, private company • Private services providers supplying mobile and value-added services, new general VADS licence issued in February 1987

187

The United Kingdom has moved rapidly to introduce competition in its telecommunications sector. It radically changed the organization of the sector with the Telecommunications Acts of 1981 and 1984: introduction of a competing network provider, Mercury; privatization of British Telecom; licensing of private providers of mobile radio, paging and cable TV; and licensing of a large number of value-added services providers — to date nearly 200. In the spring of 1987 the United Kingdom issued a new general value-added and data services (VADS) licence, under which private providers may register.

With this radical transformation of its telecommunications sector in a very short period, the United Kingdom took a lead in the transformation of the European telecommunications market — though the rapidity of the transformation was also closely related with the specific context of UK policy. More recently, France, Germany, Spain and the Netherlands have started to react to the changing conditions of the sector.

In France, since the early 1980s, a general consensus has built up regarding the need to redefine the telecommunications structure, in order to respond to the new requirements following the rapid and successful build-up of the network during the 1970s which gave France the lead in digitization in Europe.

Throughout the early 1980s, a new market-based approach towards accelerated introduction of new services was promoted, by creating commercially oriented subsidiaries of the DGT, such as the Transpac company, for the introduction of the packet-switched network. Transpac quickly developed into the largest public data network in Europe and became the basis of the nation-wide introduction of Minitels.

Great attention was paid to audio-visual policy which took more and more account of the convergence of the audio-visual technologies and telecommunications. Two audio-visual laws have been passed successively since 1980.

Major changes have occurred since the mid-1980s: substantial liberalization of value-added services with the decree on value-added services of September 1987, licensing of a second competing provider for mobile telephones, and other providers for paging systems. A broad public debate has started on new draft legislation.

In Germany, the government commission on telecommunications (the so-called 'Witte' Commission) submitted its proposals in September 1987. They aim at extensive liberalization of the German telecommunications environment and make detailed proposals for the future organization of the Bundespost to adapt to the new competitive market environment. Firm legislative proposals were presented in 1988.

Spain adopted a new telecommunications law in December 1987, moving the country a major step forward towards an open market environment. Details of implementation will be defined in the course of 1988.

The Netherlands introduced legislation into Parliament to transform the PTT into a publicly-owned limited liability company and to liberalize the terminal and value-added services market by 1989.

Italy has introduced a series of new measures to open the terminal market. Belgium has announced an extension of liberalization in the terminal market. Luxembourg, Portugal and Greece are examining the situation. Ireland and Denmark have reshaped the structure of their telecommunications organizations.

In fact, the launching of the debate in all Member States at the same time demonstrates that the same technological and market challenge is being felt everywhere.

All Member States have started to react and to consider substantial liberalization.

In the context of this on-going reorganization of the telecommunications sector, the Commission defines in the Green Paper the role of the Community as ensuring that:

'(i) the necessary European scale and dimension are introduced into the current phase of transformation;

(ii) no new barriers are created within the Community during the adjustment of regulatory conditions;

(iii) existing barriers are removed in the course of the adjustment.'

A number of common trends have become apparent. These trends are towards:

(i)   freedom to connect terminals to the network;

(ii) freedom to use the network;

(iii) freedom to provide services over the network.

In the Green Paper, the Commission builds on these emerging trends in the Member States, but it pushes further. It aims to harness the new potential of telecommunications to contribute fully to the 1992 objective.

Telecommunications is expanding into a general infrastructure for the 1992 market.

The European Community must consider the new technological and economic potential of telecommunications in the context of the obligations and opportunities which derive from the Treaty of Rome (Box 42).

Box 42

The Treaty of Rome as a framework for telecommunications policy

The Treaty of Rome sets out a comprehensive framework for Community telecommunications policy. The provisions of most relevance are:

(i)   the provisions governing competition, in particular Articles 85, 86, and 90;

(ii) the provisions concerning the freedom to provide services and the freedom of establishment, in particular Articles 52 to 66;

(iii) the provisions concerning the free circulation of goods, in particular Articles 30 to 37;

(iv) the provisions concerning the common commercial policy, in particular Articles 110 to 116;

(v) the general provisions for the approximation of provisions laid down by law, regulation or administrative action in Member States which directly affect the establishment or functioning of the common market, in particular Article 100, and after the coming into force of the Single Act, Article 100a.

Beyond these Articles other provisions of the Treaty must be taken into account, as well as case-law developed by the Court of Justice with regard to telecommunications and to other sectors, in so far as they are of relevance. The Commission has stated that 'it regards the Member States' postal and telecommunications authorities as commercial undertakings since they supply goods and services for payment' which are subject to the application of Community competition law, an opinion confirmed by the Court of Justice. [1]

In the Green Paper the Commission states that: 'In pursuing the lifting of existing restrictions, the Commission will take full account of the fact that the competition rules of the Treaty apply to telecommunications administrations, in particular to the extent that they engage in commercial activities. It may use, as appropriate, its mandate under Article 90 (3) of the Treaty to promote, synchronize and accelerate the on-going transformation.' [2]

For easy reference, the main provisions of the Treaty in the context of telecommunications are cited hereunder:

Article 90(1) provides that:

'In the case of public undertakings and undertakings to which Member States grant special or exclusive rights, Member States shall neither enact nor maintain in force any measure contrary to the rules contained in this Treaty, in particular to those rules provided for in Article 7 and Articles 85 to 94.'

Article 90(2) provides that:

'Undertakings entrusted with the operation of services of general economic interest or having the character of a revenue-producing monopoly shall be subject to the rules contained in this Treaty, in particular to the rules on competition, in so far as the application of such rules does not obstruct the performance, in law or in fact, of the particular tasks assigned to them. The development of trade must not be affected to such an extent as would be contrary to the interests of the Community.'

Article 90(3) provides that:

'the Commission shall ensure the application of the provisions of this Article and shall, where necessary, address appropriate directives or decisions to Member States.'

Article 86 provides that:

'Any abuse by one or more undertakings of a dominant position within the common market or in a substantial part of it shall be prohibited as incompatible with the common market in so far as it may affect trade between Member States.

Such abuse may, in particular, consist in:

(a) directly or indirectly imposing unfair purchase or selling prices or other unfair trading conditions;

(b) limiting production, markets or technical development to the prejudice of consumers;

(c) applying dissimilar conditions to equivalent transactions with other trading parties, thereby placing them at a competitive disadvantage;

(d) making the conclusion of contracts subject to acceptance by the other parties of supplementary obligations which, by their nature or according to commercial usage, have no connection with the subject of such contracts.'

Article 37 (1) provides that:

'Member States shall progressively adjust any State monopolies of a commercial character so as to ensure that when the transitional period has ended no discrimination regarding the conditions under which goods are procured and marketed exists between nationals of Member States.

The provisions of this Article shall apply to any body through which a Member State, in law or in fact, either directly or indirectly supervises, determines or appreciably influences imports or exports between Member States. These provisions shall likewise apply to monopolies delegated by the State to others.'

Article 59 provides that:

'Within the framework of the provisions set out below, restrictions on freedom to provide services within the Community shall be progressively abolished during the transitional period in respect of nationals of Member States who are established in a State of the Community other than that of the person for whom the services are intended.

The Council may, acting by a qualified majority on a proposal from the Commission, extend the provisions of the Chapter to nationals of a third country who provide services and who are established within the Community.'

---

[1] See Case 41/83, *Commission v Italy* of 20 March 1985 (British Telecom).
[2] Green Paper, p.186.

With the 1992 objective in mind, the Commission sets out three clear objectives in the Green Paper:

(i) a common market in telecommunications terminal equipment, in order to ensure a broad choice for the user;

(ii) a common market in telecommunications services, in order to allow telecommunications to develop into the all-pervasive infrastructure for the Community's service and technology market of 1992, which is its major vocation;

(iii) a common market in network equipment to ensure the Community's future position in large-scale information technology.

The last objective aims at the economies of scale needed for the new switching and transmission technologies of the network — development of large-scale computer technology and of advanced opto-electronics.

As stated in the Green Paper, the Community's policy in this area is closely related to the Community's R&D policy — the R&D framework programme and the RACE programme — and the opening of the procurement of the telecommunications administrations who dominate this market. Both these themes are discussed in other sections. [1]

The emphasis in this chapter will therefore be on the first two policy goals which will largely determine the future utility of telecommunications in the work-place and in homes:

(i) liberalization, in a Community-wide market, of the telecommunications terminal market;

(ii) liberalization of the provision of services via the new multi-purpose digital networks.

2. The common market in terminal equipment: a broader choice for the European user

The interface of the user with the telecommunications network is the telecommunications terminal. It is in this market that the convergence of telecommunications and computer technology will lead to an explosion of new features over the coming years. [2] The business sector will see the rapid emergence of integrated business communications systems. The home will see telephones with a multitude of new features, and with the emergence of videotex on a mass consumer basis and the projected spread of home computers — more and more connected to the communications function — data and information-based services will gradually be integrated with everyday life.

Forecasts show that the European citizen will demand a broad range of new equipment — if supply develops according to user choice.

Enquiries regarding the future spread of new telecommunications and media technologies indicate substantial penetration of new types of terminals for the 1990s, with for example interactively used personal computers reaching more than 20% of households, which corresponds to more than 20 million PCs in homes in the European Community by 1995 (Figure 18).

---

[1] See Chapter VI, Sections 4 and 8, and see also Chapter VII, Section 6.
[2] See Chapter III.

FIGURE 18

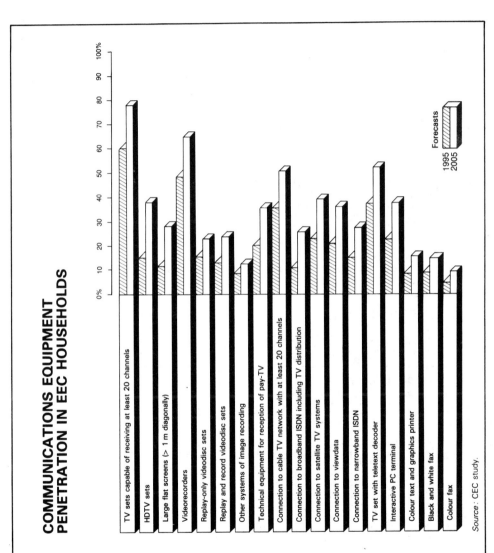

COMMUNICATIONS EQUIPMENT
PENETRATION IN EEC HOUSEHOLDS

Source: CEC study.

The terminal equipment sector will therefore be characterized by an impressive diversification of features, with rapid merging of communications, data processing and audio-visual features. Technology must be allowed to adapt to user requirements, both in the work-place and in the home. All Member States realize that this future task is very different in nature from the past, when a limited number of telecommunications terminals — basically the telephone sets and telex machines — with a limited number of features were provided mostly under monopoly by the telecommunications administrations.

The regulatory situation regarding the terminal sector is shown in Figure 19.

The trend in all Member States is towards progressive full opening of the terminal market to competition. However, provision is still currently reserved for the telecommunications administrations in most Member States for a range of equipment, in particular the first telephone set.

The trend towards opening of the terminal market is world-wide. The full liberalization of the terminal market will be an essential pre-condition for future growth of telecommunications in the European Community. In a more profound sense, it will be a test case for establishing the principle of choice for the user in the future communications society (Box 43).

Box 43

Freedom of choice for the user: cordless telephones

The introduction of cordless telephones has become a test-case in the Community for the free choice of terminal equipment by the user.

Cordless telephones introduce a new level of convenience into the home, by making it possible to move a portable telephone freely within the house or flat, without being linked by a wire to a connection point.

Cordless telephones are offered by a number of manufacturers, with multiple features and at reasonable prices. Innovation is rapid. While there is a genuine need for type approval procedures, to avoid frequency overspill into other apartments or houses — which could entail substantial disruption of other telephone users and of TV and broadcasting reception — there is no technical reason why the sale and maintenance of cordless telephones should be retained under the monopoly of the telecommunications administrations.

In the case in point, the German Bundespost tried to extend its monopoly to cordless telephones. After intervention of the Commission under Community competition rules, in particular Article 37, the Federal Government dropped its plans to extend the Bundespost's monopoly to this area. [1]

---

[1] See Chapter VI, Section 7.

FIGURE 19

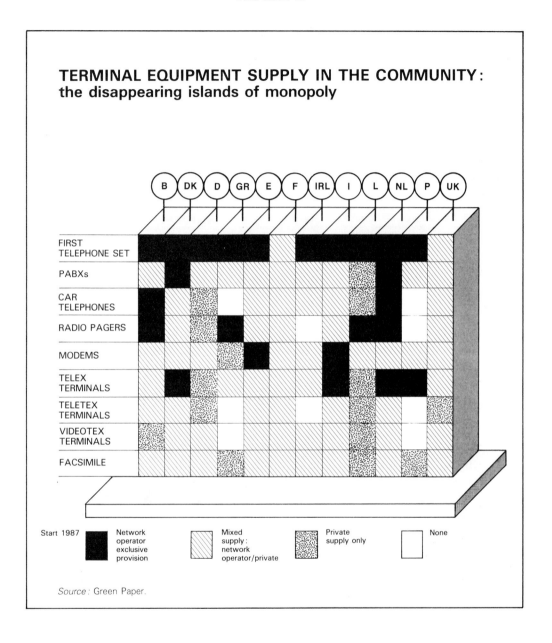

195

In the Green Paper, the Commission makes an open terminal market a clearly stated goal.

The current technological evolution towards multi-functional computer-based terminal equipment, including ISDN terminals, [1] will make the current trend towards competitive provision inexorable. However, the change from the existing solution of sole supply of certain terminal equipment, in particular the first telephone set, to a competitive environment, will have to allow for a sufficient but defined time period for the European equipment industry to adapt to the new situation.

An open Community-wide market depends on the fulfilment of two requirements:

(i) lifting of monopoly provision in those areas where it still exists;
(ii) fair type-approval procedures required for the connection of equipment to the network, indispensable to make market opening effective.

In the Green Paper, the Commission makes proposals to achieve both ends, combining the use of Community Treaty provisions and the proposition of appropriate Community legislation (Box 44).

Box 44

The Green Paper proposals for the Community-wide opening of the terminal equipment market

The Green Paper proposals concentrate on the full and strict application of Treaty rules and on full implementation of fair type-approval procedures mutually recognized between Member States.

More specifically, the Green Paper proposes the following elements of a new framework:

(i) 'The general surveillance and control function imposed by the Treaty regarding the free movement of goods and the adjustment of State monopolies of a commercial character. The Commission has made clear in the past that it will apply Articles 37 and 86 of the Treaty, as well as Article 90 in conjunction with Article 86 and more particularly the means at its disposal under Article 90(3) of the Treaty, progressively to terminal equipment, in order to support the current opening process.

---

[1] See Chapter III.

(ii) Rapid and effective application of:

    (a) Council Directive 86/361/EEC concerning the first phase of the establishment of mutual recognition of type-approval for telecommunications terminal equipment, which was adopted by the Council on 9 June 1986;

    (b) Council Decision 87/95/EEC on standardization in the field of information technology and telecommunications, which was adopted on 22 December 1986.

(iii) On this basis, Community-wide definition of the technical interfaces of the network with the subscriber terminal equipment, i.e. the network termination points (NTPs).

Clear guidelines in this respect are given in Council Recommendation 86/659/EEC on the coordinated introduction of ISDN.

(iv) Extensive application of Recommendation 84/550/EEC under which Member States agreed to open bidding on supply contracts being awarded by their telecommunications administrations to suppliers in other Member States.'[1]

'Telecommunications administrations would be able to offer terminal equipment in a competitive environment alongside other equipment suppliers. A key issue here will be careful supervision under competition rules.

The transition towards a Community-wide competitive terminal equipment market could be substantially accelerated by two measures:

(i) clear definition of network termination points in the overall context of fixing the conditions under which the network infrastructure is provided by the telecommunications administrations to users and competitive services providers (Open Network Provision — ONP; see Box 47). This could build on the guidelines provided by Recommendation 86/659/EEC;

(ii) rapid extension of Directive 86/361/EEC to full mutual recognition of type approval.'[2]

Regarding the restrictive effect of national procurement policies, rapid opening of telecommunications administrations' purchasing to Community-wide bidding is requested.

The conditions for the opening of the terminal market were subsequently defined in Commission Directive 88/301/EEC, issued on 16 May 1988.[3]

---

[1] Green Paper, p. 62.
[2] Green Paper, p. 63.
[3] See Chapter VIII, Section 3.

Free Community-wide availability of suitable terminal equipment is a pre-condition for the development in the Community of the highly diversified and user-adjusted telecommunications services which the 1992 market will need.

3. The common market in telecommunications services: allowing telecommunications to develop into the Community's infrastructure for the future information-based market

The freedom to provide services in a Community-wide market will be essential to develop telecommunications into the pervasive force for development of the Community's market which it can and should be.

Provision of telecommunications services world-wide will be determined by the two trends discussed in Chapter III:

(i) technical progress makes a multitude of new uses and services possible;

(ii) the network infrastructure can carry more and more services operated independently of network operators. Telecommunications services are becoming more and more tradable.

Value-added services will play the role of the mediator between the general multipurpose digital telecommunications network of the future and the special requirements in the work-place during the first stage, in homes during the second.

Europe must implant itself strongly in the value-added services market-place if it wants to maintain control of its future economic structure (Box 45).

Box 45

An integrated network infrastructure together with service suppliers operating in a Community-wide market: a European strategy for value-added services to face up to the challenge of the multinationals

The growing need for value-added services will only bring forth the creation of a strong European industry in this area if the following two conditions are met:

(i) the European market for value-added services needs to emerge from its current embryonic state, through demand stimulation and the end of the uncertainty, above all regulatory, which is weighing on the market;

(ii) the organization of the information-transport system must be developed at European level, especially with respect to network infrastructure and to the harmonization of conditions of access, while at the same time European supply needs to be stimulated in the area of applications.

The accelerated development of European value-added services will rely on active cooperation between basic transporters (telecommunications administrations) and the suppliers of value-added services operating in a competitive environment (telecommunications administrations or private new entrants). The European strategies that feature in the Green Paper are supportive of this approach.

The pre-condition for this is the Europe-wide market.

Many value-added services are targeted narrowly on specific user needs. As a result they need a large market to develop: for example, a service which appeals to only 1% or less of businesses may well be viable in the Community market of 320 million people where it would not be viable in any single Member State with a population of some 60 million at most.

The Green Paper recalls that:

'Given the technological development, the trend in the Member States currently is clearly towards a competitive environment for more and more of these services with correspondingly narrower interpretation of those traditional "basic services" which continue to be reserved for exclusive provision by the telecommunications administrations.'

It continues:

'The new technological opportunities allow the provision of many functions and services by users which were previously only possible technically and economically for the telecommunications administrations. The maintenance of the principle of exclusive provision therefore inevitably translates into imposing certain restrictions on the ways in which terminal equipment connected to the network such as PABXs may be used.

The European Court of Justice has explicitly recognized the right of network users to benefit fully from new opportunities offered by technological progress. [1]

The justification of continued exclusive provision of certain basic services must therefore be weighed carefully against the restrictions which this may impose on users' applications for their own use or provision of services to third parties. Major conclusions are:

(i)   exclusive provision of services must be narrowly construed;

(ii) the ongoing integration of services caused by the technological trend makes it necessary that exclusive provision is made subject to periodic review.'

Given the problem of delimiting value-added services, the Green Paper does not use the delimitation of basic services versus value-added services for the purposes of regulatory proposals. Instead it establishes a distinction between reserved services and competitive services (Box 46).

---

[1] Case 41/83 *Commission v Italy* of 20 March 1985 ('British Telecom'), see Chapter VI, Section 7.

Box 46

Telecommunications services: the stumbling block of their definition

The problem of the definition of service boundaries has been a stumbling block world-wide in regulatory discussion of telecommunications, ever since the unsuccessful efforts by the Federal Communications Commission in the United States to create stable definitions. In Computer Inquiry II (1981) the attempt was made to split services according to 'basic' services and 'enhanced' or 'value-added' services.

The traditional 'basic' telecommunications services were telephony and telex.

As technology evolved, telecommunications administrations introduced new services, some of which have become accepted as basic services in some Member States (but not in others). Examples of these differ throughout the Community but include: packet-switched data services; circuit-switched data services; teletex; electronic mail; videotex.

There is no universal agreement even within the Community Member States on what constitutes 'basic services'.

In parallel, there is the growing variety of 'value-added services', defined in the United States as 'enhanced services'.

'Enhanced services' are generally understood to be services where there are additional functions provided over and above the basic conveyance functions. Indeed, it is just this definition that has been used — unsuccessfully — in the United States to attempt to differentiate between 'basic services' and 'enhanced' (or 'value-added') services.

Throughout the US experience — notably in Computer Inquiries II and III [1] — it has turned out to be impossible to maintain a stable definition. The impossibility of agreeing on precise 'technically-based' definitions is an important result of technological development.

The Green Paper therefore does not try to define 'basic services' nor 'value-added services' for the purpose of regulatory proposals. Instead, it inverts the problem by concentrating on the very limited number of services which would continue to be subject to restrictions ('reserved services'), with unrestricted supply allowed for all other services ('competitive services').

---

[1] See Chapter V, Section 1.

The Green Paper clearly argues the case for opening the services market:

'"reserved services" are defined as services reserved for exclusive provision by the telecommunications administrations. Reserved services must be narrowly defined, in order to avoid restrictions or distortions of competition. They must be provided on a universal basis. "Competitive services" would include all other services, in particular "value-added services".'

The Commission recalls that voice telephony alone currently accounts for 85 to 90% of the 64 800 million ECU per annum which make up telecommunications revenues in the Community [1] and continues:

'(i) As far as exclusive provision of services is currently justified by the need to safeguard the financial viability of telecommunications administrations, only voice telephony seems to be an obvious candidate.

(ii) Maintaining or extending exclusive provision over other services will lead to the imposition of additional restrictions on users: restrictions which will become more and more difficult to control.'

Telecommunications services are becoming more and more tradable. The provision of telecommunications services can increasingly take place across borders in the Community, without any major technical constraint being involved. With a view to 1992 this makes the opening of the telecommunications services market a fundamental obligation upon the sector.

Article 59 of the Treaty of Rome guarantees, as a general rule, the freedom to provide cross-border services.

In the Green Paper the Commission clearly recalls this obligation and continues:

'Exceptions must be interpreted narrowly. The potential for conflict will be reduced if:

(i) comparable definitions of services which may be reserved exist in the Member States;

(ii) reserved services are defined narrowly.

In practice, given existing differences in definitions in the field of non-voice services, and the likely narrow interpretation of exceptions by the Court of Justice, reservation of services which go substantially beyond voice services is likely to lead to conflict.'

---

[1] See Chapter II.

This then leads to the central concept of the Green Paper: European service providers operating in the 1992 Community-wide market; open network provision by the telecommunications administrations to users and providers, offering services in competition (Box 47).

Box 47

A Community-wide network infrastructure for the 1992 market: Open Network Provision (ONP)

'Open Network Provision' to users and service providers is a central concept proposed by the Commission in the Green Paper, which states:

'If a series of contentious cases and lengthy conflict (which would have to be resolved by the Commission under Articles 52, 59, 85, 86, and 90 of the Treaty) is to be avoided, the Community will have to develop common principles regarding the general conditions for the provision of the network infrastructure by the telecommunications administrations to users and competitive service providers, in particular for trans-frontier provision.'

The conditions of access to the network concern mainly: standards and interfaces offered for interconnection; tariff principles and usage conditions; and provision of frequencies.

'The transition towards a Community-wide competitive services market could therefore be substantially accelerated by Community Directives on ONP, based on Articles 100a and 90(3) for technical specifications and network access respectively.

Such Directives would aim at the Community-wide harmonization of principles of access. These Directives would have to include clear access conditions by telecommunications administrations for trans-frontier service providers for use of the network, regarding at least three "layers":

(i) technical interfaces, i.e. specification of facilities and standards requirements, building in particular on Council Directive 86/361/EEC, Decision 87/95/EEC and Recommendation 86/659/EEC. This may include conditions for availability of frequencies where of relevance;

(ii) tariff principles, in particular separate tariffing ("unbundling") of "bearer" and "value-added" capabilities;

(iii) restrictions of use which may be inevitable for the time being, such as implied by reservation of certain services, e.g. voice telephony. Restrictions would have to be subject to review within given time intervals, taking account of technological developments.'

4. Strong telecommunications administrations in a more competitive environment: ensuring network integrity and an open market

The telecommunications networks and their organizations represent Europe's largest asset in the information age now beginning. In the Green Paper, the Commission acknowledges this fact. Its aims are to maintain that asset and make sure it is put to full use. The Green Paper advocates strong telecommunications administrations in an open Community terminal equipment and services market.

The Commission acknowledges the traditional public service tasks of the telecommunications administrations, in particular the task of providing universal service in order to cover basic economic and social needs. The Commission accepts safeguards in order to maintain financial viability and the capability to develop networks and services.

However, the Green Paper also emphasizes the new responsibility of the telecommunications administrations for the development of the future markets which are emerging as a consequence of the convergence of telecommunications, data processing and the audio-visual sector. According to the Green Paper, the full use of the future potential of telecommunications must include participation of both telecommunications administrations and other providers in the newly developing markets — in particular in the terminal equipment and value-added services markets.

On the other hand, the Commission recalls that any remaining service monopoly does imply constraints on the activities of those connected to this network and using network facilities. The justification of continued exclusive provision must therefore be weighed carefully against the lost opportunities for economic growth and employment which this may entail.

The Commission does not speak out in the Green Paper on the future organization and ownership status of the telecommunications administrations nor does it take a position on the question of competition in the network infrastructure itself (Box 48).

Box 48

Network competition and the future organization of the telecommunications administrations — a central subject for national debate

Since the changes in the United States and Japan, the privatization of British Telecom, and the licensing of a competing network provider — Mercury — the issue of privatization and network competition has become a central subject of national debate in a number of Community Member States.

The issue is complex. Arguments for competition, flexibility and cost-based pricing stand against the argument of universal service on equal conditions for all and the increased overall cost which could result from the establishment of a parallel network.

At the moment the positions adopted in Europe vary. The decision will depend in many cases on political and social perceptions, the geographical nature and size of the country, and actual candidates to be competitive providers.

The Green Paper does not argue a Community position. It considers that the essential objectives of a Community-wide services and equipment market can be reached with or without network competition.

The Green Paper recalls that:

'Article 222 provides that the Community shall in no way prejudice the system of property ownership in Member States. Therefore, the determination of the appropriate ownership of telecommunications administrations — in particular whether they should be in public or private ownership — falls to the Member States.'[1]

It notes that:

'Given the more limited national dimension in Europe, public service goals, required economies of scale, and the trade-off to be made between more flexibility from competition on the one hand and higher transaction costs which can result from parallel networks on the other, it seems likely that the positions in the Member States will converge on maintaining exclusive provision of network infrastructure on their territory by a single telecommunications administration or a very limited number of administrations.'[2]

From a Community perspective the following seem the most relevant considerations:

(i) Whichever organizational scheme the Member States choose for provision of the network infrastructure by their telecommunications administrations, the short and long-term integrity of the network infrastructure should be safeguarded.

(ii) Member States should ensure that telecommunications administrations provide efficient national, Community-wide and world-wide communications.

(iii) The Treaty, and in particular Community competition rules, applies to telecommunications administrations whether they have an absolute monopoly or merely a dominant position.

(iv) Exclusive network infrastructure provision must be narrowly defined. New technologies in adjacent fields, such as in satellite communications, mobile radio and cable-TV networks will need special consideration.

The Commission also points in the Green Paper to the need for the introduction of effective mechanisms to ensure cost-orientation of tariffs.

---

[1] Green Paper, p. 71.
[2] Green Paper, p. 72.

Instead, the Commission clearly focuses on issues related directly to the 1992 goal. 'The proposals concentrate on those issues which must be resolved at Community level for all Member States. They leave out questions which are important but fall to the national level, such as which status for telecommunications administrations is best suited to facing the developing competitive market environment, and related questions of finance, organization and employment relations.'[1]

Box 49

Major changes required in the role of telecommunications administrations with a view to 1992

Activity	*At present*	*In future*
Exclusive provision of network infrastructure (monopoly/duopoly)	yes	yes
Exclusive provision of limited number of basic services ('reserved services')	yes	yes[1]
Participation in competitive services market (incl. VANS)	yes	yes
Combination of regulatory and operational functions	YES	NO
Protection from 'cream skimming'	yes	yes
Acceptance of common interconnect and access obligations for trans-frontier service providers	NO	YES
Supply of terminal equipment on exclusive basis	YES	NO
Supply of terminal equipment on competitive basis	yes	yes

---

[1] In the future, exclusive provision of services will have to be defined narrowly and be subject to review. Voice telephone service seems to be the only obvious candidate.

---

[1] Green Paper, p. 184.

Regarding the essential changes required at the Community level, the Green Paper lists three central adjustments (Box 49):

(i) Progressive ending of the remaining exclusive provision of terminal equipment by telecommunications administrations. This is the direct counterpart of the liberalization of the terminal market discussed previously.

(ii) Acceptance by the telecommunications administrations of clear obligations to interconnect with and provide access for trans-frontier service providers.

This is the corollary of the implementation of the common market for telecommunications services. It makes open network provision a central future obligation on the telecommunications administrations.

(iii) Clear separation of regulatory functions from operational functions.

'This is a fundamental pre-condition for the establishment of a competitive market and the participation of the telecommunications administrations in this market.

In a more competitive environment, the telecommunications administrations cannot continue to be both regulators and market participants, i.e. both referee and player.'[1]

The Green Paper tries to achieve a careful balance regarding new obligations and new opportunities for the telecommunications administrations in the future competitive Community market.

On the one hand, the Green Paper insists on:

(i) close scrutiny of financial transfers — cross subsidies — between reserved services provided exclusively by the administrations and services provided in competition with others;

(ii) a clear cost-orientation of tariff policy.

On the other hand, it accepts measures to safeguard the public service obligations of the administrations and to lift existing restrictions which could prevent them from using the new opportunities by:

(i) accepting measures against extreme cases of 'cream-skimming' as far as compatible with Community competition rules (Box 50);

(ii) normalizing the financial environment of telecommunications administrations by proposing to subject them to value-added tax, with a parallel phasing out of the substantial direct financial transfers to government budgets which are levied on them in a number of Member States.

---

[1] Green Paper, p. 73.

Box 50

The provision of leased lines in Europe : the issue of 'cream skimming'

The Green Paper acknowledges the need for safeguards to ensure the financial viability of the telecommunications administrations, especially in view of the massive investments in network infrastructure that are going to be required in the future, in order to comply with their public service mandate.

'The biggest — and under present conditions the only real — threat is the potential loss of voice traffic — which currently accounts for 85 to 90 % of all telecommunications revenues — by the public switched network. Competitive service providers could make their leased lines available for the pure resale of voice capacity (with very limited or zero value-added).

They would thus be able to "cream off" traffic on the most profitable routes, diverting traffic away from the public switched network to leased lines hired by themselves.

Telecommunications administrations may not be able to compete with them pricewise on these high-profit routes because of their requirement to provide universal basic service at comparable prices throughout their national territory.

There are currently two approaches followed — or considered — in the Member States to avoid extreme cases of cream skimming :
(i) banning simple voice resale on leased lines ;
(ii) applying usage-based tariff elements to leased lines.

With regard to (i) most Member States ban simple voice resale. Some of them, such as the United Kingdom and the Netherlands are committed to reviewing the ban after a predetermined time period.

With regard to (ii) some Member States, such as Germany, have in the past proposed usage-based tariffs on leased lines as the main instrument of avoiding extreme cases of cream-skimming. Some are envisaging applying a mixed system of flat-rate and usage-based elements for the tariffing of leased lines, based on the principle of proportionality. Other Member States are considering the issue.

Leased circuits have traditionally been priced at flat rate and it is argued by many users that this price structure is required if the development of value-added services and the attendant innovation are to be encouraged.' [1]

At this stage, the Green Paper states that:

'The decision whether to charge usage-sensitive or flat-rate or a mixture of both tariffs for leased lines is essentially a decision to be taken by each telecommunications administration subject to the power of the Commission to investigate and terminate abuses coming to its attention. Any method must follow the principle of proportionality and not go beyond what is absolutely necessary to ensure the fulfilment of the tasks assigned to the telecommunications administrations.

Thus neither must the application of usage-based tariffs lead to excessive burdens for certain user categories, nor must a ban on resale of voice operate to bring services with only a voice element into the telecommunications administrations' monopolies.

A major potential for hindering the trans-border provision of services arises in the case of difference in policies between Member States. Potential for conflict would be reduced if a set of tariff principles governing the access to the network for trans-frontier providers were established.'[2]

Principles of access to leased lines have been chosen as a priority topic for the establishment of Open Network Provision (ONP) principles.

---

[1] Green Paper, pp. 74 and 75.
[2] Green Paper, p. 76.

Regarding tariffs, the Green Paper draws attention to the need to introduce cost-orientation (Box 51).

Given estimated total transfers of up to 15 000 million ECU per annum from the long distance network,[1] it is evident that a certain rebalancing of tariffs will be inevitable. The Community must have a fundamental interest in the lowering of excessively expensive long-distance intra-Community tariffs, not only for the future functioning of its enterprises which will operate in the Community-wide 1992 market, but also for the private citizen, given the massive growth of tourist travel between the different parts of the Community.[2]

---

[1] See Chapter III, Section 2.
[2] See Chapter V, Section 3.

Box 51

Adjusting tariff principles to the new market environment: a major challenge for the telecommunications administrations

The Green Paper draws particular attention to the need for adjustment of telecommunications tariffs. It states that:

'Tariff structures are currently undergoing major changes in all Member States, and internationally in the Community, for a number of reasons, notably the following:

(i) rapid technological development has dramatically changed the cost structure of the network. The cost of provision of long-distance traffic has fallen much more than the cost of provision of local traffic;

(ii) growing international competition is increasingly leading international tariffs to follow basic cost trends;

(iii) fair and open access of users and competitive service providers requires a clear definition of tariff principles by the telecommunications administrations.

According to a report by major international users, [1] "although comparison of telecommunications tariffs in different countries is made difficult by volatile exchange rates, the scale of inconsistencies is evident ..." The report goes on to make two central points: that charges for trans-European services are generally much higher than domestic charges (between 50 and 400% more in the case of packet-switching volume charges, for example) and that charges vary greatly and according to no self-evident logic between countries. In particular, trans-European prices look high in comparison with US prices. [2]

In its resolution of 3 March 1984, the European Parliament noted the current divergence of tariff structures within the Community, both for switched and leased circuits.' [3]

The Green Paper proposes that:

Tariff principles should include 'recognition of the fact that telecommunications tariffs should follow overall cost trends and that a certain amount of rebalancing of tariffs will be inevitable, as far as compatible with public service goals. This applies in particular to tariffs for national and intra-Community long-distance traffic.

A fair trade-off between cost-orientation and the aim of universal service on reasonably the same terms for all will have to be developed.

Regarding intra-Community and international tariffs, higher transparency and convergence of accounting rates and K-values should be sought, in order to avoid excessive divergences of tariffs and possible distortion of competition. This should show the way to the gradual emergence of a European tariff zone.

Consensus should be achieved on general tariff principles for access by users and providers of competitive services, in the framework of Open Network Provision. This should include agreement on the degree of "unbundling" of tariffs required for fair access, and general principles for the provision of leased lines.'[4]

---

[1] 'Clearing the lines — A users' view on business communications in Europe', Round Table of European industrialists, October 1986.
[2] See Chapter V, Section 2.
[3] Report of the European Parliament on telecommunications in the Community, Doc. 1-477/3, 3 March 1984, OJ C 117, 30.4.1984, p. 79.
[4] Green Paper, p. 82.

In the 1992 context, telecommunications has the fundamental function of drawing the Community closer together and of integrating more closely the peripheral and distant regions into the Community's economic and social tissue. Tariffing of intra-Community telecommunications will play a major role in this. The European Parliament 'considers it necessary, as a first step towards establishing a Community preferential area for telecommunications, to adopt a single method for determining the tariffs applied within the Community for all international intra-Community telecommunications services, based on the principal that national frontiers are irrelevant to the calculation of the tariffs'.[1]

A tariff policy adjusted to the new requirements should be one important component in the new orientation which telecommunications administrations must develop: operating in the wider 1992 competitive market environment.

5. The 10 positions of the Green Paper: adapting Europe to the new market requirements

The general orientations of the Green Paper for the establishment of the 1992 market for telecommunications are summarized in 10 positions defining the regulatory environment which the Commission is proposing for Europe's future telecommunications market. These positions are set out in Table 16.

---

[1] Report of the European Parliament on telecommunications in the Community, OJ C 177, 30.4.1984, p. 79.

TABLE 16

The proposed positions of the Green Paper [1]

The general objective of the positions set out is the development in the Community of a strong telecommunications infrastructure and of efficient services: providing the European user with a broad variety of telecommunications services on the most favourable terms, ensuring coherence of development between Member States, and creating an open competitive environment, taking full account of the dynamic technological developments under way.

A. Acceptance of continued exclusive provision or special rights for the telecommunications administrations regarding provision and operation of the network infrastructure. Where a Member State chooses a more liberal regime, either for the whole or parts of the network, the short and long-term integrity of the general network infrastructure should be safeguarded.

   Closely monitored competitive offering of two-way satellite communications systems will need further analysis. It should be allowed on a case-by-case basis, where this is necessary to develop Europe-wide services and where impact on the financial viability of the main provider(s) is not substantial.

   Common understanding and definition regarding infrastructure provision should be worked out under E below.

B. Acceptance of continued exclusive provision or special rights for the telecommunications administrations regarding provision of a limited number of basic services, where exclusive provision is considered essential at this stage for safeguarding public service goals.

   Exclusive provision must be narrowly construed and be subject to review within given time intervals, taking account of technological development and particularly the evolution towards a digital infrastructure. 'Reserved services' may not be defined so as to extend a telecommunications administration's service monopoly in a way that is inconsistent with the Treaty. Currently, given the general understanding in the Community, the voice telephony service seems to be the only obvious candidate.

C. Free (unrestricted) provision of all other services ('competitive services', including in particular 'value-added services') within Member States and between Member States (in competition with the telecommunications administrations) for own use, shared use, or provision to third parties, subject to the conditions for use of the network infrastructure to be defined under E).

   'Competitive services' would comprise all services except basic services explicitly reserved for the telecommunications administrations (see B).

D. Strict requirements regarding standards for the network infrastructure and services provided by the telecommunications administrations or service providers of comparable importance, in order to maintain or create Community-wide interoperability. These requirements must build in particular on Directives 83/189/EEC and 86/361/EEC, Decision 87/95/EEC and Recommendation 86/659/EEC.

   Member States and the Community should ensure and promote provision by the telecommunications administrations of efficient Europe-wide and world-wide telecommunications, in particular regarding those services (be they reserved or competitive) recommended for Community-wide provision, such as according to Recommendation 86/659/EEC.

E. Clear definition by Community Directive of general requirements imposed by telecommunications administrations on providers of competitive services for use of the network, including definitions regarding network infrastructure provision.

   This must include clear interconnection and access obligations by telecommunications administrations for trans-frontier service providers in order to prevent Treaty infringements.

   Consensus must be achieved on standards, frequencies, and tariff principles, in order to agree on the general conditions imposed for services provision on the competitive sector. Details of this Directive on Open Network Provision (ONP) should be prepared in consultation with the Member States, the telecommunications administrations and the other parties concerned, in the framework of the Senior Officials Group on Telecommunications (SOG-T).

F. Free (unrestricted) provision of terminal equipment within Member States and between Member States (in competition with telecommunications administrations), subject to type approval as compatible with Treaty obligations and existing Directives. Provision of the first (conventional) telephone set could be excluded from unrestricted provision on a temporary basis.

Receive-only earth stations (ROES) for satellite down-links should be assimilated with terminal equipment and be subject to type approval only.

G. Separation of regulatory and operational activities of telecommunications administrations. Regulatory activities concern in particular licensing, control of type approval and interface specifications, allocation of frequencies, and general surveillance of network usage conditions.

H. Strict continuous review of operational (commercial) activities of telecommunications administrations according to Articles 85, 86 and 90 of the EEC Treaty. This applies in particular to practices of cross-subsidization of activities in the competitive services sector and of activities in manufacturing.

I. Strict continuous review of all private providers in the newly opened sectors according to Articles 85 and 86, in order to avoid the abuse of dominant positions.

J. Full application of the Community's common commercial policy to telecommunications. Notification by telecommunications administrations under Regulation 17/62 of all arrangements between them or with third countries which may affect competition within the Community, in order to build up a consistent Community position for GATT negotiations and relations with third countries.

---

[1] Green Paper, p. 184.

Adapting Europe to the new market requirements must take full account of the two major consequences of the ongoing technological revolution which have been discussed.

The first major consequence is that the telecommunications administrations will be able, in principle, to do many more things than before. This raises the problem of how their mandate will be interpreted in future — both by themselves and by the regulators. As set out previously, in the past the telecommunications administrations had basically a public service mandate, very much centred on telephony and — to some extent — telex. Their entry into the data communications business was very hesitant, and only occurred recently. Currently, telecommunications administrations obtain, on average, 85-90% of their revenues from the public telephony service, 3% from telex — and less than 1% from public data communications.

In the future, there will be many more new possibilities for the telecommunications administrations. But this also means that they will have to demonstrate new capabilities. It will be an age of diversification and multiplication of services and it will be an age of marketing. It is clear that the old conception can no longer hold true unchanged in this new evolving environment.

The second major consequence in regulatory terms derives from the simple fact that those connected to the network will be able to do many more things than before, via this network. As shown in Chapter III, in many cases functions equivalent to those which can be carried out inside the network will be able to be executed outside the network, by means of computer-based terminal equipment connected to the network. In the case of the telex service, for example, full future enforcement of the current service monopoly would mean that the use of personal computers would have to be strictly controlled because it is now technically possible to connect them to both the telephone and the telex network: otherwise switching between telephone and telex services — and the offering of telex forwarding via the telephone network for others, at higher speeds and cheaper rates than via the public telex service — would clearly be possible. It is unlikely that such controls would be enforceable — with the consequence that a 'grey market' would more and more develop, both in the services and terminal equipment fields.

With the 10 positions, the Green Paper pleads for the lifting of restrictions now which would anyway have to be lifted by market development in the future. Opening the market now will create stable market conditions and give a clear signal to European industry and service providers. Delaying market opening until the situation becomes untenable would leave Europe unprepared for the more competitive market environment which technology inevitably will entail.

The 10 positions try to strike a balance between the requirements to safeguard public service on the one hand and to encourage market development on the other: between maintaining the telecommunications administrations' central role in future network development and their financial viability and the need to provide for more freedom for the use of this network; between the principle of universal standardized services for all and the trend towards tailoring services to individual needs, served best by a competitive environment.

Safeguards

Positions A and B aim at satisfying the need for safeguards for the telecommunications administrations' ability to develop networks and services.

Position A, Network infrastructure: the Green Paper accepts the possibility for the Member States to continue exclusive or special rights for the provision of the network infrastructure by the telecommunications administrations. It accepts it but does not take a position in favour or against. Member States, according to their own perception of economic and financial requirements may, of course, be more liberal. The situation in the United Kingdom — British Telecom and Mercury, two network providers in competition — is entirely compatible with this position.

Position A also proposes to move forward towards cautious opening of satellite communications — case-by-case analysis of two-way satellite communications and a broad opening of receive-only satellite antennas and low data-rate systems.

Position B, Services under exclusive provision: the Green Paper acknowledges that a restricted number of 'reserved' services should be able to be exclusively provided in the future, as far as 'considered essential, at this stage, for safeguarding public service goals'.

But at the same time, the Green Paper gives a strong warning. Exclusive provision must be narrowly construed. There is not much room for manoeuvre, for the simple reason that Community competition law exists and must be enforced. The Green Paper sees voice telephony as the only 'obvious' candidate for exclusive provision. The Commission makes it clear that in its view this would be entirely sufficient to ensure the viability of the telecommunications administrations and allow them to fulfil any public service mandate to which they are subject and which may, in fact, be much broader than voice telephony (Box 52).

Box 52

Public service and a competitive market — a delicate balance to be struck for the future

The major public service goal of telecommunications administrations in all Member States has been the offering of universal service, at reasonably equal rates, over the entire national territory. Regarding telephone and telex this goal was achieved in most Member States by the late 1970s.

In the Green Paper, the Commission strongly supports the goal of universal service. According to Position D, 'Member States and the Community should ensure and promote provision by the telecommunications administrations of efficient Europe-wide and world-wide communications, in particular regarding those services (be they reserved or competitive) recommended for Community-wide provision, such as according to Recommendation 86/659/EEC' providing for the introduction of ISDN.

However, the Green Paper does not see an automatic necessity that services which should be provided universally must be provided under monopoly. Out of the broad range of ISDN services only voice should be reserved or under restricted competition. Reservation of voice should be a sufficient safeguard to guarantee the viability of the telecommunications administrations, in order to allow them to carry out their general service mandate. At the same time, it must be kept in mind that any monopoly provision entails constraints for others and should therefore be kept to the minimum necessary. The task is to find the right balance.

In a European context, the concept of universal service provision is also closely linked to the introduction of Europe-wide standards. Standards are the pre-condition for universal service as a Community-wide concept because otherwise telecommunications services will be restricted to national coverage and would not be available universally in the Community-wide market. This has happened in the past in a number of new service fields, such as packet-switched data networks and videotex. [1]

---

[1] See Chapter V, Section 2.

The Green Paper recognizes that voice and data are converging in a digital environment. This means that the reservation of voice and exclusive provision is proposed to be periodically reviewed, as digitization proceeds.

Market opening for services

Position C of the Green Paper proposes free competitive supply for all other services, including the broad range of 'value-added' services.

Position C translates an open competitive common market for telecommunications services in 1992 into a clear tangible objective. It will mean abolishing the many constraints and prohibitions currently existing in Europe, concerning the provision of services within Member States and between Member States.

Community-wide inter-operability

Position D, Standards: the Green Paper pleads for strict requirements for standards for network infrastructure and major service providers to ensure Community-wide inter-operability.

Position D emphasizes the central role which the Commission, within its overall policy priorities, allocates to standards, in order to guarantee a Europe-wide market and European inter-operability of services.

Open Network Provision (ONP)

Position E proposes the development of common principles for ONP, in order to ensure fair conditions for competing service providers. As set out before, ONP is the necessary counterpart of acceptance of the monopoly of the telecommunications administrations over network infrastructure.

Market opening for terminals

Position F translates the goal of free choice for the user in buying and connecting equipment into practice.

Creating the dynamics leading to an open market

Position G proposes the separation of the regulatory and operational responsibilities which telecommunications administrations currently hold in most Member States. Telecommunications administrations cannot be at the same time both referee and player once markets have been opened. The process leading to an open market must result from the interplay of an independent regulatory authority and independent operators.

Fairness of competition

Positions H and I express the principle of symmetry of regulation, for both telecommunications administrations and private providers. In the future conglomerate sector of telecommunications and data processing, telecommunications administrations will face big multinational providers such as IBM, coming from the data-processing field. The control of abuse of dominant positions must apply to both. Regulated public monopolies should not be replaced by unregulated private monopolies.

External position

The Community's external position has repercussions on the internal development of the Community. Only a common strong outside position will allow rapid internal opening of the Community market. **Position J** expresses the urgent requirement for Europe to speak with one voice at world level, in order to meet the challenge set by the United States and Japan.

This last point leads to a more general statement. The liberalization of the Community telecommunications market must be seen in the general context. The adjustment must be based on a strong European telecommunications sector — the objective of the ongoing actions, as set out in Chapter VI. It must be seen as one — important — element in the Community's overall social, economic and external policy goals.

6. A broadened action programme: supporting the adjustment process

The opening of the telecommunications equipment and services market, as proposed in the Green Paper, is the necessary complement to the building up of a strong European telecommunications sector, along the lines of the action programme under way, set out in Chapter VI. The Community-wide opening process will stimulate the broad range of new private and public service providers which are needed to put the new digital telecommunications infrastructures — the ISDN and in the 1990s, the IBC — to full use for European society and to offer tailor-made solutions for the special needs of the customer at work and at home.

At the same time, only on the basis of a strong European position can Europe develop an open market. Only a strong European presence will enable Europe to face the telecommunications equipment and services multinationals. Only measures which ensure that the peripheral Member States of the Community and less favoured regions fully participate in the wealth which will be generated by the new infrastructure, will make it politically acceptable for all Member States to open the markets.

In the Green Paper, the Commission proposes a substantial broadening of the current programme under way in order to achieve this balance and to 'create a favourable environment for the on-going transformation'.

The Commission proposes a number of actions:

'(i) to smooth the transition towards a more competitive Community-wide market;

(ii) to promote a strong European presence in both the services and industrial fields;

(iii) to prepare the Community for its discussions of future trading relations in these fields with its outside partners, in particular in the framework of GATT.

It is envisaged:

(i) to accelerate the implementation of existing action lines;

(ii) to initiate a number of new action lines needed to complement and facilitate the transition.' [1]

The proposals are listed in Box 53.

Box 53

The broadening of the action plan proposed in the Green Paper [1]

1. Acceleration of existing action lines

Action to ensure the long-term convergence and integrity of the network infrastructure in the Community

A pan-European telecommunications infrastructure with full inter-operability is the only basis on which an open and competitive Community-wide terminal equipment and services market can thrive. Intensified industrial cooperation within the Community must ensure that European industry will fully benefit from the opening of this market.

---

[1] Green Paper, p. 186.

The main tools envisaged are the rapid implementation of the RACE programme, the decisions on ISDN and digital mobile communications and the STAR programme.

Rapid extension of the current Council Directive 86/361/EEC to include full mutual recognition of type-approval for terminal equipment

According to the current Council Directive 86/361/EEC on the mutual recognition of testing required for type-approval, proposals for full mutual recognition of type-approval must be submitted by July 1989 at the latest. The Commission proposes to accelerate this measure which is vital for the development of a competitive, Community-wide terminal market.

Phased replacement of the current Recommendation 84/550/EEC on the first phase of opening up access to public telecommunications contracts by a Directive

A Directive on the opening of the procurement contracts applying to public and private telecommunications administrations to which the Member States confer exclusive or special rights.

2. Initation of new action lines

I — Substantial reinforcement of the development of standards and specifications in the Community — Creation of a European Telecommunications Standards Institute

based on the current cooperation of the telecommunications administrations within CEPT and with CEN-Cenelec. A substantial reinforcement of resources applied to standardization is a necessary requirement for a truly open competitive market.

II — Common definition of an agreed set of conditions for Open Network Provision (ONP) to service providers and users

This concerns in particular the definition of clear Europe-wide network termination points, usage conditions and tariff principles and availability of frequencies where relevant.

III — Common development of Europe-wide services

Future intra-Community communications will depend on achieving three objectives: Europe-wide compatibility and inter-operability of those services provided by the telecommunications administrations; rapid development of intra-Community provision of value-added services; rapid development of the Community's policy on the information market.

Three objectives should be singled out as a *sine qua non* for achieving market liberalization in a Community-wide market in telecommunications:

Ensuring the integrity of the network infrastructure

Integrity of the infrastructure based on strong European policy on standards, must be a central plank of any effective market opening. Community policy on ISDN and mobile communications shows its full relevance here, as does the RACE programme, which will forge the network standards of the European markets of the 1990s and draw together the major network development lines in the Member States.

Promoting a strong European presence

A competitive environment is the only long-term option to enable European industry to face the tough competition of the world market. But Europe will also have to support the restructuring of its industry if it wants to compete successfully with the US and Japanese multinationals. Restructuring of European industries and service providers on a future-proof European instead of national basis will depend essentially on two conditions, in addition to Community-wide opening of the terminal and services markets:

(i) A European dimension in research and development. Here again the RACE programme is breaking new ground. Within only three years, it has profoundly changed the climate within the European telecommunications sector. Nearly 200 companies, telecommunications operators and research laboratories are now cooperating on joint projects on advanced telecommunications research in Europe.

(ii) The opening of the procurement of the telecommunications administrations. Telecommunications administrations buy more than 70% of telecommunications equipment in the Community. As long as purchasing continues to be purely nationally oriented in most Member States, national procurement will continue to fragment markets and to impede lowering of costs and the effective restructuring of industry in Europe. In the Green Paper the opening of procurement is given high priority (Box 54).

Box 54

The opening of public procurement: a key to a future-proof market structure

The equipment used to construct a telecommunications network infrastructure — switching and transmission equipment — is predominantly purchased by the telecommunications administrations. The total telecommunications equipment market in Europe is estimated at 17 500 million ECU (1986). Switching equipment accounts for 47%; transmission equipment for 13%; terminal equipment for 24%; other equipment for 16%.

Via their dominant position in the purchasing of switching and transmission equipment and their other equipment purchases, the telecommunications administrations in the Member States account for 75 to 90% of equipment purchases in the traditional telecommunications equipment market.

While the growing size of the computer-based terminal market and growing investments by users in their own telecommunications equipment will reduce this role in the future in relative terms, the telecommunications administrations will remain by far the largest purchaser in key areas of the market, such as public switching.

For many types of equipment — notably switching — the bulk of production costs are accounted for by the development of software, and must be paid out by the equipment companies before even the first piece of equipment can roll off the production line. It is for these products that potential economies of scale are highest and therefore savings gained by a larger market are greatest. It is in this area where the closed, nationally focused market structure of the past in Europe has done most damage. [1]

---

[1] See Chapter V, Section 2.

The main reasons for the closed market structure were three-fold: nationally oriented procurement by the telecommunications administrations, incompatible standards and abuse of type-approval for protectionist purposes, and the specific technical relationship between network operator and network supplier which results from development based on specific national technologies, and which made the 'national champion' in many cases the only feasible supplier.

Closed nationally-oriented procurement policies have led to high costs in Europe. According to estimates, prices for network equipment in Europe during the early 1980s have been as high as 50 to 100% above world market prices, depending on the Member State.

Currently, as described in Chapter V, European manufacturers have started to break up the 'national champion' model and to establish a multinational base, in order to adapt to the new requirement of scale. However, a major barrier on the way towards a Community-wide equipment market remains the closed national tendering procedures.

The Commission has made it clear that it considers the opening of public procurement as a pre-condition for achieving the completion of the internal market by 1992. Given the specifics of the telecommunications network equipment market, a step-by-step approach is called for in the Green Paper. [1]

The main elements needed are as follows:

(i)   Rapid progress towards common standards and specifications for network equipment. Open specifications for network equipment are a pre-condition for progress towards open procurement.

(ii) Full application of Council Recommendation 84/550/EEC requiring that Member States ensure that telecommunications administrations provide opportunities for undertakings established in other Community countries to tender for at least 10% in value of their annual orders regarding contracts for switching and transmission apparatus.

(iii) Close surveillance to ensure that tenderers from other Member States are not discriminated against. Article 7 of the Treaty expressly prohibits discrimination on the grounds of nationality. This surveillance must also ensure that no breach of Article 30 is occasioned.

In 1986, the voluntary and partial opening of procurement of the telecommunications administrations under Recommendation 84/550/EEC gave rise to more than 150 tender publications in the *Official Journal of the European Communities*.

The Commission has announced that it will undertake a determined campaign to introduce common purchasing procedures in those sectors which are still excluded from the existing supply directives (telecommunications, energy, transport, water).

---

[1] Green Paper, p. 92.

> 'While the Community-wide opening of the terminal market to competition should rapidly ensure open purchasing procedures under the pressure of a competitive market place, special measures will be needed to ensure fair Community-wide purchasing practices in the field of network equipment.'[1]
>
> Proposals were to be submitted in autumn 1988.
>
> ――――――
>
> [1] COM(88) 48, p. 22.

Ensuring cohesion between the centre and the periphery of the Community

Community-wide market opening will only be achieved if the Member States stay in step in telecommunications development. The STAR programme and the operations of the European Investment Bank in telecommunications investment in the less favoured regions of the peripheral Member States are major steps in this direction.

More will be needed. The development of a Community-wide competitive market for telecommunications services and equipment will represent for these regions a special potential for future growth on the one hand, and a major challenge on the other.

Special attention will have to be paid to the following topics:

(i) how to ensure that regions are fully integrated into the new information markets, on an equal footing; and

(ii) how to ensure that the growth potential is put to best use, in order to reduce the gap in economic development which currently separates these regions from the more prosperous parts of the European Community.

Only a strong and united European telecommunications sector will be able to face up to the rapidly changing telecommunications world market.

7. Uniting Europe to face up to the rapidly changing world market: the current GATT negotiations — Europe, an equal partner for the United States and Japan

'The creation of a common market for telecommunications services and equipment within the Community will help overcome its structural problems and contribute to the creation of continental-scale advantages which have so far eluded Europe in this sector. It would however be a mistake to undertake this task in a manner which would insulate the Community market from the outside world.'[1]

Europe's international environment in telecommunications over the next years will be determined by two major factors:

(i) the pressure of US and Japanese deregulation on international markets, in parallel with a major reshaping of the role of international organizations in this field: the International Telecommunications Union (ITU) and the international satellite organizations, Intelsat and Inmarsat;

(ii) the growing importance of services generally in international trade which has made services the major topic of the new Uruguay Round in the GATT.

In international telecommunications, the stakes are immense. World-wide, the new conglomerate sector of the management and transport of information — telecommunications equipment, data processing and telecommunications services — already represents more than 500 000 million ECU. The world market for telecommunications services is approaching 300 000 million ECU, the world market for telecommunications equipment 90 000 million ECU.

The multinationals are rushing to take up positions: IBM, ATT, along with new entrants in this market such as EDS of General Motors, Geisco of General Electric, ITJ and IDC of Japan.

Europe, united, on the basis of a competitive market allowing the development of the new value-added information services products which the world market will require, will be able to take its share of the cake which will be shared out during the next decade.

But the process must be based on fair rules of the game. As Mr Narjes, Vice-President responsible, *inter alia,* for telecommunications in the Commission, told the December 1987 Financial Times World Telecommunications Conference:

'We aim at an open international trading environment. But given the strong economic and industrial interests in the telecommunications field at the international level, it is obvious that an intense bargaining process will be needed, both at the multilateral and the bilateral level, in order to work out future rules.'

The major bilateral issues will have to be settled between the Community and the United States and the Community and Japan.

The Green Paper notes that 'the Japanese market remains virtually closed to European suppliers, while the Community's deficit in telecommunications with this country is steadily increasing.'[2]

---

[1] Green Paper, p. 150.
[2] Green Paper, p. 176.

With regard to relations with the United States, the Commission lists in the Green Paper a number of outstanding issues on which common positions must be sought, such as the conditions of interconnection of the European network with the new US operators and service providers which have emerged in the deregulated US telecommunications market, and which are now pushing on to the international market.

In his speech, Mr Narjes emphasized that 'there is no alternative to exposing our industry to competition, relying on European ingenuity and competence to confront non-European competitors. ...

We are having continuous discussions with the United States on telecommunications issues and we hope for a more intensive debate with Japan. We are concerned about protectionist tendencies in the United States Congress which have surfaced during recent years. If the US trade bill were to be adopted and also contains *inter alia* provisions on sector-by-sector reciprocity requirements, e.g. on telecommunications, the Community would then have to fully protect its GATT rights if they are impaired and breached.

... Interdependence must be based on sharing of responsibility and taking account of others' interests. Europe must properly participate as soon as its own interests are touched upon by other parties' agreements. We made this clear on the occasion of the semi-conductor agreement between the United States and Japan of last year (1986). We are deeply concerned by the growing number of United States/Japanese agreements which concern directly or indirectly our own interest in telecommunications, such as the recent understanding on international value-added services concluded between the United States and Japan in spring of this year (1987).'

In the long term, the international trading rules relating to telecommunications will be largely determined by the future evolution of the general trading environment for services — banking, insurance, transport, consultancy, etc., of which telecommunications is in many cases an essential carrier.

In the Green Paper, the Commission makes it clear that it therefore sees the new Uruguay Round of talks in the framework of the GATT as the major forum for determining the future framework for trade in telecommunications-related services (Box 55).

Box 55

The framework for future world-wide trade in services : the new Uruguay Round in the GATT

Since its creation in 1947, the General Agreement on Tariffs and Trade (the GATT) has developed over several 'rounds' of negotiations into the fundamental framework of world trade. The Community's position in the negotiations is represented by the Commission, on the basis of negotiating mandates from the Council.

On 20 September 1986, a new 'round' of negotiations was launched formally at Punta del Este in Uruguay. Known as the Uruguay Round, they include for the first time trade in services.

With regard to services, the general negotiating objectives are as follows:

'Negotiations in this area shall aim to establish a multilateral framework of principles and rules for trade in services, including elaboration of possible disciplines for individual sectors, with a view to expansion of such trade under conditions of transparency and progressive liberalization and as a means of promoting economic growth of all trading partners and the development of developing countries. Such a framework shall respect the policy objectives of national laws and regulations applying to services and shall take into account the work of relevant international organizations.'

The current assumption is that all services which can be traded will be covered by the new agreement. In telecommunications, this is likely to include in particular value-added services.

As to negotiations on trade in telecommunications equipment during the Uruguay Round, the main issues appear as follows:

(i)   the question of the inclusion of telecommunications equipment in the Government Procurement Code;

(ii) customs duties (especially relevant where certain countries maintain high tariffs);

(iii) issues related to the Code on Technical Barriers to Trade.

According to the Green Paper, the general approach of the Community should be based on the following overall considerations:

'(i) An evaluation of the Community's interests with regard to market opening by non-Community countries (services and equipment).

(ii) On services, taking into account the progress towards the establishment of a common European approach towards regulatory issues, preparation of a Community approach to the definition of "appropriate regulation".

(iii) In the light of the above, and taking into account the progress made towards the realization of the internal market:

(a) examination of the implications of further opening of the Community market for telecommunications equipment and services;

(b) comparison of this with the prospects for market opening in non-Community countries.'

The negotiations are likely to last for at least four years.

'The Community will need to determine a common position on telecommunications with a view to these negotiations. The starting point must be internal consensus on a concept of "appropriate" or "acceptable" regulation, a primary objective of the proposed positions in the Green Paper.

Given the close integration of telecommunications with other services, the Community's position on telecommunications must be influenced by its intention to work, in the framework of the GATT negotiations, towards a more open trading environment for services in general.'[1]

---

[1] Green Paper, p. 174.

VIII — The future: achieving together the 1992 goal

1. The Single European Act: establishing a new framework

The Single European Act entered into force on 1 July 1987. It is the most important reform of the Treaty of Rome since its inception (Box 56).

Box 56

The Single European Act

The Single European Act adopted by the Parliaments of all Member States, defined the 1992 objective for completion of the internal market. It came into force on 1 July 1987.

The Single European Act is the most important reform of the Treaty of Rome since its inception in 1957. It introduced a number of new Articles into the Treaty.

It formally established the 1992 objective as a Treaty goal (Article 8a).

It laid down the goal of the European Technology Community and the R&D framework programme as its mechanism (Article 130i).

It wrote new areas of interest into the Treaty:

(i)   research and development (Articles 130f to 130q);

(ii) an extension of social and regional policy ('economic and social cohesion') (Articles 118a, 118b, 130a to 130e);

(iii) environmental protection (Articles 130r to 130t);

(iv) certain aspects of monetary policy, providing a full Treaty basis for the European Monetary System (Article 102a).

It extended majority voting instead of the requirement of unanimity in the Council to most areas involving national barriers to internal trade except taxation.

The system of qualified majority voting which now applies in the Council sets a majority at 54 votes out of the total of 76, shared as follows:

10 votes each:	Germany, France, Italy, United Kingdom;
8 votes:	Spain;
5 votes each:	Belgium, Greece, Netherlands, Portugal;
3 votes each:	Denmark, Ireland;
2 votes:	Luxembourg.

It substantially upgraded the role of the European Parliament.

It established a firm Treaty basis for European political cooperation on foreign policy issues.

The new Article 8a of the amended Treaty reads:

'The Community shall adopt measures with the aim of progressively establishing the internal market over a period expiring on 31 December 1992, in accordance with the provisions of this Article and of Articles 8b, 8c, 28, 57(2), 59, 70(1), 84, 99, 100a and 100b and without prejudice to the other provisions of this Treaty.

The internal market shall comprise an area without internal frontiers in which the free movement of goods, persons, services and capital is ensured in accordance with the provisions of this Treaty.'

Article 8a expresses most clearly the new qualitative step which has been introduced by the Single European Act:

(i)   It has introduced a new strategic vision — the 1992 goal of the completion of the internal market of the Community, the definitive abolition of frontiers and borders between Member States.

(ii) It has produced new common goals and a new focus — thus vigorously relaunching the process of convergence of the Member States of the European Community.

(iii) It has introduced new dynamic elements to generate this convergence: a substantial extension of the use of majority voting in the Council of Ministers and allocation of a substantially larger role to the European Parliament.

(iv) It has consolidated the achievements to date.

The Single Act has consolidated achievements to date. In telecommunications this means that the actions already under way — RACE, ISDN, mobile communications, STAR — gain their full importance in the new framework. They are necessary elements for achieving a Community-wide market for all of those economic activities which will depend on information — the greater part of the Community's economy in 1992. They are a comprehensive means of eliminating regional imbalances in the Community and forging economic cohesion — another of the essential goals of the Single Act.

Finally, they introduce telecommunications as a major asset for the future European Technology Community — a third major innovation introduced into the Treaty by the Single Act.

Fair access to the new technologies for all Member States, an essential aim of the European Community, will be a pre-condition for the first two goals: the internal market and economic and social cohesion. This makes programmes like RACE and STAR and the information technology application programmes essential links in the chain leading up to 1992.

The Single Act has introduced a new strategic vision — the 1992 goal of completion of the European market. For the future regulation of telecommunications, this sets out a firm framework for the proposals put forward in the Green Paper. It defines the goals, the obligations, and the time-scale, within which to advance towards an open competitive telecommunications market in Europe. It puts clear obligations on both Member States and the Community.

The Single Act has introduced new dynamic elements to generate this convergence.

For telecommunications this means majority voting in the Council on measures falling under the new Article 100a for the harmonization of administrative provisions. This includes technical specifications and type-approval.

As important is the fact that the Single Act has created a new climate for competition in the Community — and the application of the relevant provisions in the Treaty.

But more important, it has brought in the European Parliament as a major actor, in a substantially reinforced role. The global social and economic importance which communications will take on over the next few years requires a broad political and social base for the Community's telecommunications policy which can only be supplied by the European Parliament.

The European Parliament is playing a rapidly increasing role in the formulation of policy in this area. Over recent years, the European Parliament has on increasingly frequent occasions taken positions on the Community's telecommunications policy (Box 57).

The broad support of the European Parliament for the proposals in this area testified to by its resolutions provides probably the strongest legitimacy for Community policy in this area.

Box 57

The position of the European Parliament on telecommunications

During recent years, at more and more frequent intervals, the European Parliament has taken positions on telecommunications: The European Parliament...

On regulation

'Considers that the traditional system of telecommunications administration regulation has served the public well in the past, but that it lacks the necessary flexibility to permit the development of new products and services at the necessary speed to keep pace with the rapid rate of innovation in this sector; believes, therefore, that there needs to be a liberalization of the existing equipment supply monopolies in order to permit greater freedom for individual users to connect their equipment to the telecommunications infrastructure, and for suppliers to sell their products in other Community countries;

further believes that other carriers beside the telecommunications administrations should be allowed to offer the new value-added services which are currently evolving.'[1]

On public service and competition

'Recognizes the vital public service obligations of telecommunications administrations, and does not believe that deregulation on the American model could be applied within the Community; considers, therefore, that what is needed is "re-regulation" which would permit more rapid development while still providing necessary safeguards;

recommends that the widest possible competition be encouraged for markets and equipment. The ability of Community undertakings to compete in overseas markets will depend to a large extent on their capacity to do so in the internal Community market.'[1]

On the Integrated Services Digital Network

'Whereas it is imperative to develop a European telecommunications network extending beyond the Community's frontiers if European industry is to stand up to world-wide competition;

whereas the prospective Integrated Services Digital Network (ISDN), evolving from the telephone network, will offer many additional services to corporate and private subscribers...'[2]

On data protection and telecommunications

'Calls upon the Commission to submit proposals on a practical approach towards ensuring within the ISDN now emerging throughout Europe, a consistent level of data privacy protection commensurate with the enhanced technical capabilities of this new network.'[2]

---

[1] Resolution on telecommunications, 29 March 1984, OJ C 117, 30.4.1984, p. 75.
[2] Resolution of the European Parliament on the coordinated introduction of the Integrated Services Digital Network (ISDN) in the European Community, of 12 December 1986, OJ C 7, 12.1.1987, p. 334.

2. Consultations on the Green Paper: a broad consensus

Following its announced intention to launch an in-depth debate on the Green Paper proposals, the Commission carried out a broad public consultative process. On 9 February 1988 it published its conclusions and plans.[1] This paper is referred to hereinafter as 'Implementing the Green Paper'.

According to the paper, the Green Paper proposals stimulated a very broad response from users, the telecommunications and data-processing industries and the other parties concerned. More than 45 organizations representing different interests in the field both at Community and national level forwarded written comments. In parallel, intensive discussion was carried out with the Senior Officials Group on Telecommunications (SOG-T) and with the telecommunications administrations (Box 58).

Box 58

Europe responds: comments on the Green Paper

The publication of the Green Paper by the Commission in June 1987 generated a broad public debate. By January 1988, when the Commission closed the consultation, more than 45 organizations had responded:

Aeronautical Radio, Inc.
American Chamber of Commerce
Amsterdam Informatics and Telecommunications Council
Association of European Chambers of Commerce and Industry (Euro-chambres)
Belgian Telecommunications User Group (Beltug)
British Petroleum (BP)
British Telecom (BT)
Computer Association of Large French Companies (CIGREF)
Confederation of European Computer User Associations (CECUA)

---

[1] 'Towards a competitive Community-wide telecommunications market in 1992 — Implementing the Green Paper on the development of the common market for telecommunications services and equipment — State of discussions and proposals by the Commission', COM(88) 48, 9 February 1988.

Confederation of German Industry and Trade (DIHT)
Council of Netherlands Industrial Federations (CIB-RCO)
Digital Equipment Corporation (DEC)
Dutch Business Telecommunications Users' Association (NVBTG)
Electronic Engineering Association (EEA)
Esprit Industrial Round Table
European Association of Information Services (Eusidic)
European Association of Research Networks (RARE)
European Committee for Standardization — European Committee for Electrotechnical Standardization (CEN-Cenelec)
European Computing Services Association
European Council of Telecommunications Users' Associations (ECTUA)
European Federation of Public Servants (Eurofedop)
European Organization for Nuclear Research (CERN)
European Service Industries Forum (ESIF)
European Space Agency (ESA)
European Telecommunications and Professional Electronics Industry (Ectel)
French Committee of the International Chambers of Commerce
French Telephone and Telecommunications Users' Association
German Machinery & Equipment Manufacturers' Association (VDMA)
German Postal Services Users' Association
Institute of Satellite Applications (ISA)
International Business Machines (IBM)
International Chamber of Commerce (ICC)
International Data Exchange Association (IDEA)
International Telecommunications Users' Group (INTUG)
Italian Telematics Forum (FTI)
National Council of French Management (CNPF)
Plessey
Postal, Telegraph and Telephone International (PTTI)
Round Table of European Industrialists
Shell
Society of Telecom Executives (STE)
Telecommunications Equipment Manufacturers' Association (TEMA)
Televerket: Swedish Telecom
Unilever
Union of Industrial and Employers' Confederations of Europe (Unice)
US Council for International Business
US Government

All the major contributors — telecommunications administrations, users, manufacturers, service providers and trade unions — have participated in this exercise, which has been a key condition for developing consensus on a common European strategy.

Their reactions to the Green Paper's main proposals are described as follows: [1]

(i) a broad consensus regarding the full liberalization of the terminal equipment market, with a reasonable period for transition;

(ii) a broad consensus on the liberalization of value-added services, the high-value end of the overall spectrum of telecommunications services which is proposed to be open to competitive provision;

(iii) full endorsement of the principle of the separation of regulatory and operational responsibilities of the telecommunications administrations;

(iv) general recognition of the fact that tariffs should follow overall cost trends;

(v) strong support of the principle of standards, in order to maintain or create Community-wide and world-wide inter-operability, and of a clear definition of general requirements imposed by telecommunications administrations on providers of competitive services and other users for use of the network (ONP — Open Network Provision);

(vi) broad acceptance of the principle that telecommunications administrations should be able to participate in the newly open competitive sectors, on an equal footing;

(vii) general acceptance of the need to apply the general rules of competition law to the operational (commercial) activities of both the telecommunications administrations and other private providers, in a symmetric way;

(viii) support for the line taken in the Green Paper, that, while this implies on the one hand a clear requirement for transparency of operations, in particular with regard to cross-subsidization and procurement of equipment, it should imply on the other hand a relaxation of the organizational and financial constraints imposed on telecommunications administrations which may inhibit their ability to compete;

(ix) general support for existing Community programmes, actions and proposals aimed at strengthening the long-term convergence and integrity of the network infrastructure in the Community: Integrated Broadband Communications (IBC) — the RACE programme; the Integrated Services Digital Network (ISDN); digital mobile communications.

A second category of positions also met with general support, while at the same time receiving criticism from both possible perspectives: of going too far in the opinion of some and of not going far enough in the opinion of others.

This concerned in particular:

(i) The acceptance of the continuation of exclusive provision for network infrastructure. This met with acceptance in most comments while receiving some criticism from both sides.

(ii) The degree of competition in services other than value-added services. There was broad general support for accepting exclusive provision of voice telephony, as long as it is defined as switched voice telephony intended for the general public and as long as this is subject to review.

---

[1] See COM(88) 48.

233

A number of comments held that either special authorization schemes or exclusive provision for other services, in particular telex and switched data communications intended for general public use, are required. Authorization schemes were suggested as a possible option for movement towards market opening in this area.

Generally, comments held that a broad provision of efficient Europe-wide and world-wide communications to the public must be ensured.

Regarding competition in satellite communications, a consensus still did not seem possible. On this issue, there seemed only to be a general readiness to open competition for receive-only equipment as long as it was not connected to the public network.

Regarding other major issues, further discussion and definition would be needed. This concerned in particular:

(i)   the development of a common European position on satellite communications;

(ii) the rapid promotion of Europe-wide services and development of principles for these services;

(iii) the development of a common position on the Community's relations with third countries and on international problems, in particular with regard to multilateral issues;

(iv) a further strengthening of the use of advanced telecommunications for developing the less favoured regions, on the basis of the STAR programme, and the consideration of the special problems of the peripheral regions of the Community;

(v)   the further promotion of the social dialogue and the discussion of effective means to match the requirements for training/re-training in the sector;

(vi) in this context, comments drew attention to the need to cover broader social concerns in this area more clearly, in particular the protection of privacy and of personal data and general long-term social implications.

On the basis of this reaction, the Commission concluded in 'Implementing the Green Paper' that a broad consensus on major regulatory goals had been reached on the basis of which to define a clear schedule leading up to 1992.

3. The implementation plan announced by the Commission: a strict timetable for the 1992 market, endorsed by the Council

In 'Implementing the Green Paper', the Commission links the opening of the telecommunications market strictly to the overall 1992 goal. The paper 'sets out a programme of action, both as regards measures to be taken by the Commission under Community competition rules and its general mandate, and as regards future proposals to the Council, in order to achieve progressive opening of the telecommunications market in the Community to competition. It reviews the proposals advanced in the Green Paper in the light of the comments received, establishes priorities and proposes strict deadlines for implementation.'

The thrust of the measures announced is towards progressively achieving by 1992 an open Community-wide market environment for the telecommunications user and the service provider (Box 59):

(i) full Community-wide liberalization of the terminal market; free choice of equipment to connect to the network for the user; lower costs; more innovation; more features;

(ii) progressive Community-wide liberalization of the telecommunications services market: freedom to provide value-added services; tailoring services to user needs; cost orientation of tariffs while safeguarding public service.

Additionally, accompanying measures are announced to make market opening effective: separation of regulation and operations; simplified type approval of terminal equipment; ONP for service providers and users; stepping up of production of effective standards; opening of procurement to obtain higher cost-effectiveness, following the proposals of the Green Paper.

Box 59

Implementing the Green Paper: the schedule of measures — the deadlines announced

In 'Towards a competitive Community-wide telecommunications market in 1992' the Commission announces the schedule of planned measures as follows:

(i) Rapid full opening of the terminal equipment market to competition by 31 December 1990 at the latest.

Directive 88/301/EEC under Article 90 was issued on 16 May 1988 in line with this schedule. [1]

(ii) Progressive opening of the telecommunications services market to competition from 1989 onwards, with all services other than voice, telex and data communications to be opened by 31 December 1989.

This will concern in particular all value-added services. Special consideration will apply to telex and packet- and circuit-switched data services.

Directive on the progressive opening of the services market to competition to be issued by the end of 1988.

(iii) Full opening of receive-only antennas as long as they are not connected to the public network, by 31 December 1989. Directive 88/301/EEC includes this target.

(iv) Progressive implementation of the general principle that tariffs should follow overall cost-trends. Review of the situation achieved by 1 January 1992.

A number of accompanying measures are announced:

(a) Clear separation of regulatory and operational activities to conform with Community competition rules.

(b) Definition of Open Network Provision (ONP). This will initially cover access to leased lines, public data networks, and ISDN. Directives will be submitted to the Council according to progress of definition work.

(c) Establishment of the European Telecommunications Standards Institute (ETSI).

   The CEPT has now established the Institute. It is located at Sophia-Antipolis near Nice.

(d) Full mutual recognition of type-approval for terminal equipment.

   A Directive to be submitted to the Council before end 1988.

(e) Introduction of value-added tax, where still not applied to telecommunications, by 1 January 1990 at the latest. This should allow telecommunications administrations to operate normally in a commercial environment and replace direct financial transfers to the public exchequer imposed on them in several Member States.

(f) Guidelines for the application of competition rules to the telecommunications sector, in order to ensure fair market conditions for all market participants.

(g) Opening of the procurement of telecommunications administrations.

   Proposals were to be submitted in autumn 1988.

---

[1] Commission Directive of 16 May 1988 on competition in the markets in telecommunications terminal equipment, 88/301/EEC.

Regarding implementation, the Commission emphasizes on the one hand full application of Community competition rules, with more extensive use of directives under Article 90 which allow global and more effective application than a case-by-case approach as has been followed up to now. On the other hand, it indicates its intention to make full use of the new possibilities offered under the Single European Act to reach Council decisions rapidly, particularly in the field of type-approval and ONP specifications.

In parallel with the planned measures directed towards progressive market opening, the Commission singles out in 'Implementing the Green Paper' a number of areas for which common policy should be defined before the end of 1988:

(i) *Satellite communications:* at this stage, Europe still does not have a consistent policy with regard to the future use of its sky.

(ii) *Universal service and tariff policy:* a major issue to ensure Europe-wide provision of the new services. Full Community-wide coverage is currently only achieved for telephone and telex.

(iii) *International questions:* Uruguay Round, International Telecommunications Union, relations with the United States, Japan and the Third World.

The conference of the ITU on international regulation — the WATT-C 1988 — is seen as a major test for Europe's future international position.

With the growth of the international information economy, telecommunications will become an important issue in the Community's relationship with the Third World.

(iv) *The social dialogue and social dimension:* the social dimension of achieving the 1992 market has been singled out by the Commission as an essential component of its general policy (Box 60).

Box 60

Issues for the future

In 'Implementing the Green Paper' a number of issues are set out for which the Commission aims to define common policies before the end of 1988.

1. *A common European position regarding the future regulation and development of satellite communications in the Community*

(i) Future regulation of two-way satellite communications.

(ii) Development of the earth station market in Europe.

(iii) The space segment, in particular the relationships between Eutelsat, national, and private systems; full use of the technological potential of the European Space Agency.

(iv) International satellite communications, in particular Intelsat and Inmarsat.

2. *A pro-active concept for the promotion of Europe-wide services, by a market-led approach, and definition of common tariff principles*

(i) Europe-wide compatibility and inter-operability of telecommunications services.

In addition to efficient telephony and telex, packet-switched and circuit-switched data services, videotex, ISDN, and future digital mobile communications should be available universally at the European level. This coincides with ongoing Community action.

(ii) Common tariff principles, as far as compatible with a market-led approach, with a view to seeking convergence on tariff structures.

Provision of switched and leased lines services at reasonable rates must be an essential feature of Open Network Provision.

(iii) Developing Europe-wide value-added and information services; full use of the TEDIS programme concerning electronic data interchange and the programme for the establishment of a Community-wide information market.

In addition, new initiatives towards advanced broadband services for business use based on the RACE programme.

3. *Defining a European position on the major international questions in telecommunications*

This concerns in particular Community relations with:

(i) the EFTA countries,

(ii) the United States and Japan,

(iii) the Third World.

The elaboration of a common position on the World Administrative Telegraph and Telephone Conference (WATT-C 1988) on the international regulation of telecommunications is seen as a high-priority objective.

4. *Developing the social dialogue and taking full account of social concerns*

The requirement for common analysis of social impact and conditions for a smooth transition is seen as the single most important issue in the long term:

(i) social dialogue, on the basis of joint analysis;

(ii) future skill requirements and their impact on training/re-training, in order to manage the shift in job qualifications required by the change of technology and to expand employment in new services provision;

(iii) acceptability of new services and activities, both in the business and the private sector. With the increase in the quantity of communications media and services, data protection and protection of privacy will become a major concern in telecommunications.

Access to information and protection from intrusion into the individual's private life are closely related to the fundamental human rights which underlie the basic political and cultural consensus of the Community.

Exactly a year after the publication of the Green Paper, the Telecommunications Ministers gave strong support to its major policy objectives, at their Council meeting on 30 June 1988.

The Resolution is printed in full in the Annex.[1]

---

[1] Council Resolution of 30 June 1988 on the development of the common market for telecommunications services and equipment up to 1992.

This was the first time ever that a Council of Ministers was held in order to consider purely telecommunications issues; and it was further decided to hold such meetings in the future, in the light of the increased importance of the sector.

Ministers made it clear that while the current reform should allow the full use of the new economic potential of telecommunications, the fundamental public service goals of telecommunications must be maintained. The social environment for the future development of telecommunications must be created in order to keep with the Community's overall aim of creating a common economic as well as social area by 1992. Building up the dialogue between the social partners was seen as being particularly important in this context.

While broad political support had been assembled by mid-1988 for the Green Paper policy objectives, as testified by the 30 June Resolution, agreement on the application of the various Community instruments for their implementation had still not been fully achieved. In July 1988 the French Government submitted an appeal for partial withdrawal of Directive 88/301/EEC[1] issued by the Commission on 16 May 1988 concerning the full opening of the terminal market by the end of 1990 under Community competition rules (based on Article 90(3), EEC Treaty), according to the schedule of actions announced.

The French complaint contested in part the application of Article 90 as the basis of this measure and insisted on the need to refer to Council for such directives, while confirming the policy objectives of the Green Paper and in particular the objective of the full liberalization of the terminal equipment market. Directive 88/301/EEC remains in force during the consideration of the Case by the European Court of Justice. [2]

Telecommunications will have an impact on all aspects of the Community's society. The Community's future information-based economy must therefore be seen in the overall context of Europe's economic and social needs.

4. At stake: the future structure of the Community's information-based economy — structuring Europe's market according to European economic and social needs

'Given the present situation of the world economy, the Community will no longer benefit from an external impetus. Implementing the cooperative growth strategy for more employment now means: successfully accomplishing the switch from growth underpinned by external factors to growth based on internal forces, shortening the period of con-

---

[1] See Box 59.
[2] Case 202/88.

junctural weakening and thus escaping more rapidly from the trap of slow growth extending into the medium term into which the Community seems to have fallen. In this way, the Community will once again be able to reduce unemployment, derive full benefit from the completion of the large internal market and reinforce its economic and social cohesion. In order to exploit Community strengths to the full, increased cooperation and the pursuit of ambitious Community policies remain essential. It also remains necessary to reinforce the consensus with and between the social partners on the policies required by a more intensive dialogue on all aspects of the strategy at both Community and national level.'[1]

Telecommunications will play a central role in such a global Community strategy.

In their joint opinion on the Community's 1987-88 annual economic report — in the framework of the social dialogue at Community level established on an initiative by the Commission in Val Duchesse on 12 November 1985 — the Union of Industrial and Employers' Confederations of Europe (UNICE), the European Trade Union Confederation (ETUC), and the European Centre of Public Enterprise (CEEP) argued that: 'A more rapid execution of large-scale infrastructure projects of European interest would at present be particularly appropriate in order to boost demand while strengthening the Community's productive potential. These projects should contribute notably to the strengthening of cohesion within the Community by establishing communication networks able also to promote the development of less favoured regions. Improved conditions for mobilizing private capital would enable their financing avoiding increasing the burden on public budgets'.[2]

Telecommunications is taking on a growing importance in the expenditure of private households, compared to other expenditure on communications (Figure 20). This illustrates the key role of telecommunications in both economic and social terms.

Economic processes of the importance which telecommunications have now gained cannot be based on a technocratic approach. European consensus must be searched for and developed in a broad framework of consultation.

The reactions to the Green Paper have shown Europe's willingness and capability to agree on broad common goals for its telecommunications sector and, in a broader sense, its future position on information technology. The position on high technology and ser-

---

[1] 'Using the Community dimension to reinforce internal growth', *European Economy*, No 34, November 1987, p. 14.
[2] *Idem*, p. 113.

FIGURE 20

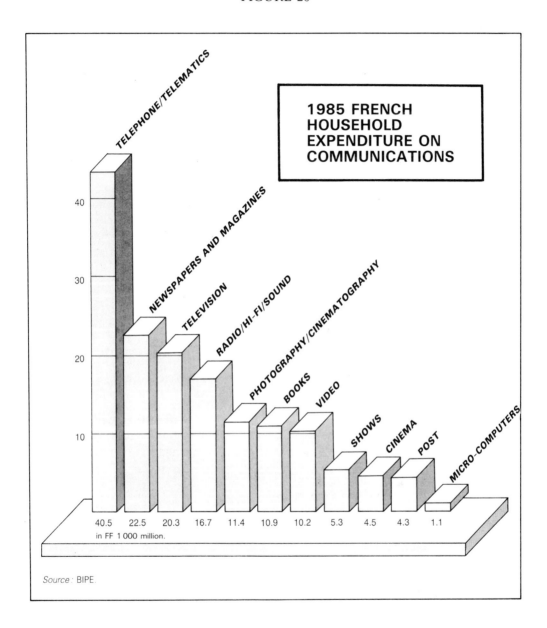

Source: BIPE.

vices will substantially influence the future long-term wealth of an economy. The position on telecommunications will play a key role in this.

The Green Paper aims at maintaining and developing major European assets for the future information age: its telecommunications network, worth some 200 000 million ECU; its telecommunications administrations, which have assembled a unique experience with their near 1 million employees in the Community; and its telecommunications industry, Europe's stronghold in information technology.

But at the same time, the Green Paper calls for opening this resource to full use by the European consumer, by the European economy, and by its social system. The Green Paper's message is clear: more competition in a Europe-wide market. Europe needs more opening of the telecommunications sector to competition in order to achieve a single Community-wide market by 1992. At the same time, only a unified Europe-wide market can offer the economies of scale which the new national competitive environment needs.

Inevitably, the future will require a balance between different interests, all of them legitimate in themselves. But as this publication has tried to show, this balance can be found by:

(i)   more competition/less rigidity *and* maintenance of public service goals;

(ii) free access by the user to more information *and* protection of the user's private sphere;

(iii) an open trading environment in the world market *and* reduction of the North/South gap, both within the Community and at world level.

The working out of the balance must be based on consensus, taking account of all interests involved. But some tasks are immediate:

(i)   the Community must rapidly adjust its internal market structure to the new competitive conditions, in order to achieve the 1992 goal. In its implementation plan for the Green Paper, the Commission has set an ambitious but determined schedule for action;

(ii) adjustment in the Community will be a base for Europe to speak with one voice on the imminent international decisions on the future international regulation of telecommunications. A major step is the World Administrative Telegraph and Telephone Conference at the end of the year — the WATT-C 1988 (Box 61). The broader medium-term framework of discussion will be the GATT;

(iii) the Community market needs rapid progress on Community-wide services. It is in this field that the cost of 'non-Europe' has been the most devastating. There are encouraging signs that effective Europe-wide data communications can become a reality soon (Box 62).

Box 61

The WATT-C 1988: the future international regulation of telecommunications

The World Administrative Telegraph and Telephone Conference (WATT-C 1988) of the International Telecommunications Union (ITU) in December 1988 in Melbourne is to discuss and decide on the future international regulation of telecommunications.

'It will have a major influence on the Community's future external relations in telecommunications.'[1]

Substantial discussion is going on in preparation for the conference.

'The role of the ITU ... should be ensured — and confirmed — by making the ITU framework flexible enough to adjust to, and to accommodate the future open international trading environment for telecommunications services and equipment which the international community needs.

For the European Commission, achieving a common position for the WATT-C will be a major political goal ...'[2]

---

[1] Green Paper, p. 172.
[2] Commission Vice-President Narjes addressing the Financial Times World Telecommunications Conference, December 1987.

Box 62

Outlook for the future: breaking down frontiers for advanced Europe-wide services — Managed Data Network Services

Managed Data Network Services — MDNS — represent a key area where national telecommunications administrations and private-sector service providers are concentrating their efforts to develop new products and services and are reinforcing their marketing strategies.

Telecommunications administrations in Europe are trying to keep abreast of the trend by widening the range of services offered to corporate customers. In the past, the fragmentation of national markets in Europe has prevented them from offering international clients the 'one-stop shopping' they are looking for in organizing their trans-frontier communications requirements.

This has given rise to the emergence of private-sector companies dedicated to managing the communications networks of others. The best known examples are American: IBM, EDS, and Geisco.

Negotiations are under way among the European telecommunications administrations to see whether the concept of one-stop shopping can be realized at European level. The main initiative among European telecommunications administrations to develop MDNS and the one-stop shopping concept is taking place in the Commercial Action Committee (CAC) of the CEPT.

MDNS could become an important base for providers of Europe-wide value-added services, if offered in an open way.

Services offered under the MDNS would range from the provision of extended networking capabilities to the provision of a physical network offering application-to-application level functionality. MDNS would be in accordance with the OSI reference model.

Envisaged as a pre-ISDN service integration concept, MDNS would seek to satisfy the individual demands of users for international data communication and related support. As such, the MDNS concept embraces communications processing without offering, but enabling, user-application processing. This would involve the provision of a data network with packet-switching capabilities, including all the facilities normally offered via the public switched data network.

In addition, MDNS would offer data communication services and facilities that are not presently available over the public-switched data network, such as extensive protocol conversion, in order to provide connectability for a range of otherwise incompatible computer systems.

The CAC is also active in working in other fields towards Europe-wide services:

(i) efficient Europe-wide data packet-switching services, correcting the deficiencies of the past;

(ii) pan-European videoconferencing services;

(iii) introduction of a 'European green number', a Europe-wide free phone service.

Telecommunications will play an important role in the determination of the emerging future world order. Europe — which maintains close ties with many Third World countries — is in a unique position to take a global view, to mediate, and to contribute to consensus. Telecommunications will play an increasing role in the Community's relations with these countries (Box 63).

The main task of Community policy up to 1992 will be to extract the full benefit of the global advantages of the internal market: the major motor of growth in Europe in the years to come (Box 64). The global benefit will only be fully realized if it is considered in the general social context.

Box 64

The overall benefit of the internal market

The Commission has outlined the overall economic effect of the internal market on supply and demand in the Community as follows: 'The completion of an area without internal frontiers creates important stimuli for both the supply and demand sides in the Community. Removing fiscal and administrative barriers, mutual recognition of technical standards and the opening of markets will have both an immediate as well as a progressive impact. For the private sector the following supply-side effects can be expected:

(i)   first, direct cost savings achieved in trade within the Community, if frontier formalities, additional inspections and certificates disappear;

(ii) the easier and less costly it becomes to offer products marketed in one Member country in other countries as well, the greater is the incentive to expand production capacities and to produce for the large internal market; the resultant economies of scale can be considerable; productivity rises while unit costs fall;

(iii) because transparency for public and private goods is greater, competition on the Community's internal market will intensify. Firms will have a greater incentive to increase their efficiency and to improve the quality of their products. In the medium term this can lead to a more efficient structure in the Community;

(iv) the large internal market finally also creates substantially better conditions for a greater European research and development effort since it opens up the whole Community as an outlet for the institutes and enterprises involved, benefiting the technological competitiveness of the Community.

The completion of the internal market can also, however, have positive effects on private demand:

(i)   if competition is wider, lower unit costs lead to lower product prices. As a result competitiveness is improved. This not only strengthens internal trade but also enables demand outside the Community to be better exploited;

(ii) the greater variety of products available in the large internal market meets the needs of enterprises and consumers and is also likely to trigger additional demand.

Completion of the internal market will also produce many cost savings in the public sector: expenditure on the supervision of national regulations will fall, and procurement opportunities will improve, if public contracts are awarded within the Community under conditions of free competition. This also increases the budgetary margin available for growth-promotion measures on both the supply and the demand side.'[1]

The Commission study of the economics of 1992[2] confirmed that the development of the common market for telecommunications services and equipment now promises major savings to the economy along with improved competitiveness. From a combined equipment and services market of around 80 000 million ECU in the EC, gains of up to 10 000 million ECU are there to be realized from the Green Paper proposals.

---

[1] *European Economy*, No 34, November 1987, p. 40.

[2] 'The economics of 1992 — An assessment of the potential economic effects of completing the internal market of the European Community', *European Economy*, No 35, March 1988.

In their joint opinion on the Community's cooperative strategy for more employment, Unice, ETUC and CEEP argue that:

'The internal market must be completed rapidly. This will make it possible to release considerable growth potential which will reinforce the positive effects which the implementation of the cooperative strategy will have on investment and growth. Completion of the internal market should be accompanied by taking account of social policy and by the development of structural policies to strengthen the Community's economic and social cohesion as it is defined in the Single European Act.'[1]

The future regulation of communications will substantially influence Europe's future economic position. The task is to structure Europe's market according to European economic and social needs. This must include developing consensus in Europe on the future position — and protection — of the individual in an environment which will be much richer in information than before.

But the overall objective is clear. The Community must make a determined move towards the 1992 goal: free choice for the user in a Community-wide market.

---

[1] 'Joint opinion of the Social Partners on the cooperative strategy for more employment', *European Economy*, No 30, November 1986, p. 109.

Conclusions

In the preparation for the information society the telecommunications sector plays a crucial role. Telecommunications services should be able to link people and machines at every moment and everywhere on earth at low cost. Technological developments show that such a prospect will be feasible, when services are implemented with adequate interconnectability. The world-wide telephony and telex services prove that interconnectability is the major factor that makes a service worthwhile for people and business.

The international component of telecommunications brings the real added-value. Although improvement of speech quality of telephony remains vital, a major future requirement for the telecommunications sector lies in the provision of data communications and proper image transmission services. And in a European Community with a common market this requirement can be specified as the provision of Europe-wide data communications and image services.

The implementation of these services and the subsequent upgrading of the networks for the introduction of the ISDN, the Integrated Services Digital Network, and at a later stage IBC, Integrated Broadband Communications, will require massive investments. The history of telecommunications shows the importance of the coordination of implementation strategies. Telex was introduced as a fully standardized international service and it has grown smoothly into a world-wide service, which now connects major business establishments throughout the world. Telephony was originally developed as a local service. Only after 1945 did long-distance telephony become a reality as a result of the invention of the amplification of electrical signals in cables. The adaptation of the different national or regional systems to a new world standard for interconnection required a period of 25 years.

Some new data communications services, such as videotex and teletex, were also introduced initially as national or regional systems. Unfortunately the system standards were not coordinated up to the level which we would now consider as necessary. When at a later stage interconnection between national services became a required feature, the technical and financial problems proved to be very complex.

It has been accepted in Europe that interconnection of networks and the inter-operability of terminals are prerequisites for Europe-wide services. The agreements made between a large number of telecommunications administrations in Europe for the introduction of Europe-wide digital cellular mobile telecommunications services and Europe-wide managed data network services, prove that the proper instrument has been found. Similar agreements could be made also for the new services based upon ISDN and later IBC. As the implementation of national ISDN services has already started in some European countries, further delay of implementation agreements should be avoided. The EC Council Recommendation on ISDN allows proper monitoring of the developments in the Member States, and lays down the ultimate date for agreement in the area of ISDN services. Such agreements should preferably cover more countries in Europe than the EC Member States and even extend outside Europe.

The interconnection of existing national data communications services such as videotex, teletex, electronic mail, and the packet- and circuit-switched public data networks still encounters major obstacles. It would, however, cause serious damage to leave the situation unchanged, as all these services prove to be of extreme value for the business world and the lack of interconnection has given rise to many delays.

Due to the importance of telecommunications services for society as a whole and as a consequence of the acceptance that networks can be provided under exclusive or special rights, network providers should be obliged to offer basic network services as efficiently as possible and at tariffs which are cost-related. The unfortunate situation that tariffs for international telephone calls and international leased lines are often high compared with actual costs in many cases, causes much friction between users and providers of services.

As this publication shows, the European Community has initiated many actions to improve telecommunications in Europe and it will take its share of the responsibility for promoting measures to ensure and regain interconnectability of services. In this way Europe should ensure a greater variety of efficient telecommunications services, in order to assist the rapid development of the 1992 Community-wide market, and Europe's preparation for the information society. The European achievement will be a true example of successful cooperation and will play a crucial role in world-wide development.

T. Schuringa,
Director for Telecommunications,
Directorate-General for Telecommunications,
Information Industries and Innovation
of the Commission of the European Communities

Annex

COUNCIL RESOLUTION
of 30 June 1988

on the development of the common market for
telecommunications services and equipment up to 1992

THE COUNCIL OF THE EUROPEAN COMMUNITIES,

Having regard to the Treaty establishing the European Economic Community,

Having regard to the Single European Act,

Having regard to the Green Paper on the development of the common market for telecommunications services and equipment published on 30 June 1987 and the communication on the implementation of the Green Paper up to 1992 dated 9 February 1988,

Having regard to the Opinions delivered by the Economic and Social Committee,[1]

Having regard to the draft from the Commission,

Whereas the strengthening of European telecommunications has become one of the major conditions for achieving the internal market for goods and services in 1992;

Whereas, as set out in the Green Paper, the current wave of technical innovation resulting from the convergence of telecommunications and computer technology has led to reviews in all Member States, and at world level, of the future organization of the telecommunications sector and its necessary regulatory adjustment;

Whereas the administrations or private operating agencies recognized in the Community and providing public telecommunications services are hereinafter referred to as the 'telecommunications administrations';

Whereas the creation of an open common market in telecommunications services and equipment is compatible with continued exclusive provision or special rights of telecommunications administrations as regards the supply and the operation of the network infrastructure and the provision of a limited number of basic services where such exclusive provision is deemed essential, at this stage, for safeguarding the public service role;

Whereas the arguments in favour of continued exclusive provision or special rights, where they exist, must be weighed carefully against the obligations of the telecommunications' administrations which will be retained but also against the restrictions which this may impose on those connected to the network concerning present and future application for

---

[1] OJ No C 356, 31.12.1987, p. 46 and OJ No C 175, 4.7.1988, p. 36.

their own use, shared use or provision to third parties; whereas this should take account of the fact that the development of trade must not be affected to such an extent as would run counter to the interests of the Community;

Whereas the substantial progress made with the Community's 1984 action programme for implementing a common telecommunications policy has laid a solid foundation for the implementation of a common approach in telecommunications;

Whereas the social, regional, industrial and trade aspects must be kept carefully in mind during the progressive implementation of such an approach;

Whereas the Community must adopt measures with the aim of progressively establishing the internal market, over a period expiring on 31 December 1992; whereas, to this end, the communication of 9 February 1988 defined an action plan for the progressive achievement of a competition-oriented Community-wide telecommunications market and the strengthening of European competitiveness;

Whereas the overriding objective must be to develop the conditions for the market to provide European users with a greater variety of telecommunications services, of better quality and at lower cost, affording Europe the full internal and external benefits of a strong telecommunications sector and the development in the Community of a strong telecommunications infrastructure, industry and efficient services;

CONSIDERS THE FOLLOWING POINTS AS MAJOR POLICY GOALS IN THE TELECOMMUNICATIONS POLICY:

1. creating or ensuring Community-wide network integrity as one of the essential elements for a common market in telecommunications services and equipment, working on the principle of full interconnectivity between all public networks concerned in the Community;

2. creating progressively an open, common market for telecommunications services, particularly for value-added services. Due account must be taken of the competition rules of the Treaty. Rapid definition, by Council directives, of technical conditions, usage conditions and tariff principles for Open Network Provision, starting with harmonized conditions for the use of leased lines, is of crucial importance and closely linked with the creation of an open common market for non-reserved telecommunications services;

3. promoting the creation of Europe-wide services according to market requirements and appropriate social needs, to enable European users to benefit from a wider range of better and cheaper telecommunications services, so that Europe can reap the internal and external benefits of a strong telecommunications sector.

   In addition to appropriate measures in the area of standardization, this approach should include definition of common tariff principles and the encouragement of cooperation between network operators and others, as far as compatible with Community competition rules; one of the aims in this should include definition of efficient pricing principles throughout the Community while ensuring general service for all;

4. developing further an open, Community-wide market for terminal equipment; for this purpose, reaching agreement quickly on full mutual recognition of type-approval for terminal equipment, on the basis of the rapid development of common European conformity specifications;

5. developing a common market on which telecommunications administrations and other suppliers can compete on an equal footing; to this end, the following are particularly appropriate:

   — clear separation of regulatory and operational duties, with due regard for the situation in each individual Member State;

   — application of the relevant rules of the Treaty, notably competition rules, to telecommunications administrations and private providers;

   — the creation of a transparent fiscal environment;

   — achievement of full opening of the markets for telecommunications supplies and works as part of the completion of the internal market;

6. continuing Community measures regarding common standards in the telecommunications sector. The establishment of the European Telecommunications Standards Institute (ETSI) is warmly welcomed in this context. However, futher efforts are needed to ensure conformity with general principles of Community standardization policy, taking into account the achievements of European cooperation in the field of telecommunications and the special characteristics of the telecommunications sector;

7. stimulating European cooperation at all levels, as far as compatible with Community competition rules, and particularly in the field of research and development, in order to secure a strong European presence on the telecommunications markets and to ensure the full participation of all Member States;

8. creating a social environment for the future development of telecommunications, in line with the Community's overall aim of improving the economic and social situation by extending common policies.

   Sustaining the dialogue between the social partners and undertaking in-depth analysis is particularly important in this context, to secure the conditions for developing social consensus concerning the transformation of working conditions and lifestyles resulting from the new telecommunications technologies.

   In addition, given the changing requirements, steps must be taken to see that workers have the right skills, to protect personal data and to provide for the individual's access, through the communications media, to an environment significantly richer in information than before;

9. integrating the less-favoured areas of the Community fully into the emerging Community-wide market making full use of existing funds. This is one of the aims of the STAR programme, which is designed to provide these areas with high technology telecommunications networks and equipment as well as developing the endogenous potential, especially in the field of services linked to this sector, thus making the best use of the growth potential of telecommunications.

   This should include examination, in particular taking into account the experience of the STAR programme, and within the context of overall Community priorities, of the case for further extension of funds available for this purpose, with a view to narrowing the gap in economic development which still separates the less favoured areas from the more prosperous areas of the Community;

10. working out a common position on satellite communications, so that this new information medium can develop in a favourable environment, taking account of the general rules of operation and exploitation of the network environment, as well as the competition rules of the Treaty and existing international commitments of Member States;

11. fully taking into account the external aspects of Community measures on telecommunications, and working out, as appropriate, common positions on international telecommunications problems.

There should be prior Community coordination, according to procedures agreed, for the purpose of defining not only key negotiating positions of concern to the Community in the international organizations dealing with telecommunications, in particular the various conferences of the International Telecommunications Union, but also a common position on those aspects of the Uruguay Round which cover telecommunications;

NOTES WITH SATISFACTION:

that substantial progress has been made with the Community's 1984 action programme approved at the Council's meeting of 17 December 1984 for implementing a common telecommunications policy, and applying Community law with the aim of creating a Community-wide market, particularly in the following areas:

— establishment of standards, and steps towards the mutual recognition of type-approval for terminal equipment;

— development of advanced telecommunications technologies, with the launching of the RACE programme;

— access to modern telecommunications for the less-favoured areas of the Community, with the launching of the STAR programme;

— coordination of technical plans and strategies for the introduction of new services, in particular the Integrated Services Digital Network (ISDN), and pan-European digital public mobile communications;

GIVES ITS GENERAL SUPPORT:

to the objectives of the action programme set out in the communication of 9 February 1988, which relates to the opening of the common telecommunications market to competition up to 1992, having regard also to Articles 8a and 8c of the Treaty, introduced by the Single European Act, and to the strengthening of European competitiveness, while safeguarding the public service goals of telecommunications administrations.

In this context and in the spirit of the conclusions of the Council of 17 December 1984, under which it was established, importance is accorded to the role played by the Senior Officials Group on Telecommunications (SOG-T);

INVITES THE COMMISSION:

to propose, where required, the measures necessary for pursuing the achievement of these goals, to be taken in priority areas on the basis of the appropriate Community procedures, in particular for the creation of the common market for telecommunications services and equipment and taking appropriate account also of the external dimension of these measures;

INTENDS:

to meet henceforth periodically on telecommunications issues, in order to pursue, together with the European Parliament, the Commission and the Economic and Social Committee, the rapid completion of the internal market for telecommunications services and equipment up to 1992, according to the goals set out and bearing in mind Article 8a of the Treaty and any adjustments and derogations which may be agreed upon on the basis of Article 8c of the Treaty.

Glossary

AIM	Community information technology and telecommunications application programme in the area of health care ('Advanced Informatics in Medicine in Europe') (EC programme)
Bell Operating Company (BOC)	The 22 companies born out of the divestiture of AT&T; term also often used to refer to the seven regional holding companies which group together the original 22
Bellcore	Bell Communications Research Inc.
Broadband	Transmission at speeds equal to or greater than 2 Mbit/s
CCH	Coordination Committee for Harmonization (CEPT)
CCIR	International Radiocommunications Consultative Committee (Comité consultatif international des radiocommunications) (ITU)
CCITT	International Telegraph and Telephone Consultative Committee (Comité consultatif international télégraphique et téléphonique) (ITU)
CCTS	Coordination Committee for Satellite Telecommunications (Comité de coordination pour les télécommunications par satellites) (CEPT)
CEC	Commission of the European Communities (institution of the European Communities)
CEN	European Committee for Standardization (Comité européen de normalisation)
Cenelec	European Committee for Electrotechnical Standardization (Comité européen de normalisation électrotechnique)
CEPT	European Conference of Postal and Telecommunications Administrations (Conférence européenne des administrations des postes et des télécommunications)
CLTA	Liaison Committee for Transatlantic Telecommunications (Comité de liaison pour les télécommunications transatlantiques) (CEPT)

Conformance	Conformity of a product with standards or technical specifications
Council	Council of Ministers of the European Communities (institution of the European Communities)
CSDN	Circuit-switched data network
CUG	Closed user group
DELTA	Community information technology and telecommunications application programme in the area of training ('Developing European Learning through Technological Advance') (EC programme)
DFS	German telecommunications satellite (Deutscher Fernmeldesatellit)
Digital mobile communications	Cellular mobile radiotelephone system using digital technology
Downlink	Unidirectional communications link from a satellite to an earth station (antenna)
DRIVE	Community information technology and telecommunications application programme in the area of road transport ('Dedicated Road Infrastructure for Vehicle safety in Europe') (EC programme)
EC	European Community; the 12 Member States are as follows: Belgium, Denmark, the Federal Republic of Germany, Greece, Spain, France, Ireland, Italy, Luxembourg, the Netherlands, Portugal and the United Kingdom
ECMA	European Computer Manufacturers' Association
ECS	European Communications Satellites
ECTEL	European Telecommunications and Professional Electronics Association
ECTUA	European Council of Telecommunications User Associations
EDI	Electronic Data Interchange
EFTA	European Free Trade Association
EN	European standard
ENV	European pre-standard
ESA	European Space Agency
ESPRIT	European Strategic Programme for Research in Information Technologies (EC programme)
Eutelsat	European Telecommunications Satellite Organization

EWOS	European Workshop for Open Systems
FCC	Federal Communications Commission (US)
GAP	Analysis and Forecasting Group (Groupe d'analyse et de prévision) (sub-group of SOG-T)
GSLB	Special Broadband Group (Groupe spécial large bande) (CEPT working group)
IBC	Integrated Broadband Communications
IEC	International Electrotechnical Commission
IEEE	Institute of Electrical and Electronic Engineers
Inmarsat	International Maritime Satellite Organization
Intelsat	International Telecommunications Satellite Organization
ISDN	Integrated Services Digital Network
ISO	International Standards Organization
ITSTC	Information Technology Steering Committee
ITU	International Telecommunications Union
LAN	Local Area Network
MAC	Standard for enhanced transmission of television by satellite
MDNS	Managed Data Network Services
MHS	Message Handling System
Modem	Apparatus allowing the connection of data terminals to the telephone network
Narrowband	Transmission at speeds up to 2 Mbit/s
NET	European telecommunications standard (Norme européenne de télécommunications)
ONA	Open Network Architecture — US concept
ONP	Open Network Provision — concept set out in the Green Paper
OSI	Open Systems Interconnection
PABX	Private Automatic Branch Exchange
Paging	Non-speech, one-way, personal selective calling system
PSDN	Packet-Switched Data Network
PSPDN	Packet-Switched Public Data Network
PSTN	Public-Switched Telephone Network

PTT	Postal, Telegraph and Telephone administration. Traditional but inaccurate term for telecommunications administrations
RACE	R&D in Advanced Communications Technologies for Europe (EC programme)
R&D	Research and development
R&TD	Research and technological development
ROES	Receive-only earth station for reception of satellite telecommunications
RPOA	Recognized Private Operating Agency; included under the term 'telecommunications administrations'
SMS	Multi-service satellite system (Système multiservice par satellite); category of service offered by Eutelsat
SNA	Systems Network Architecture — IBM proprietary communications standard
SOG-T	Senior Officials Group on Telecommunications (EC)
SOGITS	Senior Officials Group on Information Technology Standards (EC)
SPAG	Standards Promotion and Application Group; group of European industrialists, now established in Brussels with its own staff
STAR	Special Telecommunications Action for Regional development (EC programme)
TEDIS	Trade Electronic Data Interchange Systems (EC programme)
Telecommunications administrations	Term used for traditional telecommunications administrations together with Recognized Private Operating Agencies
TRAC	Technical Recommendations Application Committee; committee set up by the CEPT to establish NETs
TVRO	TV receive-only, domestic apparatus for the reception of television via satellite
Type-approval	Confirmation that a product is authorized or recognized as suitable to be connected to a particular public telecommunications network
Uplink	Unidirectional communications link from an earth station (antenna) to a satellite
VAS	Value-added service
VSAT	Very Small Aperture Terminal; satellite earth station with very small antenna
WATT-C 1988	World Administrative Telegraph and Telephone Conference of the ITU, to be held in December 1988

ECU conversion rates
(June 1988)

Belgian franc and Luxembourg franc	43.45
Danish krone	7.90
German mark	2.08
Greek drachma	166.20
Portuguese escudo	169.60
French franc	7.01
Dutch guilder	2.34
Irish pound	0.78
Italian lira	1 542.00
Spanish peseta	137.40
Pound sterling	0.66
United States dollar	1.18
Japanese yen	150.70

Note: The ECU/dollar rate has varied greatly in the course of the 1980s. This gives rise to unavoidable problems in the preparation of comparative statistics, and should be taken into account when interpreting them.

European Communities — Commission

Telecommunications in Europe
by Herbert Ungerer with the collaboration of Nicholas Costello

Luxembourg: Office for Official Publications of the European Communities

1988 — 259 pp. — 17.6 × 25.0 cm

The European perspectives series

ES, DA, DE, GR, EN, FR, IT, NL, PT

ISBN 92-825-8209-4

Catalogue number: CB-PP-88-009-EN-C

Price (excluding VAT) in Luxembourg: ECU 10.50